Something Worth Saving

by
Bettie P. Mitchell

Published by Good Samaritan Ministries
7929 S.W. Cirrus Drive, Bldg. #23
Beaverton, Oregon 97008 U.S.A.

ISBN 978-0-9852786-0-1

Library of Congress #TXu 1-826-530

First Printing 2011
Printed in the United States of America

Scripture quotations in this publication are taken
from the New Jerusalem Bible.

Permission to tell personal details of any client's story was
granted prior to printing this book.

Additional copies of this book can be purchased online at:
www.createspace.com/3748949

Dedication

This book is dedicated to the Glory of God.
He took a slave of sin, and through the
Pearl of Great Price, purchased her freedom.

Dominion

I know God in my breath, and my breath cries out to Him. God receives the fullness of my emotions – Spirit and Truth. Through the breath, He has connected us to Himself. He listens for our breath.

I know His humor and suffering – we share in it together – never alone. I know the God of Job and the Father of Abraham. He made all of the generations to know each other – we don't know that. He made our intimacy for all of the generations. He waits for us to find this profound truth of Divine Intimacy.

He gave us land that our feet may be holy. He gave us seas that we would know the depths and breadth of His character. He gave us animals so we could have dominion over them instead of dominion over each other.

TABLE OF CONTENTS

Appendix I

Appendix II

CHAPTER 1

We Come Forth Through the Generations

Denton, Kansas, never had more than 200 people when it was jammed full. In the Northeast corner of Kansas, it had a pool hall, a grain elevator, and a railroad track going through town. My father was the second of four children born to my grandparents. He was named Roy William Roberts.

Grandpa Norman was a stubborn cussed man. He loved to swear. In fact, he knew very little English besides swear words because he had little education. He could barely write. I don't know if he could really read. He talked through his teeth, so you always heard this sound that was going through his teeth. It was hard to discern exactly what he was saying. Every day, after his retirement from mule trading, selling things at the auction and some farming, he would go up town to play pitch with the men.

When my grandmother asked him what he wanted to eat, he always said "beans and eggs." Banality was a strong spirit throughout this man's life.

Astonishingly, grandpa's four sons liked him. They showed him respect. They believed in him. In some ways, I learned more in Denton, Kansas, than I learned anyplace else that could be called home.

My grandmother, Carrie Boettiger Roberts, had a little more education. She could write letters. She was thoughtful of others, and she was the town patcher. Anyone who needed anything patched would give it to grandma Carrie, and Carrie patched her best for each hole found in that clothing. She had curly hair. Her birthday was two days after mine. She made her dresses out of flour sacks, and she only changed them every two weeks. She did have a Sunday dress, but she seldom went to church. She sat in her rocking chair and patched. She cooked on a kerosene stove. There was no running water in the house, although there was a bathtub where they could pour water for a bath. The pump outside and the outdoor two-hole privy lasted into the mid-50's. My grandfather's well-stated philosophy was that he did not understand why people ate outside, and went to the toilet inside the house. There was no changing him once he made up his mind!

Over my youth, I spent many months in Denton, Kansas. When my parents wanted time alone, they dropped me in Kansas. Denton, the farm, and the whole area became a safe-haven, a place where I could be free.

When I was three years old, I ran away in Denton. I crossed the railroad tracks into town. My cousin, Beulah, who was ten years older, chased after me. I had such a fit; she had to carry me all the way home. Denton definitely was part of my homeland.

My father, Roy Roberts, weighed less than two pounds when he was born in 1906. They put him in a little box behind the stove to die, and he lived. It was really a miracle. He was never physically strong, although he loved to play sports.

My father was closest to his grandmother, Almira Roberts. According to the family, she was married to a man who was nearly hopeless. He was an angry veteran from the Civil War, maimed and crippled from that experience. She liked my father, Roy, a lot. She read him the Horatio Alger books. She taught him to think beyond the world of Denton, into the bigger picture of the world. Because he had almost died in that little box, he was her special friend, and

2

she was his mentor.

My great grandmother, Almira Roberts, was noted for giving talks throughout the Midwest on the Civil War. She was one of the founders of the Methodist Church in Denton. A stained glass window in the church is in her honor. She was a Christian. She went to church, and she taught my dad about Jesus.

My father was a very intelligent man. He was creative too. In his later life, he was an inventor. At age 18, he went to Business College in Chillicothe, Missouri. While he was there, he came down with tuberculosis. Tuberculosis forced him to move to Colorado Springs, Colorado. He lived in a bed at a sanitarium where he read the whole Bible for the first time. No one in the family ever visited him.

My mother, Laura Wilma (Lee) Costin, was raised in Ohio, first in Bellefontaine, but later in Toledo. Her father, Edwin Glenn Costin, was her first grade school teacher. She was his only child, and they adored each other. Later, her father became a lawyer, and a claim agent for the New York Central Railroad. According to the stories in the family, he went to many train wrecks.

My maternal grandmother's maiden name was Amanda Ellen (Nellie) Gray. When she was born, her mother died. Her grandfather was very angry, as he had not thought much of the marriage anyway. When she was three, her father died, and her grandfather became her sole living parent. When she was nine, her grandfather died. That left grandma to be a maid in a distant cousin's household where there were nine children. Nellie had to do the wash, wring it out, and hang it before she could go to school. It was more than her little heart could bear, and this affected her entire life. She always said, "I didn't want children." She had been too much of a parent at too young an age.

Grandma Nellie told the story of riding in a covered wagon into Oklahoma during the Land Rush. The territory of Oklahoma was opened for land claims. My grandmother was not highly educated, but she was an amazing housewife. Both of my mother's parents read their Bibles daily. When they received money from a wage grandpa earned, he would cash the check, and, first, before anything, he would put the tithe in the desk drawer, ready to be given to the church.

My grandfather taught a Bible class of men. There were 150 men in the class, and that will come into the story later. I want you to remember it.

When my mother, Laura, was in her early teens, after some major health problems in childhood, she too contracted tuberculosis. The doctor ordered that she and her mother go to Tucson, Arizona, where she would spend much of three years in recovery. During that time, most of her friends there died of tuberculosis.

One of the things my mother hated about her parents was they always chaperoned her every time she had a date. They protected her like she was in a hot house, and they had the key. Even in her late teens and early 20's, they still felt it was improper for her not to have a chaperone when she went out. My mother had a wild streak, and did not exactly take to such a controlled life. But, she made the best of it, and she did love her parents.

My mother and father were both born in 1906. My mother's parents were married in 1900. If you visited our house today, you would find their marriage bed in one of our bedrooms. It was kept. When I was in 9th grade, my mother and I removed eight coats of paint. It is a memorable bed – much shorter than an ordinary one.

After my mother was old enough to get out from under her parent's pressure, she moved to Colorado Springs, Colorado. This was a resort town for those who had tuberculosis, or for those who needed special air for lung problems. She loved Colorado Springs. She loved being there un-chaperoned, and she was free to develop her own life. She had several suitors. She often went dancing at The Broadmoor, the swank country club in the United States. The

Broadmoor was the top of the top.

My mother and her mother were fabulous seamstresses. They made everything. My mother was particularly gifted at making hats, lampshades, slipcovers, and every kind of clothing there was!

My mother took this talent and used it to be one of the best-dressed women in Colorado Springs. Thus, my dad, Roy Roberts, noticed her and began to pursue her, although three other men were pursuing her at the same time.

Now, pursuing my mother was a little bit out of his league. She was way beyond Denton, Kansas. As he had a little competition, he wrote my mother telling her that if they married, he'd buy her a nice house. The other men didn't offer her a house. My parents decided to get married. They began a trip to Toledo, Ohio, to visit her parents, but along the way, they decided to get married, eloping exactly at midnight. They went to the door of a local Justice of the Peace. They were married on June 1, 1930.

The point of all of these details is very important because my parents were so opposite it was incredible! I would say, honestly, that my mother had delusions of grandeur. She always told her mother, "When I grow up, I will never wash my own clothes, I will have a maid." She sometimes trimmed her clothes in ermine fur, wore silks and high-heeled shoes, and she was a knockout in style.

My father was very basic. He liked handling money, and he became a teller at the bank in Colorado Springs. He had the most beautiful handwriting I've ever seen. He could sign his name in a half a dozen ways, and each one was a work of art. Later in life, he tried to teach me handwriting, but it was absolutely impossible for me to improve my basic writing skill.

After a little period of time, my parents decided to visit my father's family in Denton, Kansas. My mother packed very carefully in order to make a good impression upon his parents and family. The problem was she didn't know anything about Denton, Kansas, and how they dressed there. So, she packed her silks, her high-heeled shoes, her ermine-trimmed dress, and she went in high style to visit my father's family. The shock at that meeting, although I was not present, must have been the most terrific style shock Denton ever had. Even in my later childhood, it was discussed as an historic event in this little Kansas town. She did not know her husband's mother made her own dresses out of flour sacks, and had never used perfume or deodorant in her entire life.

My parents were both 24 years old when they married. Four years later, I was born.

When I was 11 years old, my father and I made a trip to Denton to visit. He picked up a new Pepsi Cola truck in St. Louis, as a way to pay for the trip, and drove it to Portland. As we were driving across the country, going through Colorado, he looked up at a mountain on the left-hand side, and said, "That's where you were conceived. Right on top of that mountain. Your mother and I were camping by a stream." I thought, "Wow!" In that truck, on my lap, was the antique clock from my grandparent's house in Denton. I carried it on my lap the whole way from Kansas to Oregon. The truck went 40 MPH, and it took a long time to get to Oregon. This was the closest time I ever spent with my father.

It was told that when I was born, my father was playing a baseball game, and didn't come to the hospital until later. That seemed to be a great crime, as it was discussed by my mother's parents; but, that was my father. He had four passions – work, sports, gambling, and some womanizing.

My mother had four passions – learning, music, travel, and the arts.

My mother was a very gifted pianist and organist. She bought a grand piano when I was seven years old; paying for it out of money she made cleaning apartments. She moved this grand piano into our apartment. That piano tells a large story of the prominence of music and her passion for it in our lives.

There is one more notable story about my time in Colorado before I was three years of age. I ran out of the house, while my mother was getting dressed, and fell into an uncovered street sewer system. I would have been washed under the street and drowned, but a dog caught hold of my dress and saved my life. A man saw the dog and came and lifted me out. The story was in the newspaper. I have the article so I know it's true.

When I was three years old, my parents went on a vacation to Oregon. They fell in love with Portland.

Now, in 1937, we came to live in Portland, Oregon. My father found his first Oregon job at First National Bank, Sixth and Morrison Branch. He loved being a banker. As we had little money, we lived in a rooming house. It was funny living with strangers, but I got used to it.

My mother gave me a lot of freedom. When I was five, I got to walk two blocks to the store to buy bread and a hostess cupcake. She not only gave me the money, she gave me the trust. This is a huge part of who I am, "Trusted to Go."

I remember the first day of kindergarten. I was totally terrified and wanted to run home. My mother let go of me, and I made it through kindergarten. When I was about to begin the first grade, we moved into our own apartment. The building is still in Portland: 2634 NE Broadway. We lived on the bottom floor. My parents were the managers of the apartment building. War was looming when I was six.

One of the high points of my childhood was when my Uncle George came to live with us. He was with us less than a year, but it was the first time I had somebody with me besides my parents. He was an uncle, but a brother too. He was 14 years younger than my dad. We stayed close until he died in his 80's. He went into the Army Air Force and became a pilot. The war began to get close to home, and I became involved in the daily war story.

When I was in the second grade, I became seriously ill with streptococcus infection. I had to stay at home for many days to recover. I can remember the doctor coming, and I can remember lying in a big bed.

The first day I went back to school, I had to walk ten blocks each way to and from school. I stayed all day. I missed all the words on the spelling test because I had never seen the words before. My teacher, Miss Lawrence, said I had to stay after school and write the words ten times each before I left for home. Many years later, the Lord told me she was my greatest teacher. Can you believe that?

As a child, I was not upset. I was eager to learn. But when I got home so late, my mother was terrifically upset, and it was the last day I went to that school for several years. It was decided by someone that I should go to a special school for children with health problems. Only years and years later did I learn it was a school for children with pre-tubercular conditions. The school was called Mills Open Air.

By this time, the war was on for all of America. There were blackouts every night. We had black shades across all of our windows. No light was allowed outside. We had only a little gas each month, as everything was rationed, and I had to go to school several miles from where we lived in our apartment. So, as a seven year-old, I got on a bus every morning, took another bus, then a streetcar, and finally, walked a quarter of a mile to school. Every night I reversed the process. I did this alone, without anyone helping me. It was the way it was during World War II, and I was a World War II child.

Mills Open Air was a strange school. All the windows, the length of the room, were open all the time, year around. You got used to it, but, boy, in the beginning, it was pretty cold! I was required to wear long stockings and a garter belt, which I hated. We had to take naps every day on cots which we had to get out of a cupboard. We had to drink milk at 10:00 a.m., eat healthy meals, and of course, we had to learn. Later in this book I will talk about education, but for now, you have heard that I was at Mills Open Air. I was there for three and a half years.

I did have health problems. When I was seven years old, I weighed 40 pounds. People would shake their heads. I was never allowed to be vaccinated. I was too thin. It was a very hard time, and my health was precarious.

I was a "failure to thrive child." This probably came to pass because there was so much anxiousness and violence in our family. There was too much love and too much violence, and it switched around almost daily. I was a nervous child, so nervous that my hands sometimes dripped when I walked. I did not have sweaty hands, I had wet, dripping palms. It was often one of my greatest sources of embarrassment.

The first major health problem I clearly recall occurred when I was four years old. I had been vomiting for several days and my parents decided to take me to the Doernbecher Children's Hospital. They took me up an elevator and I was put in a bed in a room by myself. My parents were not allowed to visit me for four days. In addition, they took all food and water away from me and put me on IV's. For a four year-old, that was pretty traumatic. I remember vomiting in the bed the first night. I didn't know how to get a nurse so I layed in the vomit until morning. But, what I remember most is, after four days, they gave me fresh orange juice and toast with butter on it. That was, to this day, the best meal I have ever eaten.

The doctor said I was vomiting because my mother was giving me too much fat and not enough sugar. This led to some suckers here and there, but more importantly, it led to less vomiting. However, the whole problem was still there. Here was a child with huge anxiety, a suffering child, trying too hard. I was sick to my stomach almost every morning. If I could talk my mother into it, I would take my breakfast toast and throw it into the bushes on the way to school; otherwise, if I didn't eat what I was given at breakfast, I had to eat it later in the day when I came home. Oatmeal, later in the day, is not very good. In addition, even in my teens, I was vomiting consistently at the beginning of every relationship that involved a date. I vomited on the first day of school each year. I believe you can get a picture of a child who is very troubled, very intense, and yet I can say I was very precocious and talented. More about that later.

My mother and father fought all the time. I don't know that they ever agreed upon anything, except that we would have a family meeting once a week and we would discuss what we wanted to do on family night, which would always be on Friday night. It was so significant because I always had a voice in the family's decisions. This was powerful, and it was this balance of power that taught me the significance of the absolute balance of power between children and adults. Again, it goes back to trust.

I almost always voted for the movies, and to this day, I love movies. I love the imaginary world, the mystery, but I also love to read. Often I would read under the bed covers with a flashlight until past midnight. I found out as much as I could from those books. What was the world to be in my life?

As I got a little older, I walked ten blocks, a couple of times a week, to the YMCA. My assignment was to learn to swim. I hated having my head in the water, as this usually resulted in major earaches. Everything was to improve my health. God bless the people who worked on my strength.

My mother attempted to teach me two things, both of which I hopelessly failed. She attempted to teach me to play the piano. After five years of torture and complete lack of success, we both gave up. One of my greatest sorrows is that I could not play the piano the way my mother did. I loved music.

The second thing I failed completely was sewing. Sweaty hands make rusty needles. It just didn't work!

I know I was my mother's project. She made much of each thing we did together. We went to the movies downtown once a month, and to Jolly Jones for vegetable soup on the way. I can remember skipping down the street in downtown Portland singing. I can remember many of those movies. It was a powerful time for significant growth. World War II became alive in the news reels. I watched intently. I was always interested in the bigger world. I felt personally connected to the war.

My mother was convinced that I needed to be developed in many different ways, and she helped to give me a musical education that would produce a child that favored music over sports. She knew the situation with my dad was hopeless because it would always be sports, but perhaps, through their child, music could live. We went to every concert that ever came to the Portland Civic Auditorium, and we went to all of the operas. These were the most incredibly intense and powerful times for me. I was experiencing people's greatest talents, people from all over the world. I heard Marian Anderson sing. She was a great Contralto Negro (now called African American) voice. She was a concert soloist, famous all over the world. When she went to the Benson Hotel to stay, they turned her away because she was a Negro. I heard the greatest sopranos, altos, tenors, baritones, pianists, the worlds' greatest violinists; but, I loved opera the best because it was filled with passion, creativity, story, and glorious music.

Then there was church. We went every Sunday, to Sunday school and church. We went to a big church downtown called The Disciples of Christ, or The Christian Church. The sanctuary had beautiful stained glass windows, and those windows had a deep affect on my life, especially the one of Jesus praying in the garden.

Underneath it were the words, "Not My Will, But Thy will be done." Since my mother always said I was a strong-willed child, I felt those words were probably written to impress upon me something that was important. What was going on in the church was not very interesting or important to me. It seemed to be "form," but not "substance," to put it into adult language. But what was going on in that garden, in that life-sized window right in front of the sanctuary, where my eyes could not miss it, which was really important to me! I'll speak more about church later. But, for now, it is important to know that on the way to church, we were always fighting. If we sang, we sang in all different keys, and sometimes all different songs. On the way home, we were fighting, but in Sunday school and church, we had to be very, very good. We had to wear gloves and hat. We had to take our purse, and have money to give. When we left, we always had to shake the pastor's hand and tell him what a good sermon it was.

Now, politics was another conflict! My father was a Republican. The entire family in Denton, Kansas, was all historically Republicans. A story was told that when my dad's grandfather, James Roberts, saw a wagon going by his house, he would shout out, "Republican or Democrat!?" If they said "Democrat," he cursed them and sent them on their way. If they said "Republican," he invited them to dinner. In those days, your party defined who you were in the community.

My mother was a liberal Democrat who thought her vote was none of my dad's business. She once swore that she voted for the third-party socialist, Norman Thomas, who was a candidate in four elections.

My dad always stayed up on election night to hear the results. If a Democrat won, he loudly declared the country was going to hell. I was expected to be a Republican, whatever that meant.

My politics eventually became "One nation, under God,

indivisible, with liberty and justice for all."

My mother read to me every night. Sometimes she had me read to her. She had me give her massages because she had pain. In my childhood, she had five major surgeries, and lost several babies in miscarriage. My mother and I were close, but there was terrific tension between us.

Now, the subject of sports was another story. My father often sold tickets at ball games. In order for us to see him, we had to go; therefore, my mother took the tickets at most of the games. I spent the whole game wandering around. I watched the game for awhile, then, I went under the bleachers to pick up cans. I turned them in hoping to get money for them. This happened at least two nights a week. My mother figured out that if she wanted to see my dad, she'd have to live in the sports world with him, but his world was always linked with work. In the summer, we did baseball and softball, and in the winter, we did basketball, still always working. Can you imagine that? You had to work to do sports!

It was told to me that when I was a baby, my father was gone almost every night. He played ball two nights a week, and he played poker three nights a week. When my mother was furious and wanted to go out, she would hand me to him, and say, "You take her to the ball game." So, he would hand me to some stranger in the crowd, and I would be there for the whole ball game while my dad played ball. I have some memory of this.

I was a failure at sports. I still can't, even to this day, throw a ball overhand. I tried and tried and tried. I thought maybe I could be a pitcher because I could throw it underhand, but it just didn't work out. I wanted so much for my father to be proud of me.

During World War II, my father worked two full-time jobs at the bank, 16 hours a day. His first job was as a teller, and at night, he headed the accounting department to process all of the business of the day. If my mother was going to be gone, she sent me with my father to the bank. I would sit in the dark area outside the room where my father was working. He would give me a pen and some paper, and I would sit at a bank desk during all of those hours waiting for him to be ready to go home. It's strange to admit this, but I liked it. I liked the feeling of a desk, a position, something that signified work. It later served me in good stead to like that desk, to like that paper, and to use it.

During the War, on our summer vacations, we lived at lookout fire towers. There were not enough men in the country to do the firefighting or to watch for fires. My dad was 40 and flat-footed. His battlefield of victory was the Home Front work.

When I was 11, I lived through the hardest year of my childhood. Two very significant things happened. My mother's parents moved from Ohio to live with us in Oregon. They had never told my mother that was what they planned to do. When they retired, they simply announced they were moving out to be with us. My mother was horrified, suffering her own health issues, and a nervous wreck. It was a disaster for her. It was one for me also. The second shocking event was that, as my mother was recovering from a major hysterectomy, a lawyer called and asked if my parents wanted to have a baby to adopt – a baby girl. My parents talked briefly and the baby girl was with us two days later. She was named Arabelle. I was almost 11, she was a baby. There had been no family meeting about either issue. Family meetings had stopped.

The best time happened, immediately after this time, when we moved to Grants Pass, a town of about 5,000. This was a town small enough that I could go anywhere, enjoy myself, have absolute freedom, and I didn't have to take any busses. We lived in a motel for two months until our new house was finished. My father had finally bought my mother the house he had promised her 16 years earlier. It was exciting to have our own house. There was a secret passageway behind a wall bookcase in my room. I was upstairs, and that was good. There was only one problem: My grandparents were in the room right across the hall, and I could hear them talk. They were not happy with my father, and they were worried. While we lived there, my grandmother broke both ankles and an arm. My mother had the baby, and her mother to care for. She ran up and down the stairs caring for her mother. It was a very hard time in my mother's life, and a year of complete separation for us. The freedom had a price. The home brought us a lack of a home.

I went to Junior High. I had skipped one year of school so I was a year younger than everyone. I loved school. I had my first really good friend, Anita. We only lived in Grants Pass for two years. Those were the good days of my childhood. Then, suddenly, my father was transferred to Portland. He had given too many veterans loans to buy houses. He was removed from being assistant manager of the Grants Pass bank. We were back in Portland in a rented house.

I always lived in an adult world. I also lived in the world of the elderly. As a child, on N.E. Broadway, there was nothing but businesses. I made friends with people who operated the businesses. I made friends with two elderly families: Mrs. Anthis, down the street, and The Craigs, in our apartment building. I loved to visit. I would go to where they lived and I would play. One day, Mrs. Craig invited me to lunch. I will never ever forget that day. She had the most beautiful sterling silverware. She had beautiful crystal, beautiful china, and she brought it out for my lunch! As I recall, we had a grapefruit (I don't know what else we had....), but it stood out, and I knew that Mrs. Craig thought I was really special. Later, when our first baby was born, I took Michelle to Mrs. Craig's on the way home from the hospital. I laid Michelle, on the bed beside her, shortly before Mrs. Craig died.

I did not understand the world of children very well. In the early years, my mother discouraged me from having any friends. I seemed to provide her security and protect her from loneliness.

60 years, although we did not see each other for 49 of those years. It was God's provision. Where would I go? What was happening to me?

I lost the deeper sense of connection with my mother. She was distracted by my sister and her parents. She had two outside jobs. The marriage continued to distract her, and we seldom found time to connect.

Learning to drive was a really big challenge for me. I had five accidents learning to drive. The first accident occurred the first day. My mother took me out on a very busy street that was on a hill at the light. She expected me to change gears on the hill, go through the light, and come out okay. Well, I slid backwards, and, of course, into a car.

How I finally learned to drive is an interesting story. I didn't learn to drive until I was 19. An old lady in her 70's said, "I'll teach you to drive!" She was kind of a crazy old lady. We called her Aunt Mary, but she wasn't really an aunt. She took me out in rainy November weather, sang to me, and taught me to drive with confidence. Aunt Mary was a great blessing!

I talked to practically no one, for I did not know what to say. It was as if I was waiting. But upon what was I waiting? Time would soon tell.

At the end of my 16th year, something very unusual happened that had a profound effect on my life. It was a "God-Calling Event." I was sitting in church, studying my stained glass window of Jesus, when all of a sudden, without any introduction or warning, the Lord told me, "Go up and give your life to full-time Christian service."

In those days, this was not something women did. It was a shock to me, and to the church. The pastor called the elders. They laid hands on me and prayed. I went back to my seat. Not a single one of them ever spoke to me again. This became a very painful loss, which caused me problems for many years. Why was I left alone? Why was I not helped or counseled, as I desperately needed it? One day I overcame my fear, and made an appointment to see the pastor, but the conversation did not refresh or provide for anything. It was an hour, and then the time was over. It was not the hour that my heart desired!

I believe, at this point, I will tell you something really important. For years and years and years, the memory of this time stayed inside of me. One day, the Lord showed me something about this time of the first call. This is what He said: "I put everyone to sleep. You gave your life to MY service, not theirs, and I took charge of YOUR life, and did not give them a chance to influence you at all."

I've often found that the Lord has a different perspective than I do. He has a way of looking at things that changes the way I see. When God made it clear to me, I rejoiced. The absence of human counselors brought the Wonderful Counselor, the Holy Spirit.

My 17th year was the hardest of my life. I finished high school just before I entered my 17th year. I had to prepare to go to college. I had to work hard, hard, hard to get the tuition money together.

The year started out to be challenging and somewhat interesting, as it was very different to go to Lewis and Clark College. Here was a place where there was little disciplined structure. You went to class, or didn't go to class by your own decision, and no one else's. I must admit, I wasted some time going to the Shack instead of going to class; but generally, I was a dedicated student, and I soon discovered that I wanted to learn, not waste time.

At that time I had a boyfriend, but he wasn't the right person for me, and I was not in a good place with him. He did not go to college. I was changing.

The best part of college was when my girlfriend, Anita, from Grants Pass, joined me at Lewis and Clark. She came unexpectedly, and we took our first year of college together. This was a huge miracle, because now I had a friend again. In May, of our first year of college, Anita was Maid of Honor at my wedding.

One day, Anita and I were walking on the campus. A girl passed us who was smoking a cigarette. I turned to my friend, Anita, and said, "Isn't that terrible? I would never smoke!" What a fatal statement!

Now the Lord is into humbling us, and when we say "never," He will give us a temptation that will be almost a killer. One week later, a man I wanted to like me offered me a cigarette, and I began to smoke. I tried to increase the cigarettes every day so I could be a true smoker. I lost my sense of reason, lost my balance, and smoked for 17 years. It was one of the worst decisions I ever made in my life.

I will tell you the outcome of it. Seventeen years later, I was smoking 2 ½ packages of cigarettes a day, and drinking 8 to 10 cups of caffeine coffee each day.

As my 17th year continued, I became less and less balanced. I found myself lost in a nightmare of inner pain. In such a time, I turned to men, thinking that being loved by a man would solve my problems. It was the absolute wrong decision. But my decision did turn out well in the end!

I went through a date rape and an abortion. My mother tried to kill the baby at home, and then took me for an illegal abortion. This was the most devastating event of my life. It left me in a fatalistic position. I felt, from deep within, that God would no longer accept me into His Kingdom, and that my future, fittingly, would be in hell. I also believed my mother was perfect and I was from the evil one. I profoundly believed this for the next 17 years, which led me to greater and greater levels of acting out, massive depression, and finally, to a psychiatric hospitalization at age 33.

Then, something unusual happened which changed the picture again. It was February; I was 17 years and 8 months old. At college, I ran into a man I knew at the "Shack" snack bar. I knew him from a couple of years before. He was in an Army uniform. I walked up to him and I said, "I think I know you." We sat down, talked, and decided we did know each other. We were sitting with his friend, Dick. We talked for a little while, and then the men flipped a coin to determine who would take me home. Jerry was the one to take me home. This journey home was very unusual. We went straight home. We parked in front of our house. It was day time. We began a conversation that is still amazing to me. We talked about getting married, how many children we might have, what we might name them, and where we would live. We had not had a date. We had only had this hour's conversation together in our lives, and here we were, planning a marriage. He took me to the door. My mother briefly met him. He didn't even come inside. I went in, and the next morning, my mother said, "That is the man you are going to marry."

We dated for five days, and then he went to Fort Bliss, Texas, to Officer's Candidate School. His dad had died when he was eight. His dad had been a 2nd Lieutenant in W.W. I. Jerry's mother expected him to be an officer. He didn't make it. Jerry came home the middle of April, and we dated two more weeks. He was ready to be shipped overseas. It was 1952 during the Korean War.

There is one more part of the story. Jerry and I went to church together the latter part of April before he left. He gave me an engagement ring as we went out to the church foyer. I said to him, "I will only become engaged to you under three conditions: 1) you will be a baptized Christian; 2) you will go to church with me the rest of our lives, and 3) you will never deny me sex.

There is one humorous event during the final week of our dating. When we were dating those last two weeks in April, there came a night when I couldn't remember Jerry's last name. I spent the whole night trying to recall what his last name was, not knowing that two weeks later we would be married and it would be my last name for the rest of my lifetime. I've always had a problem with names. I still do!

After his April leave, Jerry reported to Fort Lawton in Washington. We talked on the phone. He had no idea which day he would be shipped out. He suddenly appeared at our house at midnight, having driven his mother's car. He had cracked the block on the way down and his brother-in-law was with him. He wanted to see if I would go back up to Seattle with him. There was no warning of this at all. It just happened. I said, "No, I won't go, unless we're married." So he said, "All right, let's get married." Now, at 17, my dad had to sign papers or I couldn't get married. My Dad went to the kitchen, flipped the coin in my presence, and signed the papers. I would be married to Jerry. I often laugh and say "by two flips of a coin, the rest of my life was decided." Was this a divine event? Had it been planned from the beginning? Most of me believed it was, and part of me was torn by the circumstances.

I want to say to you that Jerry kept our agreements. If I had known it would work so well, I would have asked for a little more. I often pass that advice along. What are you adamant about, and what agreements will you make before you get married? Agreements before marriage are life and death essential!

We married May 3, 1952, at the Christian Church in Vancouver, Washington. We married in Washington, as they did not require a three-day waiting period.

Now, since the decision was made for us to get married at 2:00 a.m., Wednesday morning, and we were going to be married at 8:00 p.m. Saturday evening the same week, there was considerable pressure to put everything together. I would be married in a pink suit. Jerry was married in a suit he bought at Goodwill for $5.00.

At the church, I waited for my husband-to-be to show up. Since the wedding was at 8:00, and he had not arrived by 8:00, I was pretty nervous. Finally, at 8:15 p.m., he came in, but the best man did not arrive at all. A tenor singer, Dean Lieberman, sang "Always "and" Because." During the time the singer was sitting behind the altar, the candles began to explode and the rug began to catch on fire. The soloist stamped the fire out and took care of the problem.

There were 50 guests at our wedding. The reception was the next day. When we got into the car to leave the wedding, we discovered Jerry's suitcase was missing. He had left it at home in the rush to get to the church, after hitchhiking all the way from Fort Lawton, near Seattle, to Portland the same day. Being without a haircut, his aunt put a bowl around his head and cut his hair. In that chaos, no suitcase.

We kept calling Jerry's mother's house, but she did not return home. We decided to go to a dance at Lewis and Clark College. We went to a drugstore and had a soda. We went to my parent's, and while we were there, there was a prankster phone call. It was my mother and father's friend, Jimmy. He sounded very official, asked to speak to Jerry, and informed him that he was AWOL and needed to return to base immediately. Jerry turned white as a sheet as he was AWOL. He was supposed to return to base at 2:00 a.m., and he would not be returning to base until the following night. Needless to say, we were relieved when we found out it was not a legitimate phone call.

Finally, Jerry's mother returned home, we got the suitcase, and we checked into the Multnomah Hotel.

The next day, after our reception, we drove my parents' car to Seattle.

When we married, we had only five dollars. Through a loan from my parents, we spent only one whole night together. Tuesday was our final night in Seattle. Jerry had to report at 2:00 a.m., daily. On our fourth night of marriage, May 6th, Jerry announced he was shipping out for overseas the next morning.

We called our mothers and asked them to fly up so they could drive me home in my parents' car. Our "goodbye" was a family event. It was a very shaky event. We had started something. How would this turn out? I went openly into the relationship, and I gave much to it.

My husband, Jerry, ended up stationed in Japan instead of Korea. He worked at military hospitals there. We corresponded weekly. He went through one period when he didn't write for two months. I called him five times. Each, three-minute phone call, cost $20. It took 24 to 36 hours for the operator to locate Jerry on the base. He began to write again. We were o.k. Those five phone calls, 15 minutes in all, were the only times we talked together for two years.

Jerry came home on the day of our second wedding anniversary. The Oregonian newspaper called me and said the ship was arriving in Seattle. I drove up, and he was shocked I was there. After five days, we were back in Portland. Jerry was officially out of the Army. After my wedding, my parents decided I would pay all of my way through college. In order to do this, I sometimes worked three jobs. I worked with 30 men as an assistant bookkeeper for four businesses. My office was in a very poor part of town. The second job I had was still working at the theatre, and the third job was working part-time at Meier & Frank department store over the holidays. In addition, I took 20 semester hours a semester, for my goal was to graduate, or nearly graduate, by the time Jerry came home from overseas. I received $90 allotment each month from the government. I put this money into a savings account. I bought and paid for a used car, and bought some furniture. When Jerry came home, I had saved $2,000 and paid my way through college. This is only told to you so you would understand I worked hard. I tried very hard to do what was right, and to be a good wife.

Our marriage was traumatic for many years. Jerry and I both had severe emotional problems. I was fighting depression; he was fighting his own emotional illness. Jerry was born in 1929. Before his first birthday, Jerry had a double mastoid operation, double pneumonia, abdominal surgery, and whooping cough. This was before antibiotics. In the hospital many weeks, he was not expected to live. This left Jerry with a lifetime anxiety disorder and a lot of pain in the spiritual realm.

When Jerry was home two weeks, I was pregnant with Michelle. It was a horrifically difficult pregnancy and I was in the hospital five times with no health insurance. We managed to pay the bills. That summer, Jerry went to school and worked at Safeway. I went to school, and worked downtown. I drove 75 miles each day for us to manage this. I was sick every mile. At five months pregnant, I weighed 90 pounds. In August of 1954, I received my Bachelor of Science degree. I had decided to become a teacher, because I had married a teacher. Jerry and I would both spend many years teaching school – elementary grades, and later, Junior High.

We had three daughters. Michelle, our oldest, had really serious health issues. I had vomited the whole nine months I was pregnant with her. When she was born, my life of vomiting ended. I was free, but she had severe projectile vomiting of most of her meals, until she was three. This led to her serious under-weight issues. Our middle daughter, Laura, never walked, but only ran. Our youngest daughter, Jennie, born nine years after Michelle, was nick-named "Ran" because she became a track star. It was a handful. Jerry and I committed ourselves to being good parents and to quality teaching with integrity.

During those early years, from the time Michelle was age seven, until she was age 18, I led a Campfire group, which grew to 15 girls. We had Campfire Saturday mornings every two weeks, at our house. One night we had a slumber party and a girl named Judy put her knee through the patio door and broke it. At the same time, my husband was trying to repair the broken dishwasher. It was two o'clock in the morning.

There was a lot of creative joy with the girls, and enough trouble to keep me on my toes. We made it through their Campfire years.

There are some things I learned that I will share with you in the chapter coming. It is important that I've laid the ground work; so that you might understand the distance I had to travel to be well enough to fulfill the call when the Lord said "Go up, and give your life to full-time Christian service."

CHAPTER 3

Facing the Darkness Within Us

I did not know I was in a battle for my life at 17 years of age. I had given up and did not expect God to be forgiving or merciful. I had not experienced mercy as a child, and I did not understand that He works in the darkness to bring the light.

Deep, profound insecurity was central to my being. I kept trying to manage an unmanageable life. There were wonderful days, days of adventure, courage, bright days, but there were even more dark days.

My depression deepened year after year. Still, outwardly coping, I was meeting obligations. We went to church every Sunday, and usually Sunday school, too. We did what seemed to be the right things to do, but my husband and I were lost in the abyss of anxiety, depression and our own inner illnesses.

I think I've said enough that you get the idea. It felt like a losing battle, and the darkness continued to grow. Finally, after 16 years of struggle with a life that was headed for hell, and with a God whom I loved, but who could not return love to me, something had to give, and something did!

My breakdown became more profound. I found myself hopelessly running away. I turned to my husband and said, "Put me in a mental hospital." Praise the Lord, he did!

The lessons I learned in the mental hospital were some of the most valuable lessons of my lifetime. I was there 12 days, rooming with a woman who had slashed both her wrists to the bone. She was soon going on trial for the murder of her husband.

There was no treatment plan, only drugs. Group therapy never took place. I was in the hospital to find myself!

Thus, I did make a decision to work on a treatment plan that I developed myself. I took a sheet of paper, and drew stick figures of my mother, my father, and myself. I put this picture in context of my childhood, my development, and my present dilemma. I enclose, on the next page, a copy of this picture that you might see how carefully I had to spell out the solution for my recovery.

I could see that my mother was too large in my life. My father was too small and ran away. I was too dependent upon my mother, and thus remained in the insecurity of profound fear. I was very small. I had never put myself in the kind of inner responsibility that needed to take place now.

I asked for my father to come to the hospital and meet with me. When he came, his first words were: "Why are you doing this to me?" I asked my father if he had ever told my mother he loved her. His answer was: "Hell no. Why should I lie?" They had been married 37 years.

As I worked on my treatment plan, I discovered the need for balance. I was 33 years old. I needed to get down from mother and grow up myself. I needed to get to my father for some answers. It would mean my peace and my freedom to prefer neither my mother nor my father. I was blessed to have each. I had to keep myself responsible for my own life and my own behavior. This is exactly what happened, and within a few years of working this plan consistently and effectively, I had balance, and wellness.

The second significant decision I made in the mental hospital was as follows: One day, I said to some of the women that were there, "Let's go in the laundry room, behind the door and have group." There was no place to find out who we were and what

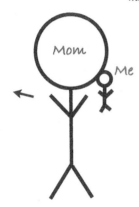

The problem I found in myself at the Psychiatric ward.

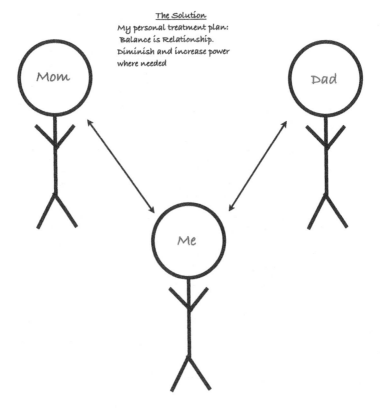

was going on. This was the rudimentary beginning of something I later called group therapy. It was powerful. We began to share one another's burdens, and at least show some basic concern for one another's wellbeing.

One must keep in mind that in those days, psychiatrists gave pills, counselors were rare, and pastors, in my experience, did not know how to help, or did not want to get involved. (Perhaps, the pastors were struggling with their own imbalances.) How could anyone help another balance if they, too, were unbalanced?

This was an extremely important event, to go to the hospital, to search out and to find myself. I did not care for the psychiatrist at all. He had no interest in me, and I wasn't well enough to have much interest in him. Bless my mother, she called my OBGYN, Dr. Thomas, and, without charge, he came to the hospital and met with me over his lunch hour. I considered that meeting one of the great miracles of my lifetime. My doctor significantly gave me respect. He raised the life of a human being from the dead.

The third, and greatest decision I made in the psychiatric ward was to throw myself upon God's mercy. I loved God profoundly. I had been taught, from early childhood, I could not be forgiven. My mother always said, "I would like to forgive you, but I cannot." My life had grown darker and darker, and I was engulfed with spiritual sinfulness. In that hospital room, I made a core decision that I would do what was right in God's eyes. I was not asking for salvation. I was not asking to be saved. I was asking to do what was right in His eyes. Thus, I had a new relationship with God that would affect all the days of my life. God would be the final judge of who I was, and where I would go. I began to love God with all my heart, soul, mind, and strength. He slowly took me unto Himself.

I took medication for about three months, and then I was ready to go off of it. I never saw the psychiatrist again, but I had the direction of my healing well in hand. Patiently, slowly, I required of myself to learn and practice this profound balance, *"You must love the Lord your God with all your heart, with all your soul, with all your strength, and with all your mind, and your neighbor as yourself."* (Luke 10:27)

During the next year, the darkness was a little less. I had some calmness, but I was still quite withdrawn from what was going on around me. I could seem to cope, but I was still lost. My hidden inner love of God stayed profound.

In 1968, my mother suggested that we go together on a trip to the Middle East: Turkey, Athens, a five- day Greek island cruise including Patmos, Cairo, and Israel.

Believe it or not, this journey to the Middle East was $1,750 for guides, meals, and plane fare – total!

When I was ten years old, my parents encouraged me to buy a life insurance policy. I paid $30 a year for 20 years. I had that policy and I cashed it in. It paid for a lot of the journey ahead. It was a turning point. At the time, I was still barely at "survival" level.

Something in my spirit began to awaken, but it was extremely slow. I was a chain smoker. I had dark circles under my eyes, and I looked like a survivor of a concentration camp. I knew what I was. I still did not know who God was.

The night before, on the way to the Island of Patmos, where St. John wrote the book of Revelation, my mother and I decided to read the whole book of Revelation for the first time. I read most of it to her out loud. The next day, we took donkeys up to the place where Saint John agonized to give us his final glimpse of the power of the mercy of God.

We flew into Israel late at night. The following morning, a guide named Shmuel Sternberg picked us up at the hotel and drove us, seeing sites along the way, up the coast towards the Galilee. Our first stop was at Caesarea on the Mediterranean, the Roman city where Pontius Pilate once lived and ruled Judea. There is a great amphitheatre there and our guide, whom we called Sam, went down on the stage and sang the famous aria from the opera, Pagliacci. This was a remarkable event for my mother and me, as we had shared the love of music and the opera in my childhood. It became a signature event in each of our lives.

We finally came to the Jordan River. It was October. It was evening. The moon was out. The guide, Sam, asked, "Do you want to stop at the Jordan River?" We both said, "Yes." When we came to the Jordan, all three of us took off our shoes and went into the water. This is the watershed experience of my entire lifetime. Everything and all that happened later, evolved from this defining moment. My life would be before the Jordan and after the Jordan River.

We were just standing in the water. We sang a couple of hymns, and then we sang Brahm's Lullaby. We got out of the water. I got in the car and something inside of me completely broke. The wall between God and myself was gone.

Without any warning, I came to know that Jesus had allowed me to stand in a place where He stood, in the Jordan River. The light came in. I was forgiven. But more than that, I was accepted. I was accepted exactly as I was. There were no requests for changes. There were no endless lists of things I should do or shouldn't do. I was completely free of a lifetime of fear and shame.

There are no words to adequately describe the powerful fall of that wall, and the intimacy with God and Christ that followed. God became my Father; Christ, the one who set me free. I began to softly cry.

Three days later, we were in Bethany, East Jerusalem, at the Tomb of Lazarus. We walked into the tomb where Lazarus had been raised. I asked the first question of my Father in Heaven." Was this really the tomb of Lazarus?" He answered gently, "Go and find out."

Here was a profound God who didn't say "yes" or "no," but let me find what is lost. My faith would be developed and empowered through that freedom.

When I got home, I was a different person. I cried for joy for one year. It poured out of me endlessly. My husband did not know what to make of it. But I knew what it was. I knew my character was permanently changed.

No matter how hard the road ahead, I knew I would never have to go back into the life of hell.

When you've been one way for a long time, often people do not expect to see you any other way. I did not look for the approval of others, for I had the approval of my Father in Heaven; His blessing, His peace upon me. I was no longer dependent or needy.

One day, our church called and asked me if I would teach the Gospel of John for an adult Bible study. I had not even read the Gospel of John. My familiarity with the Bible was almost non-existent. When I had tried to read it from the standpoint of being in hell, I could not understand the Bible at all.

It was a great blessing to discover how much the Word of God could influence my life and the lives of others. I will always be grateful for this first assignment given in His Word.

There was a man in that Sunday school class who really enjoyed the class. Ten years later, he wrote me a letter saying he had been praying for me every day for ten years. God chooses whom he chooses.

I loved teaching school. I became a lover of children, a lover of learning. I began to have experiences that lifted me up instead of creating experiences that pushed me down. My own experiences had pushed me down. I grew and grew and grew and I became a better teacher. My love for children would be profound!

It is very significant that I was a substitute teacher for 18 years. It is key to my training. I learned what it would be like to substitute for Jesus, instead of trying to be the teacher. I learned what it was like because I learned how to be a good substitute for hundreds of teachers. I taught almost every day. I learned to teach the way the teacher wanted me to teach. I learned to give full measure, and running over. If there were papers that needed to be corrected, even papers I hadn't assigned, I corrected them. I corrected them all. I tried to leave the room in better order. I always taught the children how special and important their teacher really was. I taught for the teacher, not for myself. Later, I would see clearly this was the training Jesus had offered me, "You will teach for Me. You will never be the teacher, for I am the teacher."

Who is our teacher? Is it not the Lord Himself? It is He who has made us. It is He who will train us, and it is He who raises us up.

In 1968, 1972 and 1974, I made trips with my mother, our daughter, Michelle, and a couple of friends to the Middle East, always including Israel. I was growing in my understanding of Biblical lands. Sam Sternberg and his family became lifetime friends. In 1972, I left our 17 year-old daughter, Michelle, with his wife, who spoke no English, and his daughter, Etty. She stayed a week with them and then flew home by herself, having to get a hotel and change planes in Brussels. I went on to Italy, continuing to learn, to seek and find.

My gratitude had started, but truly, it needed a great deal of development, for I still felt negative and conflicted in many areas of my private life. I still struggled with my pernicious need to be right. I never saw it that way, but I'm sure others did.

Breaking free of bondages is never easy. It would be fair for me to tell you one very powerful breaking of bondage. One day, I realized we went to church because my mother taught me to go to church, but I was not going to church because I longed to go to church, or because it was deeply and profoundly important to me or my family. Our attendance was human obedience, not a divine call.

I met with the family and we decided we would not go to church, but have church at home. In the spiritual realm, I decided the Lord would have to give me longing for the church. I was not rejecting the church, I was desiring to long for it with all of my being, so that when the church was given back to me, it would remain of great value and never compromised in me again.

Every Sunday my mother would call and say, "Did you go to church today?" I would say, "No." She would say, "I didn't bring you up that way." Two years passed, and the Lord heard my prayer. He gave me a profound love and honoring, not only of my own church, but of the church as a whole. I began to know the church as something beyond my personal borders. I began to know it, not as an institution. I began to know the church as the intimacy of the sword of the spirit, the healing of divisions.

Around this time, I had a very significant dream that I have never forgotten. I was walking along a long trail at the Oregon Coast, and there seemed to be a little glen off to the left of the trail. I went over and looked into the glen. There was a glowing church, as if it was solid gold. The Lord spoke to me in that dream and said, "This is my church."

I struggled to understand people other than myself. I really thought, from my childish mind, that everyone was good. At least, I wanted them to be. But, I discovered that everyone is an individual, and that it is not easy to find balance and courage in each of our relationships. Sometimes, I was deeply disappointed, and other times hurt, and I'm sure at times, I was hurtful to others. I did not hesitate to learn the cost of friendship. There is a bigger picture here – something very important. It would take me a long struggle to understand the bigger picture. Jesus did not say you shall love your friends as you love yourself. He said, "You shall love your neighbor as you love yourself." Slowly, this began to be written on my soul, and breathed into my spirit until I had no listlessness in my spirit. Most of my neediness for friendship was completely over.

I want to say one more thing that was not resolved for several years, but I believe it belongs in this place of resolutions. As I developed and strengthened in ministry, I had this longing, this need, to have one special friend who would hear my cry and understand me. I said to the Lord, "You had your John, and I need mine." I'm not talking about a male, I'm talking about that one supportive friend that will go through the crucifixion with you. After ten years of discussion, the Lord finally spoke to me very firmly and said, "Everyone is your John. I never want to hear any more about it." This was the empowering WORD. Everyone was my neighbor!

Before I finish this chapter, the question remains, where do you fit in? I have offered some testimonies. They seem to be about Bettie, and here and there, they seem to be about God. They are about God! But, where do you fit in? The lawyer asked very, very deliberately, in the Parable of the Good Samaritan, "Who is my neighbor?" Jesus told a story and finished the story by pointing out the question is not, who is your neighbor; the question is, who are you in relationship to your neighbor? This book is about a relationship between us; you, the reader and myself. What will come to pass in this divine relationship?

CHAPTER 4

The In-Between Years

As you know, I came home from the Holy Land with a permanent new relationship with a Living God. I still had to live with myself. I smoked a great deal. We had three daughters. I led the Campfire group. I dealt with the pain of marital and relational issues, and I continued to substitute teach, grades one through nine.

About a year after my return, I became convinced that I needed to quit smoking. I had never tried to quit smoking. I had smoked a great deal for 17 years. I had never learned to be effective with my own "no," as my mother slapped me whenever I said no.

I became convinced that one does not just quit smoking, but one must have a treatment plan, as I had discovered, for my family issues, in the psychiatric hospital. Thus, I developed a quit-smoking treatment plan as follows: I would give my cigarettes to the Lord for Christmas. During the following six months, I would keep an open package of cigarettes on the kitchen counter, and speak to that package every time I wanted to touch it with a powerful "NO." I determined I would never quit again. I would not have a small puff if someone offered me a million dollars. I was giving up cigarettes unto the Lord, permanently, for my lifetime.

I followed my treatment plan. Late Christmas Eve I was weeping over the loss of cigarettes for they had become such a part of who I was. I suppose I had separation anxiety. The first four days were very difficult. I found going to the movies and spending several hours there, where I couldn't smoke, was helpful. My determination was very great, and my "NO" was very powerful. The addiction to cigarettes was finished. Rubbing ice on my arms and eating raw apples gave small relief. "Not my will, but thy will be done," gave the greatest relief. Shortly thereafter, I was freed from an addiction to coffee.

God broke through my barriers. He came to me bringing a true baptism of the Spirit. It was only a beginning to permanent change. There were many areas of my life that needed to change, or develop. There was still pain, the continued pressure of the programming of my past. My desire to be free of the encumbrances of long years of depression was the antidote of all pain. Healing increased daily.

"*If God is for us, who can be against us?*" (Romans 8:31) Sometimes many are. They knew you as you were, but they don't know you as you now are. Inside of me was a great struggle and longing to know the Kingdom of God.

Around 1970, I was at another low point in my life. Things were falling apart in my marriage. I was bewildered as to how to handle the problems I faced.

I went to the Oregon Coast, and spent two days alone. I was not at the coast to walk the beach, but to know the will of God and His travail over my spirit. I was there to be trained. I was on an inward journey. "*Not my will, but His will be done.*" (Luke 22:42)

I cried most of the first day, and finally fell asleep that night. I had one of the most significant dreams of my lifetime.

In the dream, I found myself in a large railroad station waiting room. There were groups of men sitting on different benches. Each of them had a Bible in their hand. Group after group, drew me close, and told me the importance of the Word of God. They said they had known my grandfather, who had taught them the Word. They held the Bible up for my eyes to see. Later, I found an actual large photograph of my grandfather's Bible Class. He taught 150 men in that class. He worked for the railroad.

As I was coming out of the dream, I heard the distinct words, "Read the Book of Job."

I had to find a Gideon Bible and obey the voice, as spoken to me. I read the entire Book of Job in one day.

The Book of Job is long, and much was going on in the book that I did not understand. It was an act of obedience to press through to the finish. I did not speed read. I looked for what the story meant.

I became, impressed by the Spirit, urgent to know the Word of God. As I had awakened from the dream, I was also told to study the Old Testament. When I returned home, I spent several weeks trying to locate a class in the Old Testament. There seemed to be none available. All I could locate was a course in the New Testament at Portland State University. But the words I had heard were specifically that I was to take a course in the Old Testament. I spent several days trying to decide what to do. I still had young children. Finally, it was pouring down rain, and it was the last day of registration. I drove, by faith, with the children, to Portland State. Walking into the gym where registration was held, I was immediately asked what course I was seeking. I told them I was looking for the course in the New Testament because that was what was cited in the catalog. Only God knew I was looking for the course in the Old Testament.

Unbelievably, the registrar's voice spoke up and said, "There has been a mistake in the catalog. The course is not in the New Testament. It is "The Old Testament and its Historical Background." If I had not chosen to go, the events to follow in my life would not have occurred. So much is at stake when the course of blind faith is chosen.

Dr. John Phillip King came from Oregon State once a week to teach this class at Portland State University. He had been a Southern Baptist Pastor, left that work, and decided to be a college professor, teaching Biblical Form Criticism. I might note that Form Criticism tends to evaluate the scriptures to seek the nuances which make them difficult to accept literally. The word criticism is not used to reflect upon the Word of God. Form criticism was a popular theological movement at that time. Largely, German scholars had many theories.

Now, Form Criticism did not heal anything inside of me. But by God's grace, I was patient. My mother and I were taking the class together. She was as anxious to learn something as I was. We were seeking to know God.

Professor King said, "Open the Bible to Amos, Chapter 1," and he began to read to us Amos Chapters 1 and 2, the Courtroom of God over nations. He did not read it the way the Bible was read in church. He read it from a different realm, a realm I had never heard in my life. The words came to life and became the power of God filling our ears. When he came to Amos 2, verse 6, "Yahweh says this: For the three crimes, the four crimes, of Israel, I have made my decree and will not relent: because they have sold the virtuous man for silver and the poor man for a pair of sandals." These words exploded inside of my body. Here we were in a class of more than 25 people we did not know; but, it was irresistible, my mother and I stood and clapped our hands. It was my first experience with Biblical joy.

When I heard the words, from God's mouth, spoken by Amos, I went into a shock that was profound and permanent. Where were the classes to develop that kind of faith in God? How could one find them? Where were the teachers that knew the voice of the Lord was true, powerful, and unending in His call for change? It was this shock that led me to decide to go on and take a course in the New Testament, and a third course about Jesus. After that, what would I do with what I learned? Theories died in that class as God's voice penetrated the very core of my being.

I decided to teach what I learned in the Old Testament class weekly to someone else the next day. I taught two seniors in their home. I taught from the realm of faith, not theory or speculation. This is very key. Often we learn, store it, but never do anything with what we learn. My goal was not only to learn, but to pass on the Word of faith to others. The Word must become life and bring about permanent repentant change. Later, I would call these faith actions.

Evidently, I was such an effective teacher, that the woman, whose name was Elda, asked if she could take the class with me when it came time for the New Testament. So, in teaching the Word of God, my first students were senior citizens. They were people usually left alone, childless, but kind and hospitable.

I have an adamant faith that we are all to teach the Word, but no one has told us. Perhaps we can only comprehend a small amount of scripture, but if that becomes life, then it becomes life-giving. It needs to be passed, not only to this generation, but forward to all generations.

I became a Bible teacher when the classes were over because something needed to be released in others as well. I started a class at our church. I taught the 60 weeks of Old Testament and New Testament over a two year period. It would reinforce what I had learned, and it would give me an opportunity to develop the hunger to learn more. It also provided structure. I was not doing biblical devotional reading. I was doing biblical life-changing reading and teaching. The classes were life changing for each of the 30 people who attended them!

At the end of that two-year period, I made a profound decision. I would take the training out of the church, and put it into public education. I would seek to find a way to do this. I wrote up a curriculum for three classes: Old Testament, New Testament, or Historical Background of the Middle East. I presented the curriculum to the Portland Community College coordinator for adult education. He shocked me when his first choice was for me to teach New Testament. I had never expected this course to be accepted. I had only believed I must set out and propose it. It became the first Bible training in public education in Oregon. By faith, I assured him, as I walked out the door, "there will never be problems from these classes." And, there never were!

It could be shocking to the reader that I did not teach the first two classes of the Bible at Portland Community College; my husband did! I was in the Middle East. Before I left, I said to him, "You need to find 12 people who will register to take the class, or they will cancel it." Knowing little or nothing about the Bible, he found 12 people, and when I came home, I was blessed to see his genuine commitment to make a difference with me.

However, when he said there was a pastor in the class, I about freaked out. What did I know about the Bible compared to a pastor? It was very scary for me!

Now, the Pastor had a long history of not doing well. His wife was in the hospital at that very time. They were very poor. They had two children and almost nothing.

By the Lord's grace, God did His work in their lives through some gifts. It was hard to co-sign on a car for them, but I also sought the day they would buy their first house. On their first Christmas, we brought a table, chairs, food and gifts.

They gave me a Christmas gift. It was a homemade gift, a small piece of wood with four nails in the wood and some Christmas decorations on the wood. This gift was a place to hang keys on our wall. In this way, they received peace, and I began to cherish keys to the Kingdom of God as we shared in one another's lives. Twenty-five years later, they came from Texas to visit and express their gratitude.

I studied the Bible 20 hours a week for 10 years. This included other materials that would help me: a Bible Atlas, a Bible dictionary, and some Bible Commentaries. When I assigned the students to read the Book of Jeremiah for the following week, I always read the same book in its entirety. This was difficult, as some of the books were very long. I did not read to prepare my lesson. I read to place upon myself the reading assignment I had given to others. It was my way of balancing with these students.

My husband had to tolerate a lot during this period of time. He wanted to go to Trailblazer basketball games, but I had to read the Bible lessons. I worked out how I would do it. I would take the Bible to the basketball game, and I would read the lesson during the basketball game. That may sound very rude and peculiar, but Jerry and I knew that it was important to be together and to also do what the Lord laid on my heart to do.

The third year of teaching the Bible class at Portland Community College was a turning point. Suddenly, 25 people showed up from one church. Instead of having one class, I would have two classes, and eventually, three classes each week.

There are three stories I want to share about the years of Bible teaching. The youngest students who attended the Bible class were 6 and 8 years old. They sat in front. They paid attention. Even though they were sitting for more than two hours, they were fully connected. My love of children, and their love of being there, was the greatest of gifts to each of us. Later, they would go into full-time Christian work, and be an influence upon many.

The second story is about a woman whom, when she introduced herself, said she was an atheist. She had decided to come to study the Bible and see what it was all about. The class was very accepting of people with different viewpoints, and no one ever pushed an agenda or a spirit of evangelism on anyone. It was a place of learning, and a place of rest.

At the end of the 10 weeks, I always asked the class, "What was the most important thing you learned this term?" When it became her turn, she had the softest look in her eyes. Something had been born in her. Her soft voice said, "God has a Name, and His Name is Yahweh." Her faith in that Name would permanently touch my faith in that Name as well.

The third story is about a man from India, a Hindu, a professor from a university in India. He was working on a research grant in Oregon for three years. He came only to the New Testament classes. He would interrupt the class very often to ask questions. Since I had travelled most of the biblical lands, I showed many slides.

I did not see the man then for a year. Finally, on the last day of class the following year, as I was about to leave the school, he walked in the door. He said, "I have become a Christian, and I'm going back to India. I want you to give me a copy of all of the slides you showed in class; for it was in this way that I became convinced that Christianity is the only historically-based religion in the world. It is not about myth, but about true and honest history." He said he was going back to his country to give this message to the other professors there.

This was a difficult assignment for me. I was getting ready to leave for the Middle East again to lead a tour, and I had little time to choose the slides, get them copied, and get them to him. I invited him over to our house. We went through all of the slides, and he picked out the ones he wanted. I helped him with the locations, and the messages within each picture. Before I left, the material was in his hands. Off to India went a teacher of the Word of God.

My husband, Jerry, attended all of the Bible classes annually. He had been the first teacher.

In 1975, I came to know about the baptism of the Holy Spirit. Our family belonged to the Congregational Church in Beaverton, and the Holy Spirit was not a topic that ever came from our church training. I had never heard of it. I knew nothing about the Holy Spirit. I had two close friends who were sisters. Their first cousin was Dr. Bob Frost.

Bob was a professor at a university in California, as I recall, a science professor. Bob Frost was famous by 1975 as a charismatic speaker, encouraging people to receive the baptism of the Holy Spirit. He was speaking at a church downtown, and his cousins, my friends, asked me to go with them. We sat in the front row.

It was the first time in my life I had ever heard a man of faith speak. It isn't that I was ignorant of faith, I was searching for it. I had found nothing but opinions and educated guesses. He was a simple man of great faith, and his great faith and simplicity brought something into me that no one would ever take away. He had received the baptism of the Holy Spirit and the gift of tongues while making peanut butter sandwiches for his children. This impressed me greatly.

I asked to meet Bob at my friend's house after the public meeting. I asked him many questions. I believed I must have received the Holy Spirit in the Jordan River in 1968. As Bob and I looked at the gifts of the Holy Spirit, I saw that I had many of those gifts. What was the gift of tongues? Was it that I did not have the Holy Spirit?

Dr. Frost assured me that I did receive the Holy Spirit in the Jordan River in 1968. The gift of tongues is listed as a lesser gift, but he said it was really an important gift because it opens up the Word in a powerful way.

I agreed for he and his wife to pray over me to receive this gift. It did not come easily. I did not suddenly speak in a full language, but it did come. Later, I would ask the Lord, "What is my language?" He said, "The language you were given is too deep for words." Later, while in the Holy Land, I noticed all the words coming out of my mouth were coming from deep inside me, no longer from my head. The change was permanent.

Some years later, my husband, Jerry, and two of our daughters, received the Baptism of the Holy Spirit.

Because we, as a family, went to a liberal congregational church,

I began to hunger and thirst for a place of anointed faith. We were not led to leave our church. Two of our pastor's children committed suicide during the time he was our pastor. It was not the time to go find another church, but it was time to find the lamp of spiritual freedom in a spirit-filled church.

I decided, every three or four months, I would go to a church in Portland – a mixed race African American church called Maranatha. It became rather humorous because I would say to close friends, "Are we going to Maranatha tonight?" And we knew we were to go to Maranatha. Each time the power of the Holy Spirit touched us, and brought us hope.

Now, in 1975, something unexpected happened to me at Maranatha. I would not understand it until years later, but this was the introduction moment of my future work in Africa.

A pastor, Wendell Wallace, was there, and he was praying for people at the altar. It was two days before Christmas. My husband and I sat together on the main floor. I decided to go up for prayer. I was the last one in a long line. Ninety-five percent of the people who went up were African Americans.

When the man in front of me went to the altar, Pastor Wallace asked him what he was seeking, and the man said, "A triple portion of the Spirit of Elisha." Pastor Wallace had a very large bottle of oil in his hand, and he took that bottle and poured the oil all over the man's body. All over his head, and down his body, the man dripped oil. I was standing several feet away, perhaps two yards away. All of a sudden, I found myself flat on the floor, without any warning. I had fallen without any pain, and I was lying, a white woman, in the midst of a sea of black faces, with my arms outstretched, "Slain in the Spirit."

"Slain in the Spirit" is not a religious term; it is a holy event when God wants to get our attention. He has to get us out of the way entirely, and He has to put us into a place where He can bring us to His rest, to His holy place, the temple of the Living God. It is not a voluntary event. I did not volunteer to be "Slain in the Spirit." It happens to you unexpectedly, and it is something that does not happen over and over again, but only at a moment God has chosen for this to take place.

Being a Congregationalist, I knew nothing about being "Slain in the Spirit," but as I lay there on the floor, I could have lain there for the rest of my life. It was the difference between this world and the world to come. I knew my arms were out-stretched, and I began to chuckle, for I thought to myself, "This must look very strange having this white woman lying on the floor of the church with her arms outstretched in the form of a cross." I remember thinking that because it was a shocking event to me; perhaps it was to others as well.

These are the In-Between Years. The year to come would bring The Call.

CHAPTER 5

The Call

In 1974, my mother and I were in a Romanian restaurant in Tel Aviv with Sam Sternberg (Bar-El), his wife, Fannie, and their son Avi. We had been to visit the Sinai Peninsula and the famous Mt. Sinai. Sinai was a land that was captured by Israel during Six Day War. The bus was full of Israelis who wanted to see first-hand the land they had won in the war. As we drove through the Sinai, we found the remnants of a very huge battle that had taken place between Israel and Egypt in 1973. We were the only Christians in a bus full of Israelis.

On this first visit to Mt. Sinai in 1974, I discovered how difficult it was to climb the mountain. 3,750 steps up and down, later I would learn it was five miles up and five miles down. No wonder I hardly made it!

In those days, Mt. Sinai was a very desolate area. There were no tourist facilities. You stayed at the ancient Greek Monastery that was built in the 300's. You were with the monks that were there. You started to climb at 1:00 in the morning. We got back about 11:00 a.m. I will talk more about Mt. Sinai later, but this was my first Sinai experience. The climb reached into my life and became a permanent part of the lessons I needed to Mature in the Faith.

Back to the dinner with the Bar-El's in the restaurant. Sam leaned over towards me and said, "I believe now you're ready to lead tours." It was my third trip to the Middle East. I had studied and worked hard to understand the region, its culture and historic background. Opening the Bible in each place, I discovered much more than just words I discovered the life of the Word!

With his words, I was a little taken aback, as I didn't expect to lead tours. I still was shy and not very socially developed; however, his words stuck in me and I decided to lead a tour to the Middle East in 1976. The tour would visit the places that had the most power in my conversion to a wealth of faith.

Now, it is one thing to decide to lead a tour, but something else to build a group that would travel together, and be willing to be gone for three weeks on a long and difficult journey. Finally, after many challenges to my faith, I knew, without a shadow of a doubt, we were going. The tour group was made up of twenty-six people, which included seven men. My husband, Jerry, agreed to help me lead the tour. Twenty-six of us left for the Middle East to travel to Syria, Jordan, Israel and Rome.

Now what made the group unusual may sound strange to your thinking, but as I saw it, there were thirteen Pharisees, and thirteen sinners in this group. Some had come from very fundamental religious beliefs (long hair for women, arms covered, no jewelry), the others came from a life of "do what you want," sometimes a reckless freedom. It was a great challenge to be with these twenty-six people, and to stand as a bridge between them. Each one received this unusual gift from God, Himself.

Our trouble began on the way to Syria. As we were due to arrive in Damascus, Syria, very late in the evening, my husband came to me and said he was sitting next to the editor of the Christian Science Monitor, who had just told him there was a gun battle and a terrorist incident at the New Semeramis Hotel the day before. Now it just so happened, we were going to the New Semeramis Hotel for four nights.

I alerted the seven men in our group in case we might run into great difficulty. We got off the plane, headed into Damascus, and opened the hotel doors into a shocking mess.

Having flown over twenty hours, not to mention the lack of sleep before we left, it was a very big assignment to put ourselves together and do what was best for everyone. The room assignments were unusual, as many of the doors were off the rooms, and in a couple of the rooms, the sinks had been shot off the wall. Curtains were on the floor. The life-size cardboard stewardess sign standing in the lobby had been shot full of holes. In spite of all of this, we came together and did what was good and right to help one another. It was the beginning of twenty-six people working together. It was God's provision for us to be healed of our divisions.

This is the story of what happened. Two days before, five terrorists had entered the hotel and held all of the guests staying there hostage. The Syrian government sent in a brigade of soldiers to rescue the hostages, and to capture the terrorists. As we understood, they were successful, and the terrorists were hanged, in the square in front of our hotel, the day before we arrived.

After two days at the New Semeramis, there was a bomb threat to blow up the hotel. We were relocated to a local flophouse in Damascus.

As we headed to Jordan, the agent in charge of our group informed me we would be staying outside of Amman, in Dibbin National Park. There was no room in Amman for us to stay. This was fifty miles off course from where we were supposed to be. They were rather primitive facilities, and they looked as if they had not been used for a long time.

In exchange for this inconvenience, the agent said he would provide cars for any of us who wanted to go to Petra the next day. He said he would be there early in the morning, and that it was a long, hard journey. Three carloads of people left Dibbin National Park late in the morning. (Middle-Eastern time seemed to be late or later.)

Due to the fact that the driving would be long, and the fall day short, the drivers decided to drive more than 100 mph. They also decided to stop periodically to have a drink. It seemed to be alcohol, and I was very nervous about what was going on. There were five of us in each car, and my husband was in a different car than I was. A young mother, Linnea, and I were sitting in the back seat of the first car. She and I were fervently in prayer. Suddenly she turned to me, and cried out. She said the Lord had asked her if she would be willing to give up her only son. She struggled greatly. He was her little boy at home, just over three years of age. What God had asked was more than she could bear. We bore it together; kept this in our hearts, and deeply pondered what this meant.

When we arrived at Petra, we saw the area, ate a light dinner, and then started back to Amman. I was in the first car and we arrived back at 8:00 p.m. The agent arrived and he and I anxiously waited for the other two cars. They did not arrive. Finally, at midnight, the second and third cars did come. There had been an accident. The second car had blown a tire and gone off the road, nearly into a ravine. One of our women had some injuries. The car had to wait for the Jordanian military to come, pull them out, and get the car operable to continue the journey. The other car stood by on the road and waited. Can you imagine waiting four hours, knowing the conditions? It was the beginning of learning there is nothing you can do in many situations, and this must lead to absolute trust in God Himself.

The next morning, we headed out at 5:00 a.m. for the Jordan/Israel border. We were to cross early into Israel. When we got to the border, we found many tour busses loaded with tourists and luggage. We sat on the bus and waited.

Unexpectedly, we were going to wait until nearly dark that night, and then we would have to return to Amman. The Jordanians had decided to cause a border incident because the Israelis had closed the border for two days for Yom Kippur. Jordan closed the border to create inconvenience for the Israelis and their tourists. These were "border games," and on our side, the games were a stark reminder of the reality between Israel and her neighbor.

It was more than 100 degrees all day. We still had a woman with some undetermined injury, a very tired group of people, and no access to food or water. The buses turned on no air conditioning. The heat and the hours pressed down upon us. The Lord was melting our people into one group. It was no longer who was "right." The greatest test that any of us face is to know God is right. Trust Him!

In the later morning, I was able to take our people into the waiting hall where the military leader was sitting. He seemed to be in charge of the border. He had a large fan in his office, and we sat in there for a considerable amount of time. While I was in there, I looked intently at this man. I don't believe I was staring. I believe it was beyond staring. I was examining him without saying a word. Later, he examined me.

In the middle of the afternoon, this same man came to me and said, "If we allow some to cross the border, would you like to be one of the groups crossing?" I said, "Yes." Later, I would be ashamed of this, but at that moment, I did not understand that which would come upon me.

One or two buses did cross into Israel. As we were going towards the Allenby Bridge to cross the Jordan River, two busloads of Palestinians pulled ahead of us onto the very narrow bridge, the border between Israel and Jordan. There were negotiations taking place. If those buses were allowed to cross, then the others would be allowed. We were stuck on the bridge for two hours.

In the meantime, inside our bus, we had been over-loaded with two other buses full of people. We were sitting three-deep, and the luggage was piled in the aisles. Some people were lying on the luggage. The door was shut. The air conditioning was not on, and claustrophobia was pushing in on us.

I finally pushed outside to find out what was happening. In this way, I was at least able to come back and report the situation that seemed to be taking place.

After long hours of negotiations making little progress, we were taken back to the Jordanian border, and we were released to go back to Amman.

Our agent, knowing what we had been through the night before, suddenly appeared. This was a great blessing. I said to him, "We must get back to Amman immediately because we must find a place to stay. These people cannot sit up all night." He said, "I know a very old hotel, and we will get you there." In the meantime, I left my husband in charge of the bus, and I jumped in the agent's car. Three Jordanian military jumped in the same car with their weapons thrown across their laps, one of them, the man who had asked if I wanted to cross the border. As we were hurtling up to Amman, it was already night, and I asked myself, "What in the world am I doing here with a car full of strangers carrying their weapons?"

The agent kept his word, and we came to the old Philadelphia Hotel. They received us. The dining room was closed. There was no food prepared, so they told us we could go into the kitchen and cook if we wanted. We could also make breakfast in the morning before we left, if we wanted to do so. Something was given to compensate for what was lost. We willingly went into the kitchen.

In the morning, we found out that all of the other tourists held at the border were put in hotels where they sat in lobby chairs all night. The event was big news on Jordanian T.V. We were the only group to have beds. In the morning, one of our couples reported there had been an attempt to break into their room, through a window, during the night.

Now, you can imagine that the border was chaos the next day, for there were all the buses from the day before, and all the buses to cross that day. At this point, twice as many people were trying to cross the bridge as in any normal day. I had never come into Israel across the Allenby Bridge. I knew not what to expect on the other side, and my eyes keenly peered in the distance to see if our Israeli bus was there with Sam Sternberg (later, Bar-El) and our driver, Abraham Winberg.

Our Jordanian guide, Little Joe, hopped on the bus, and asked us for the tip. I wanted to tip him over, for he had done nothing but allow us to be exposed to difficult situations. God's grace prevailed over my unwilling spirit, and we gave him grace, a generous tip, kindness from our hearts, and a blessing.

Can you imagine the absolute joy of crossing into the Holy Land? It had indeed become Holy ground. Our bus was waiting. The driver gave us each a drink of water as we got on the bus, and the air conditioning was on--OH WOW!

Daniel, an orthodox Jew, was on the bus waiting for us too. He was part of our tour group, but he had not been allowed to go into the Arab countries, so he could only meet us in Israel. Daniel was the last one to join our group.

It was decided that we would head for Mt. Sinai instead of Jerusalem. After that long wait at the border, and the long two days before, we were suddenly heading again into the wilderness, rather than into the city. I can't tell you how long that drive was, but the roads were not good at all. This journey was an unexpected provision for us to rest on the long ride into the Sinai.

We got to Mt. Sinai late in the evening, had some very basic food given to us by the servants of the Monks, and bedded down in the hostel inside the ancient walls of St. Catherine's Monastery. Cats wandered freely in and out of our rooms.

Arise we must! By 2:00 a.m. we were on our feet and on the

trail up the holy mountain. Small flashlights and big darkness are very challenging on a tough trail. When we were about halfway up, again something very hard happened. Linnea, the young mother of twenty-six, who had suffered from asthma all her life, had a severe asthma attack, and one of her lungs collapsed. Here we were, at about 5,000 feet, with a life and death situation. There were only narrow stairs to carry her down, if necessary, and a primitive first aid station at the monastery was available.

Rita and Darrel Owen came up to Linnea and took her situation to profound prayer. The air came into her lungs, and the healing took place. She climbed to the top, nearly 8,000 feet, and down again safely.

On the way to Sinai, I shared my weakness with the group. I told the story of the head of the border asking me if we wanted to be among the ones to go across. I told him "yes." This was my weakness. For who are we to be more favored than others? I was not willing to lay down that favor. I felt great shame, but great power in being honest with the group. Spiritual bonding was taking place. Our guide, Sam, looked at me with great respect, which has led to our 42-year friendship.

After the climb, we left Mt. Sinai, and went on with the rest of our tour of the Holy Land.

When we arrived at the Jordan River, there were several to be baptized. One was my husband. He had a lifetime terror of water, and he practically died of panic from that terror on the flight over the ocean to Syria. I spoke to him quietly and said that I was going to hold him under the water an extra length of time for his healing. I did as I said, and when he came out of the water, he was free, for the rest of his life, from the fear of water.

Baptism is a very individual experience. When each one was baptized, they were not only baptized for the remission of sins, and to be accepted into the Kingdom of God, they were baptized as individuals, and the words given were to them alone.

When it was time for Linnea's baptism, she went down into the water, and came up transfigured, glorified. I will never forget what happened to Linnea on the whole journey, but most of all what God did to comfort her in the Jordan River.

Finally, it was time for the tour group to have a last night together in Israel at a special banquet. We invited the wives of our guide and driver. When they came in, we applauded them. We felt great joy. We knew the great sacrifices they made year in and year out for their husbands to go out on journeys with tour groups, and not be available to their own families.

Our final stop on the journey was Rome, and from there, my husband took the tour group home. My mother and I flew to London.

What was I doing in London? I was exhausted, overwhelmed, and really wanted to go home. Two days of rest in London were to prepare us for an archaeological study trip to Iraq with Dr. Joan Oates of Cambridge University.

We entered Iraq and studied the Biblical archaeological sites. Iraq is a vital part of the Old Testament stories.

After two or three days in the Baghdad area, we took an overnight train to Mosul. Meanwhile, at the hotel, I was handed a special letter from America.

I opened the letter on the train, and went into great shock. The letter was from the man who was taking my place teaching the Bible classes. He informed me that Linnea's son died two days after she arrived home. The message was brief. This sacrifice had begun on the way to Petra, and the boy's death occurred.

As we came into Mosul, we were in the ancient city of Nineveh. Here was the biblical city where Jonah challenged the Assyrian King.

We came to the walls of ancient Nineveh; walls 12 kilometers long, partially rebuilt, and very high. I was the only person who climbed to the top of the walls. As I stood on the walls and looked out, I found myself not looking at a biblical archaeological site at all. I was looking at children. Yes, children were up there playing. They had their schoolbooks clutched under their arms. In Iraq, at that time, all learning was by rote memorization. Only half of the children were allowed into schools. Every Iraqi child knew six English sentences. We had talked to many children along the road.

As I looked at the children, suddenly my entire mind was interrupted. It was an utter absolute interruption of my mind.
The Lord spoke to me. He said, "Do you see these children?" I said, "Yes, Lord." He said, "Here are the children, where are the teachers? I want you to go home, quit your teaching job, and teach nothing but my Kingdom." I said, "My husband will never agree." He said, "I will take care of that." I said, "All right, I will do it!"

Slowly, I climbed down the path from the wall. The children lined up at the top, watching me. Miraculously, they left a space – a space for the teachers. I know this is true, because I have the picture I took of them that day. When the picture was developed, there was the prophetic Word of God in the children's action.

I did not speak to anyone for several days before and after this event. Later, I would say to the Lord, "Why me?" He said to me, "It is not about you; it is about the prophet Jonah. At the end of the book of Jonah, I asked Jonah a question, 'Am I not to feel sorry for so many people who do not know their right hand from their left hand, let alone all the animals?'" The Lord said to me, "Jonah did not answer My question. You have come. You showed up. The question goes to you." This was a call that had nothing to do with me, and everything to do with God. I was completely shocked. I had not been praying for a new ministry. I had not asked for direction in my life. I was not seeking or questing after a sign or a wonder. I was studying biblical archaeological sites and noticing the lives of children. This call was an absolute, and the response from my side would be when my husband agreed. God had initiated. I received. This must be passed to all generations, for this is the essence of the Gospel. God is merciful.

Three days later, we were in a town called Irbil. It had been a city for 8,000 years, and a most unusual archaeological site, for it had been rebuilt century after century, town after town, one on top of another. Underneath the mound, were 22 civilizations. On top of the mound was the current Irbil, still occupied, still built up. As we walked through the streets of ancient Irbil, my attention was drawn to a little child who was perhaps three years old. She was standing alone in a pile of rubble. She had a small sack in her hand.

The Lord spoke to me a second time. He said, "Do you see this child?" I said, "Yes, Lord." He said, "When I look at the world, they are like this child. They are looking for what is worth saving, but in all the debris of history, no longer know what is valuable and what is not. This is whom you will teach."

Again, the interruption was over, and the assignment had been clarified: "Teach nothing but the Kingdom of God." "This is whom you will teach." As we value the individual we help them find the value of the Kingdom of God.

A week after the time on the Walls of Nineveh at Mosul, we were at Ur. Our Father Abraham and Sarah left Ur nearly 4,000 years ago. We found ourselves, early in the morning, walking out on a large excavated area of ancient Ur. It had been uninhabited since the early years, after the time of Christ. The most visible and impressive site of Ur is the Ziggurat. Ur was a sacred city to the Sumerians. Even as Jerusalem is a Holy City to the Christians and Jews, Ur was a holy city set aside for worship and praise. The Goddess of Ur was named Sin.

As I walked out on the excavation site, down the streets of the houses, the Lord spoke to me a third and final time. He said, "Every thought in your brain is negative and judgmental." I said,

"Yes, Lord." I had been listening to my mind, and it was the truth. He said, "I want you to take each thought, bring it to me, and ask me My thought. In this way, I will change your mind, and break the power of sin that rules your life." I said, "All right, I will do it!"

When I returned home, I told my husband what had occurred. He told me I must do what the Lord had asked me to do.

I wanted to learn more about Robbie's death. I was grieving. As I met with Linnea, this is what she told me. She was home for about two and a half days. Robbie was not sick. During the night, he called her name and she went into his room. It was as if he said "goodbye." Later in the night, he called his father in, and the same thing happened. In the morning, he had passed away. The autopsy later showed there was no cause of death.

In the next two weeks, seventy-two adults and children in their neighborhood received Christ.

It is one thing to be called; it is another to take action. In the next chapter, I will talk about the action.

CHAPTER 6

The Action

I must say, in this book, that many people have asked me how I hear God. There is a difference between hearing God on a daily basis, and being directed by the Holy Spirit, and what happened to me in Iraq.

In Iraq, there was a complete interruption of my mind. It was as if you are listening to a radio or television program, and there is an announcement made that says, "I interrupt this program to make an important announcement." THIS INTERRUPTION WAS ANNOUNCEMENT AND PRONOUNCEMENT. It was absolute, and, therefore, it was clearly implanted, permanently.

Again, I want to say it, so that there is no confusion. He interrupted my life at Nineveh, Irbil, and at Ur. His interruption was a pronouncement desperately needed across the world. After the pronouncement, the life inside of me, the programming, the things I was thinking about, went on as usual. The pause, the silence, the pronouncement, this interruption, was what The Call is about. It was initiated by God, and not sought by myself. If God initiated it, He had to help me develop the work He wanted done!

After my husband said, "You must do what the Lord has asked you to do," I knew this was the will of God. This was definitely a divine appointment, or my husband would never have agreed. It fulfills the scripture, *"When two or more agree, then it is so."* (Matthew 18:19) It puts me under my husband's authority. I was in submission to God's will, and to my husband's will.

It was November, 1976. I needed to finish out the year of substitute teaching I was to do. The work of Good Samaritan Ministries began in 1977. I worked on a Master of Religion Degree at Warner Pacific College. I had started just before I left. In 1979, I finished the degree. Since God, at Irbil, had highly called my attention to "the individual" as the focus of this ministry, this was the direction I took.

I began to meet with people at our home. We had a small bedroom no longer used by the children. It would suffice as an office. It had a door and privacy. This ensured the safety of the people coming.

I was totally unprepared for what happened. Indeed, I was in shock for several years.

A few people did not seek help. An avalanche of people came. Somewhere, deep in the spiritual realm, I knew they came because they heard that I knew God. They wanted to know God, but all they knew was the absolute disaster of their lives.

From 1976 to 1981, I lived the divine assignment given to me at Ur. In my mind, I spoke my thoughts to the Father, and asked Him His thoughts. I asked Him what He had to say. It was a profound time of His intervention in my mind. I was never right once in the whole five years, for His thoughts were far higher than mine. His purpose was beyond my understanding. He corrected my thoughts, and at the end of five years, the power of sin turned off. In my obedience to be corrected, the power that created sin again and again and again, was finally broken.

I found much confusion about our personal sins, and the difference between personal sins and the power of sin itself to rule us. This was not about my personal sins. This was not about my past. This was about breaking the power of sin so that it could no longer control my life. He was gradually giving me trust and the power and authority to teach nothing but the Kingdom of God.

At the end of five years I said to the Lord, "I have nothing else to say." I felt Him smile. He had more to say. He worked on my subconscious mind in dreams, and continued to change me.

When meeting with clients, whom I considered sent to this house by the Lord Himself, I was taught everything I needed to know. I was shown hopelessness, confusion, destructive forces, and the power of the lies and manipulation that live inside human nature. I was totally and absolutely shocked at His hand in this work, and by 1979, there were eight to ten people coming to our home to see me each day.

I sat on a terribly uncomfortable kitchen table chair. The whole set only cost $70, so you can imagine what the chair was like! I took out paper when someone was sitting with me. Together, we began to study their life. At first, this brought me tremendous shock. I began to see trauma, intense levels of suffering, children barely surviving, untold abuse. God did not send the "nice" people here. He sent those who had little or no hope. It was they that needed to learn nothing but the Kingdom of God.

At the end of a year and a half, sitting on that chair, I cried out, "God, I cannot do this!" In my suffering, I nearly fell off the chair. He laughed. He said to me, "You never asked Me who would help." I asked Him, "Who will help?" He gave me the names of twenty people, most of whom I knew little, or not at all.

In reaching the twenty people, I asked them to pray if they were to come and help. Sixteen of them called and said they would help. This was the beginning of Good Samaritan Ministries. This was the beginning of shocking training, and redefinition of the Word "a servant of the Lord Jesus Christ."

As I was finishing my Master's of Religion Degree, I knew we were taught nothing of what had happened to people. We were taught nothing of the power of sin and how it took over a human life, and completely controlling that life. We were taught doctrine and theory, but life had not come into the training at all. I finished with straight As, Suma Cum Laude. The divine training I was receiving was quietly changing my mind inside of me. No one knew of this hidden work of His Spirit but the Lord and myself. It was the Father. It was my Father and your Father who was my final teacher, THE EDUCATOR WHO KNEW.

When I graduated, with my Master's degree in May, 1979, my husband asked me, "Now what are you going to do?" I said to him, "I have asked the Lord, and He told me He would give me the answer in October." That satisfied both of us.

I forgot about it, because it seemed to be taken care of. One Saturday evening in October, we had two pastors and their wives for dinner. We were sitting at our table talking and sharing, when suddenly, without any introduction or warning, and without any discussion, we knew as in a flash of lightning, "Good Samaritan Ministries." In that year, 1979, this flash became a legal non-profit organization.

I do want to add two parts of the naming to the Good Samaritan story. There were earlier signs of this naming. In 1978, I was teaching at the Christian Renewal Center for a week's camp. I had a lesson all prepared to teach in the evening. I was dishing up my dinner, and there was a divine command, "Teach the Parable of the Good Samaritan." Later that year, on a trip to the Holy Land, a woman named Beverly came back to the bus with a piece of pottery in her hand from the Inn of the Good Samaritan. The inn is on the road between Jerusalem and Jericho. It is an ancient caravansary. The piece of pottery she brought was of a broken heart.

Who came to the house? I could say the poor, the lame, and the weak, and that is the truth. Many who came were absolutely embroiled in a life of sin and disaster. To sum up some of the people who came to our house, a small, three-bedroom ranch-style house with a family room and two baths, I will give you somewhat of a list: a murderer who had never confessed his crime; two former Nazis; the mentally ill; the ex-prisoners of long penal-system abuse; young couples with several children and inadequate education and drastic need to grow and develop their family and their own lives. The sexual perversions were obvious in many. There was more than one rapist who came during the season of work in our house. There was an alcoholic, who was in the final stages of alcoholism, drinking more than a fifth a day, and sniffing lacquer thinner or gasoline. There were drug addicts. Perhaps, the most memorable person who came to the house was a ten year old child, who came with her mother on a Saturday night. The child was nine months pregnant, ready to deliver. The next morning, I was to preach at our church. This was not something I usually did. It was the first time I had preached in the twenty years we had been at our church. The things I saw, the stories I heard, the anguish of the people moved me way beyond – way, way beyond – all the way beyond a normal Christian life. I was torn with compassion, and I took great pity on the sheep without a shepherd. There must be strong warning to us about the needs of too many. Will their lives be saved?

The action continued to grow. One day, I asked one of the clients who had a Bible training degree if she would be willing to get some special training, and come to help me with the counseling, listening to the needs that had overwhelmed me. She said "yes," and she did. She saw individuals, sitting on our king-sized bed. I continued in the small room.

My vision was so small that, originally, I told my husband I would just work in this one room. I did not realize the whole house would be involved in the work. People sat on our front-room sofa, waiting to be seen. Needs were pouring in hour by hour. Women came in to type, clean house, and to serve lunch to any present. Lunch was whatever we had in the cupboard. As many as were there at noon, were fed. There were no special purchases for the lunches; we just ate what we had. I was led to put a collection box by the front door. When the people left, they could put money in the box, but it was never requested or expected. The money never went into the house or the ministry of my hand. It went into the needs of the people who came. What was put in was a small amount. The needs were much greater. Whatever was lacking, we added unto the provision from our own resources.

Often, people needed money for gas, rent, or bills that were terrifying to them. In one particular season, we replaced a woman's teeth. She went from completely rotten teeth, to teeth that would keep her well and beautiful.

Now, you might say, "there must have been many donations for all of that to happen." I want to say, that is not the truth. That is not the truth at all. In 1980, the Lord gave me a word and told me that we needed to give up Christmas that year. This was a big shock to me, as Christmas was a really important holiday, and I had always been exhausted to do my very best to make Christmas special. Giving it up; what did that mean? How did one go about giving up Christmas when it is a central season and event in the life of a Christian?

Our youngest daughter, Jennie, was still at home. We decided to make a trip to California. I bargained with the Lord for little bits and pieces of Christmas, but in the end, He took everything away from us. Even on Christmas day, we could find a place to stay, but no food.

As I was digging through my purse, on the way to California, I found a necklace of olive wood beads that I had bought in the Holy Land for, perhaps, 33 cents. I asked the Lord if I could give the beads to someone for Christmas. He made an exception and said yes I could, as long as He showed me who was to receive it.

I kept looking and listening, seeking who would receive the gift.

Finally, it was Christmas Eve. We were in a restaurant. In the center of the restaurant was a table with a woman eating dinner alone. She had on an overcoat and her hat was pulled down on her head. It was around 80 degrees outside. Her overcoat did not seem to represent warmth to her, but a life that had totally been lost . The Lord said, "This is who will receive the gift."

I went up to the table and told her about the beads. I told her that the Lord decided to give them to her. She said, "Oh yes, I've been in the Holy Land. I know all about these beads." Then, all of a sudden, out of my mouth came these words, "The gift is not these beads, the gift is God has seen you and decided to spend Christmas with you."

We came home on New Year's Eve. As we approached our front door, in the screen, there were two things: a shawl and an envelope. When I opened the envelope, there was a check for $1,000 for the ministry. The Lord spoke to me. He said, "If you believe this shawl came from heaven. It will be the mantle of Elijah."

I could tell you many stories about the shawl. I shared the shawl, and many lives were affected. In fact, today, the shawl is in the hands of a very sick woman who has had it for many years. Years ago, her husband came to the office on a motorcycle, and said, "My wife needs the shawl." He zipped it up in his jacket, and went off twenty-some miles away, to take the shawl to his wife. The shawl was not a personal building-up of the ministry of Bettie Mitchell. It was an act of kindness to the lives of many. It brought comfort, and faith was increased and empowered in many. It was God's gift. He saw us and decided to spend Christmas with us. Note: Since I first wrote about the last receiver of the shawl, the woman has died. The man requested that her funeral be at Good Samaritan Ministries. The worn shawl that had even been through a fire was cleaned and returned.

I must tell you the story of Carl. Carl was brought to our house by a man who had been a Chaplain at Folsom Prison in California. Carl was a mentally ill three-time loser rapist. He had shown up at the retired chaplain's house in Beaverton. The chaplain did not know what to do with him. He had heard of me, so he called and asked if he could bring this man over to see what was possible. The Chaplain said, "If something does not happen to Carl, he will end up in prison for the rest of his life. Do what you can!"

Carl came every week for over a year. Can you imagine your husband leaving for work, you're alone in your house, and you're sitting with a three-time convicted rapist?

Carl and I studied his life. We took a look at everything. We worked well together. His mental illness was obvious, but very slowly, and very gradually, shifts came into his mind that brought small breakthroughs. He was on a lot of medication. I was most concerned about the Valium he was taking, and I asked him if he would be willing to have me help him go off the Valium, as it was very addictive. He said he would be willing to do it, and he did.

One day Carl came to the door at dinnertime. I had seen many people that day. I was totally and completely exhausted. My husband was not happy when the doorbell rang. I went to the door, and it was Carl. What happened next is a good shock for all of us. Out of my mouth came these words, "I don't care if you're Jesus Christ himself, I will not see you today." Then, I shut the door in Carl's face.

Within a few seconds, I knew exactly what I had done. I knew it in the deepest part of my being, like I knew The Call. The words again became a part of who I was. The Lord had sent Carl to be my teacher. I was not his.

One year passed, and Carl came to the door again. In my entire lifetime, I have never felt a greater desire to welcome a person than on the day Carl came back.

We met again for a short while, and one day, Carl said to me, "I need $400 to buy a car. Will you loan me the money?" Now that was a tough decision because it would be money that came out of our family budget. There were no special funds. There was just what we had to live on. The other part of the decision that was tough was that I knew Carl had no way of paying it back. Nevertheless, I wrote the check, and gave Carl the $400. A few weeks passed, and Carl brought me $100. That $100 was the largest donation ever made to this ministry. In a short time, Carl came again and said, "I'm going to be leaving, and you'll never see me again. I thank you for all you did to help me." True to his word, I have never seen Carl again, but to this day, I am totally alive to who comes to the door, and who sent them.

The Chaplain has stayed in touch with Good Samaritan Ministries. The Chaplain recently wrote me that he was dying of cancer, and he wanted to write me one more letter.

I never expected to leave the house. In fact, it was the last desire I could possibly have. Although it was very inconvenient, it was also very private for people, and it gave them the sense of security that they needed. One night, at nearly midnight, a man came. I might say that the man was 6'4" and that he knew of me through a time I had spent with him earlier. He, my husband and I, went into my office. We're talking about a room that is 9x10 feet. Joe said, "You are the craziest woman I have ever met, but the Lord has told me to give you offices." I said, "I don't want to move out of the house." My husband said, "Nevertheless, you will move out of the house and into the offices." The matter was settled.

I was a little person who knew little. Each day, what was needed for that day was given. I did not pound on God's door. I did not demand anything. I sought nothing, but to live out the Action of the Call. There came a knowing what to do in the most difficult situations.

There were times when shocking events would wake me up

again. I'll tell you a funny one. I was in a town in Central Oregon, speaking at a Women's Aglow luncheon. I stood up, and suddenly I was knocked to the floor, Slain in the Spirit. While I was on the floor, I was under the table, and I was aware that my feet were sticking out. All I could remember was the Wizard of Oz and those red shoes. I thought to myself, "How funny I must look with my feet sticking out from under the table." I was able to stand and give my talk. God would continue to remind me, not your will, but His will be done.

Two sets of offices were provided for us in the next four years. We continued to have little funding, and much need. But, I never looked at money as being the real issue. The real issue was the spirit by which we learn to give. I never took any money for myself. It was many years later that I took a small salary. If you give, and you don't count the cost, then truly, you have begun to learn to give.

The next few chapters will take you to a different place. What did I learn?

CHAPTER 7

On Education

During my school years, many of my teachers had never been married. They devoted their lifetimes to being educators. My first grade teacher had an astonishing influence on my life. Her name was Miss Marias. She discovered me. I don't know how she did it. All I know is something inside of me was awakened. There was a great creative part of me, and I wasn't afraid to use it.

One day, I asked Miss Marias if I could go into the cloak room with the other children who were finished with their lessons and work on a play we could give to the class. She allowed us to do this, and it soon became a weekly event, to put on a play for the class. She allowed me to develop the play with the children, and to bring costumes where they were needed. I remember that I often played the old witch so that someone else could be the special heroine. I did not desire to draw attention to myself as a child, and the lesser part seemed important to me. I don't remember any of the plays; I just remember the permission to have them. I remember the faith the teacher had in me and her encouragement; yet, she did not single me out. She allowed me to be educated.

Towards the end of first grade, we were having an assembly for the parents, and the other children in the school. A third-grade rhythm band was performing. I, who was a first grader, was chosen to lead that band. It would be my first experience on the stage.

My mother designed a beautiful costume. I did not feel much

terror at all. It seemed to be natural to do what I was asked to do. When the rhythm band was finished, I had to turn, face the audience, and bow. My hat was not on securely, and it fell off my head. At that moment, everyone laughed. At that moment, fear entered my life. There was a great loss of my natural talents. What remained was much less of me.

I do know that the children were kept in, and I do know this brought shame on me as well. I don't believe anyone ever talked to me about the incident. This stayed inside me in that secret place where children keep significant memories, particularly the memories of events that are too hard for them.

One day the Lord spoke to me. He reminded me about Miss Marias and what a great teacher she had been. But then He said, "You know, your second grade teacher, Miss Lawrence, was your greater teacher. She was hard on you. She made you toughen up." Of course, my mother didn't agree with that assessment. But, looking back, it was very significant that God said she was the greater teacher to change my life.

Two significant events occurred in the fourth and fifth grades. I had the same teacher. Her name was Mrs. Rychard. I was in one of those classrooms at Mills Open Air, where one whole wall of windows was open all the time. Besides desks, we had the cots, as we had to take daily naps.

One day, Mrs. Rychard decided to have me skip half a year of school. She felt that I was ready to do more helping with teaching, and that it would be good for me to be in the fifth grade instead of the fourth grade. There were two of us in the fifth grade, myself, and a boy named Frank Lynch. I liked Frank a lot. I think he liked me too. After that year, I saw him again in the 9th grade. He was only at Grant High School two days. It was good to see him again.

Mrs. Rychard was a firm, strict teacher. She got education into us. It wasn't that we had so much fun going to school or so many exciting days. Our education was the steady influence of learning; even paced, quiet. Personal growth and development could occur in Mrs. Rychard's class.

I remember as a third grader, she spanked me in front of the whole cafeteria. I wet my pants. I didn't cry. Looking back on it, I respected Mrs. Rychard because she did that. I had been hitting other children, and so she swatted me. It was a valuable lesson. I placed much value on Mrs. Rychard as a teacher, but greater than that, she placed much value on my life. For thirty years, I did not see Mrs. Rychard, but for thirty years, she wrote me a personal letter every Christmas.

I never intended to be a teacher. I thought I would be a nurse. Later, I believed I would go into religious education and do full-time Christian work.

When I suddenly, at 21, found myself a public education teacher, I found it was a very hard world. I was given a degree in education, but I was taught nothing about educating. My only teachers who taught me anything about education were Miss Marias, Miss Lawrence, and Mrs. Rychard. Teacher education was completely inadequate when you had to face children, and work with them as individuals and a classroom.

One truth I gradually came to understand was children always know whether you like them, or you do not like them. It only takes them a few minutes to figure that out. From that point on, they are with you, bored, or against you. It is the greatest truth I know about public education.

I taught full-time for one year, a fifth and sixth grade combination class at a country school. Then for 18 years, I was a substitute teacher. I loved being a substitute teacher. I loved the variety of the ages, the revisiting of the education process at many grade levels, and the challenge of developing rapport and interaction, on an immediate basis, with a child and a classroom. I found great intimacy with children, being a substitute teacher. Wisdom came to me to uphold the teachers for whom I was replacing for a time. Later, I was greatly empowered by my substitute lessons, to remember, we only substitute for Jesus. He is the real teacher.

It is good for me to tell funny stories because I learn so much from them. Perhaps you can learn from them as well.

One day, I was teaching 8th grade science in a middle school. The students were doing a lab, and one of the students reported to me that a boy in class was sticking some of the girls with a needle. I chose to wait until the class was leaving, and then I said to the boy, "Would you stay behind? I'd like to talk to you for a minute."

We sat down, and this is what I said to him: "You are the only person in this school I don't like. Is there anything you can do to help me with my problem?" (There were 900 children in the school). From that day, this student stayed close to me. He always greeted me in the hall. He respected that I owned the problem, and didn't blame him. He respected me because I told him the truth. It was a great lesson. It is important to ponder this lesson because it tells us much about bonding with personal integrity.

Nick L.

I was on a sixth-month assignment to teach low math to seventh and ninth graders, as well as eighth grade history. Nick was one of my students in the seventh grade math class.

Nick was often absent. If he was in school, he was late. I was very concerned about him. I called his mother and asked about him. She went into a long tirade about the school and how bad it was. I said to her, "I'm not calling about the school. I'm calling about Nick being in my class. I want him in my math class." For a while, Nick was faithful and came regularly. But, suddenly, he stopped and went back to his old ways.

I made another call to his mother, this time at 11:00 on a

Saturday night. We went through the same conversation, but this time she heard me: "I'm not calling for Mountain View School, I'm calling for Nick, and I want Nick in my class."

By the ninth grade, Nick was given an award as the most improved student at Mountain View School. He came to Mountain View, and he came to my math class. He got an A.

Jim Beardsley

Another student was in the 9th grade low math class. The student's name was Jim Beardsley, but I always called him "Beardsley," or "Beard." I loved nicknames for students.

One day, a boy came to me after class, a tall good-looking boy, who struggled so hard with math. He said, "Mrs. Mitchell, the boys are tormenting me and beating me up after school. I can't take any more." I told him not to worry; I would see what could be done.

I called "Beardsley" out in the hall, and we had a very significant conversation. I told him the problem, and I asked him if there was anything he could do to help solve the problem. He said, "Mitchell, what you are asking is very difficult." I said, "Don't worry about it. If you can't do it, I will not report you to the office. I'm just asking you if you might be able to help." He said, "I will take care of it." And he did!

Later, when Beardsley was in his 20's, he called me on the telephone and asked if he could take me to breakfast. I was really surprised, and, of course, went willingly. He told me about his life. We had a good breakfast. Then he asked if he could take me to breakfast the next month, because he would like to talk some more.

The following month, he asked me about my life, and about Christ. I was really surprised. After the third breakfast, he asked me if I would baptize him. He didn't want to be baptized in a church, because he knew none of his friends would come, and he wanted everyone of his friends to see that he was becoming a Christian. I said, "All right Jim, I will do that." The baptism was in a swimming pool, and, indeed, his friends came.

Beardsley and I became very close friends. We didn't see each other very often; in fact, it was rare. But, we were tight and close because we could trust each other.

One day, "Beardsley" came to my office. He told me he had terrific pain in his feet, and that he was afraid he would not be able to continue to work. I looked at him, and I said, "Beardsley, take off your shoes and socks and lay your feet in my lap." I laid hands on his feet and prayed.

It was several years later that I learned his feet were instantly healed during that prayer.

As I worked at Good Samaritan Ministries, I was often given pictures of the people I saw. I decided to put these pictures up on my wall in the office so that I would see them every day; I would remember them. Because I would keep them in my sight, I would pray for them. More and more pictures were brought to be put on the wall.

Once in awhile, Beardsley would come in to see if his picture was still on the wall. As he had children, I added theirs. Once in awhile, Beardsley would bring in somebody he had met on the street, someone who needed help. He would leave us alone, but trust that the help would be given.

Gradually, Beardsley began to make sure that I was all right. As I got older and older, he made sure more often. He would come by and check on me. He would protect me by kindness and his merciful spirit touched my heart.

One day, I said to Beardsley, "I want you to be one of the pallbearers at my funeral." He will be the only non-family member. If he can be there, "Beard" will show up.

True education takes place on the inside of a child. When I was having so many mental and emotional problems, I wrote out the story of the first seventeen years of my life. I wrote about what happened on the inside of me. I gave it to my parents to read. I don't imagine my father ever read it. My mother handed it back, and said, perhaps, she had made a few mistakes. I felt so sad, for I was lonely to know and be known.

It took me a long time to be an educator. It took the kindness and mercy of many teachers along the road, and it still does.

A TEACHABLE SPIRIT

Having a teachable spirit; now, what is that? It has to do with training hard, and being given His wisdom as we grow. There are things we take into our spirit that should never be there at all. That's not a teachable spirit. That is unwise input bringing us into the wrong direction.

Love to learn. Every day, remember, you know nothing. A new day comes, and you learn; because, in knowing nothing, you are open to new ideas, new thoughts, new development, and breakthrough. It is really easy to get stuck on old material. For example, we probably have all memorized John 3:16, and the Lord's Prayer. We may know it by heart, we may say the words, we may believe them, but are we still learning from these scriptures? If we are still learning from them, that is a teachable spirit.

A truly teachable spirit learns from everything. A teachable spirit judges no one, but uses good judgment to find the kernel of truth, even in the most difficult situations.

For example, where did we learn to forgive? Are we good at it? Could we be better at it? Are we learning more about it every day? Is it a road we take to truly know the extreme power of the sacrifice of Jesus to forgive sin? A teachable spirit will stay close to that, and each day, a little more of the power of forgiveness is grasped until it matures and becomes a part of who we are.

Education keeps its own hours. It can come in the middle of the night, early in the morning, or suddenly, when we're confronted with something we've never had to deal with before. Expect education to go on your entire life.

When my grandmother was in a nursing home due to dementia and other illnesses, she shared a room with another lady. Every day, the husband of the other lady came in to feed her. The Lord spoke to me. He said, "Do you see this man feeding his wife?" I said, "Yes, Lord." He said, "For years and years and years, she fed him and took care of him. Now it is his turn to feed her and take care of her." Education happens when you're open to it, when your eyes, ears, heart, and very being are connected to the Living God, and to His purposes around you.

Does everyone have a potential to be teachable? The answer is yes, but most don't know this. When you are a teacher in a classroom, or in a family, or wherever you are, you must remember we are all teachers to one another. Your children are your teachers. Your family members are your teachers. Teachers are around you, and the Holy Spirit brings inside of you, the greatest teachings from many resources. He has chosen for you to learn and know.

One of the things I love about Jesus is He kept a teachable spirit. He noticed things that other people would not have even dreamed of noticing. He noticed the widow putting her mite in the offering box. He noticed who she was, and what that offering represented to her. He noticed the greatness of her offering. That widow, at that moment, was His teacher, bringing to Him a profound lesson that would influence the entire world for the rest of history.

The whole world is our classroom, and everyone in it influences us. Many people hide from being educated. They don't want to be exposed. They hide in their opinions, or just plain not caring much about others. I believe it is important that we never hide from learning. As I met with people in the counseling office, I learned every day from them. They were great teachers. The Lord used them to change me, hone me, and wake me up. We could weep together! We could laugh together! We could learn together!

Paul writes in 1 Timothy 2:12, a woman should not teach. It is an interesting scripture. The truth of the matter is, Jesus is our teacher, and as we have a teachable spirit, the teaching occurs in and through us.

THREE KEYS TO EDUCATION

If you are to be a teacher, there are three keys to learning you must keep in mind at all times: Subject, Timing, and Relationship. These are keys to people learning on the inside, not just garnering information on the outside, but receiving into their spirit: discernment, knowledge, wisdom, and understanding.

There needs to be great bonding in learning. If others know you are learning at the same time they are, and if they influence you as much as you influence them, the teacher among us is Christ.

Timing may sound like a strange part of education, but even the timing of one sentence spoken slowly, carefully, and deeply into us will deflect chatter and too much information.

You might say, "I've never had a teacher that really reached me." I can relate to that, for there weren't many, were there? The ones that fully really reached us, first of all, taught us to love the subject they taught. They left a lifetime impression of what they taught, and you could become an integral part of the expertise of that subject. Jesus, the Master, IS our Teacher. His lessons must leave a lifetime impression on all that we know, and often correct what we think we know.

IT'S ALL ABOUT BALANCE: SUBJECT, TIMING, RELATIONSHIPS. It is not SUBJECT, timing and relationship.

These three are equally important.

THE JESUS PRAYER

When I continued to look at Jesus and the apostles who wanted Him to teach them how to pray, there were several new thoughts I gradually understood. The apostles wanted a prayer that wasn't very long. They knew Jesus prayed all night, and they really didn't want to do that. They wanted to sleep. He knew they needed something that would steady them, keep them together, and bring them into unity. When He said "Our Father who art in heaven," those words would influence all of history. Our Father who art in heaven... "Our" is a very inclusive word. It is a training word that must never leave us.

Jesus would like to teach you this Word, "Our Father." But, you would have to realize that when you pray, you are praying with Him. Not only that, you're praying with everyone. You're praying across humanity. We are being called deep in the spirit to "Our Father who art in heaven." When Jesus prayed all night, He prayed for us and with us!

LESSONS AND CHANGES

Each child, each person, must have the courage to decide how well they are going to do in everything they set out to do. This happens when a learner is inspired!

You have read that I did music very poorly, and it was not good. Today, I can sit down and play a concert for 1,000 people. I would walk on the stage, go to the piano, play the first note I learned, Middle C, slowly get up, and leave the stage. One note is a symphony. There are great teachers in the world. Are you one of them? If you think about it, you will find your stories. You will find what you want to say. You must find your own voice, never opinion – always

84

by His Spirit. We must remember that if His goodness and mercy do not teach us, evil will.

Once at Good Samaritan, I taught a class that everyone loved, and everyone learned much by the experience. That class was called: "What is This Coming Out of Your Mouth?" Each person was to listen to everything coming out of their mouth all week. When they came back to class the next week, they were to share what they learned about what was coming out of their mouth. I will never forget what one woman said, "I learned that I talk all the time, and I must be driving people crazy, for I seldom let them talk." Each week, breakthroughs occurred. I told them not to worry about what was coming out of someone else's mouth. Don't worry about that at all. Each week; you just pay attention to what is coming out of your own mouth. They didn't get hurt. They didn't become filled with anguish. They became teachable. Everyone said it was the very best class ever. I only taught it one season. It is strange how there is an opportunity, and then it is gone.

We saw, when Jesus came, there was opportunity, and then it was gone. Jesus, however, being a great teacher, said this to us, *"And look, I am with you always; yes, to the end of time."* (Matthew 28:20) We are included.

For five years, I tried to remember God first thing in the morning. I set a goal to wake up thinking of Him. At the end of five years, I could do it less than half the time. At the end of the five years, the Lord said to me, "I always think of you, and you never have to try to think of Me again." From that moment, God knowing me would live on the inside of my life.

Jesus taught us how important story-telling is. The story never drew attention to Him, but it drew attention to the Kingdom of God. Speaking in parables is a gift you can develop. Don't be afraid to do it. Try it out. See if you can do it. See if it works. Use it on a child and see if they get it. He spoke to us in parables. We can speak in parables too, for He said, "we can do anything He has done, and even more!"

In school, I learned a certain number of subjects. The subjects were limited: Latin, American History, English, Geometry, Chemistry. You get my point. The educator from above helps us integrate learning. As we put it altogether, the whole becomes part of our life. Some teachers just teach subject matter and give grades, but the true teachers teach you to love the subject. They don't give grades. They challenge your enthusiasm and encourage you out of being a mediocre learner. They inspire you and that inspiration lasts for a lifetime.

One day, I was teaching in another 8th grade math class. A student flunked his test. I spoke to the student as he went out the door and said, "I want you to come in after school and take the test again." The student showed up for the second test, but oh was that boy mad! He was furious! He sat at his desk and he was seething on the inside, playing with his pencil, doing nothing. Finally, I did something shocking, even to me. I picked up my pencil, threw it across the room and yelled, "You make me so damn mad!" Suddenly I thought, "What just came out of my mouth!? I'll surely be fired." Do you know what happened? That boy picked up his pencil, did the math test, passed it, and from that day onward, I later found out, even through high school, he got straight A's in math. That boy saw how much I loved him, that I would even risk my own life.

When I counseled young people, I asked them if they set their own goals for grades. Shockingly, none of them did. Usually their parents set the goals. This won't work nearly as well! A child or an adult must learn to set their own goals. Again, we can inspire this to take place. Jesus did, "If someone asks you to go a mile, go two."

We're in a lifetime training program, and we shall be challenged to love our neighbors as ourselves. It is easy to go to another scripture, but our eyes must stop, for this is about something far more important than even we know. It is about the secret of all the learning that will ever take place in the history of the world.

God is our Father. None other is. Jesus said, *"You must call no one on earth your father, since you have only one Father, and he is in heaven. Nor must you allow yourselves to be called teachers, for you have only one Teacher, the Christ."* (Matthew 23:10) The Holy Spirit will teach you all things, and will bring those things to mind.

People are always saying to me, "I can't hear God." The Holy Spirit does not do casual talk, but challenges all our thoughts and actions. You may not want to hear what God has to say to you. He has rarely agreed with me. He always challenges me to His higher purpose.

We have a vast amount to learn about love. God plants love inside of us. It is a flame that must never be extinguished. We can give our face to others, a face that never loses its kindness. In depression, in negativity, we go only into the death of the spirit. Suddenly, we have no neighbors, we have only ourselves. We become a pathetic lot. Left to our own devices, we will accomplish little. But then, suddenly, it comes into us that everyone in the world is our neighbor. I remember the day that happened to me. I was alone, driving a car into the city. Suddenly, I became aware of all the other cars and all of the other drivers on the road. From that day, I was aware that my neighbors are everywhere. There is no loneliness. We are with God, and we are with all of us.

CHAPTER 8

Experiential Learning

Jesus was an experiential teacher. He didn't take the disciples to textbooks, or tests. He took them daily, hour by hour, into fieldwork and travel.

As education has become more academic and scientific, experiential education is more urgent. We have to bring experience into the classroom, and we have to develop opportunities for more experiences outside the classroom for the learners.

Early in our marriage, Jerry and I decided travel was important to each of us. Since we were both teachers, we wanted to see, experience, and know the United States. Over many years, we went to all 50 states. We took each of our children to a great number of states. We experienced our country as a family.

I will always remember standing outside the home of Martin Luther King, in 1970. I told my husband I was going to knock on the door. He said, "I'll wait out here and make sure you're o.k." As I knocked on the door, I was welcomed into a large and busy office filled with teaching materials that could be used to break prejudice, and bring reconciliation to the races. This country needed a new history!

One summer, we decided to have a transportation experience. Jerry and our oldest daughter, Michelle, took the bus from Portland, Oregon, to Kansas City, Missouri. Jennie, Laura, and I flew to Ohio to visit Aunt Jennie. We then took the bus to Kansas City, and hooked up as a family. We all rode the train home from Iowa.

While we were on the train to Oregon, our daughter, Laura, met Sister Mary Diane. We are not Catholic, and Sister Mary Diane was; but, Laura made a powerful contact with her, and in the years to come, Sister Mary Diane came to visit us and wrote Laura very special letters. Meeting people and getting to know them, reaching out beyond the borders of our comfort zones and into the bigger picture of humanity– these were significant goals for our family's experiential learning.

When we travelled as a family, we took very detailed books that would explain, along the road, the towns and cities we entered, how they got their names, what the locals did for a living. We learned the stories of many towns. We would stop just outside of town and read. Then, we'd visit. Sometimes we would stop and interview people along the street. We would ask them what was important about their town, what they liked about it. We studied the ideas shared with us of structures of historical significance; but, we also studied daily life in that town. Our children were developing the deep down comfort of expanding their boundaries to be inclusive of ideas and people.

On some of these journeys, while Jerry was driving, I read the New Testament aloud. In fact, I read it twice on these family journeys. I would have to admit that I left out the Book of Revelation. It seemed too complicated for their years. Then, after the reading, about two or three hours later, we would have what was called an M&M quiz. There would be one M&M questions, two M&M questions, sometimes three M&M questions. For those who don't know, M&M's are small chocolate candies. Everyone in the car was included in the quiz. It was a great adventure! The questions were about what we had learned or experienced earlier in the day. Some of the questions were biblical. Some of the questions were about stops we'd made in that state, and things they were learning along the road. It brought us to a lot of discussion. This sharpened our memories.

My husband is a person who likes to collect adventures, and to develop some consistency around them. Therefore, he decided we, as a family, would visit all of the covered bridges in the Northwest. It was fun and interesting. We learned about the differences in their structure, and about their history in each region.

This covered bridges experience had such an impact on our daughter, Laura, that later, in her late 30's, when Lincoln County was going to tear down the oldest covered bridge in Oregon, she was inspired to get the county to give Laura and her husband, Kerry, the torn down bridge's pieces. They had a bridge expanse across the stream in front of their property. She and her husband deeded the front half of their property and the bridge itself to Lincoln County. Because they rebuilt the covered bridge, they now have visitors from all over the world who come to see the oldest covered bridge in Oregon. The Drift Creek Covered Bridge became a designated Oregon and a national registered historical site. The bridge and the cover fit exactly. Troubled youth, in a special program, helped with the rebuilding of the old covered bridge.

Then, of course, we had the summers of ghost towns. The children LOVED this. They thought it was fabulous to walk into these old towns and visit the rustic old buildings. They would imagine and reconstruct stories that reflected this earlier period of history.

When my husband announced our theme would be "National Parks," that was very challenging! It led us to visit many states. We were fascinated with the tremendous learning available in each of the National Parks, and we took advantage of Rangers and programs to develop our vision of environment.

My husband and I are both historians. We visit not only National Parks, but also national historical sites. We walked in the homes of most of the Presidents of the United States. We studied each President's life and family.

Aside from Abraham Lincoln, I discovered my favorite President was Andrew Johnson, who became President after Lincoln was assassinated. Now, why would I choose Andrew Johnson? He was acquitted from impeachment by only one vote! Certainly, President Johnson was not one of those favored, and admired by our country. When I learned about his life, I saw something extraordinary about the United States. Andrew Johnson also was born in a log cabin. He was made an apprentice tailor when he was eight years old. He never went to school, or learned to read and write. When he grew up and got married, his wife taught him to read and write. He went from illiterate, to literate. He was determined to learn, and he had a great wife who knew how to teach him.

When suddenly he was thrust into the Presidency, he looked at the priorities of Lincoln, and he made them his priorities. When he was no longer President of the United States, he ran and became a United States Senator.

I've always found that if you know a lot about a person's life, you will have a great advantage in seeing who they really are.

Now, travel planning became an integral and accepted part of the events of each year in our family. We all participated, and we all learned from those significant journeys together.

When our oldest daughter, Michelle, was 14, we left the two little ones in Denton, Kansas, with family. Michelle took a bus from Kansas City to Dallas, Texas, where she hooked up with Dad and Mom, who had been in other states. We were in Dallas to study the assassination of John F. Kennedy. We learned the story, fresh and first-hand. The story became less historical, and more real. We went out to Irving, Texas, to the home of Lee Harvey Oswald. We went to the cemetery and interviewed the man who buried Lee Harvey Oswald. He said that five grave markers had been stolen, and that Oswald's mother came to visit his grave each year. We interviewed the head nurse at Parkland Hospital, who was in the room when President Kennedy died. Of course, we went to the site of the assassination, and other historical parts of that story in Dallas.

These journeys we made over the years developed historical context for each family member. When Jerry and I went into the classroom to teach, we had something to teach that was rare and experiential.

In fact, last night, I accidentally ran into one of my former students from Mountain View Intermediate School. Paul is now in his 50's. He said, "I always remembered you as a teacher who made us see, know, and understand. We knew; we all knew you knew the Lord, and you were there for us." Now is that not a miracle, since I was only a substitute teacher in that building?

Since many families could not travel, I decided Good Samaritan Ministries would offer weekly summer tours for children and adults in the general area of Portland, and its environs. We did this for several summers. One year, we even had a city bus that took us around. The driver was a member of Good Samaritan Ministries. He played the guitar and his harmonica for us.

Some of the significant experiential stops we made in those summers were to different churches and synagogues, the Oregon Historical Society, a mortuary and a crematorium, behind the scenes at the zoo, some of the nature trails, Shriner's Hospital for Crippled Children. These are only a few of the places we visited.

I'll always remember the visit to the mortuary, because we had a woman with us who was absolutely terrified of death. When we went into the mortuary, she was freaking out, but, of course, she went in with us. In a little while, after we talked about death and what it was like, what would happen, how we move from this life to the next life, and after we saw the coffins, I said to this woman,

"Just lie down on the floor here – you're dead." I covered her with a shawl, and she experienced being dead. When she got up off the floor, the fear of death was totally and absolutely gone. It never returned.

We made a family trip to Mexico. Again, we made it a unique travel experience. Since Michelle was grown, Laura and Jennie, our younger ones, went with us. We went first to Disneyland and then drove to Phoenix. We left our car with friends. We took the bus to Nogales, U.S., and Nogales, Mexico. We had absolutely no reservations in Mexico. We had a gallon and a half of water, our luggage, and ourselves.

When we went to the train station, my husband said, "We want to buy four tickets to Mexico City." It was late in the day. We were very tired. The ticket agent looked at us and said, "We don't have any tickets to Mexico City. It's out of the question--there is no way for you to go!" I sat on one of the suitcases and began to cry. Finally, the ticket agent called my husband over and said, "Well, we can send you to Guadalajara." We got on a train for Guadalajara. We arrived there at 11:00 at night with no hotel reservations, two very little children, and two exhausted parents. We found our way to a hotel. They said they had no room. We asked, "Where can we go?" They pointed down the street and said they might have room down there. We went down the street, and for $5 a night, we had a hotel room. Of course, it wasn't much, but it was a bed for each of us. After a few days in Guadalajara, we caught a train to Mexico City. We learned that if we needed a hotel, we needed to call for the hotel before we arrived. If we only arrived at the hotel, they would always have no room. So, from the train station, we called a place we selected from a travel book we had, made reservations, and shortly thereafter, showed up at the hotel.

When we went down to the Great Pyramid of the Sun, south of Mexico City, we discovered a shocking surprise. We all climbed countless steps to the top of the pyramid and then countless steps back down. Jerry and I stopped and breathed, stopped and breathed, because the elevation was quite high, not to mention our condition was not tops. Our youngest daughter, Jennie, was about seven years old. We watched in amazement as she climbed to the top and back down without stopping. It was our first indication that she was an athlete.

We joined the Oregon Archaeological Society as a family. They gave us professional training to do scientific archaeological digs. We did organized digs of an ancient Indian village site one summer on Sauvie Island. The next summer, we dug the original pioneer store of Fort Vancouver, Washington.

We worked together as a family. We had to build and bring our own equipment. We had to work all weekends. This required incredible energy and discipline. All finds had to be properly marked and scientifically recorded. We made fabulous finds and discoveries as we mapped the story of our "dig."

This two-summer hobby led to my pursuit of studying Biblical Archaeology. This ultimately led me to Iraq and the Walls of Nineveh.

Be challenged to develop experiential learning for your own families.

Our family loves the United States. We love every state, every part of the story of our nation, and every journey made by previous generations. Jerry and I are both patriotic in a healthy sense. We don't rebel against the law. We marvel at the opportunity this country has to develop the law.

We believe one of the most dangerous decisions any country or any family can make is to divide against itself. Abraham Lincoln said, "A house divided against itself cannot stand."

The greatest need our country has today is to inspire and challenge our own people. Presently, we are in the midst of the war between dictatorship and democracy in the Middle East. Everyone is angry and complaining, disappointed and horrified. Everyone has the potential to bring healing inspiration to thousands of people. Inspire to develop freedom. Anger begets anger; inspiration begets inspiration. It is not what we have, but what inspiration we give that creates the beauty of the earth and everything in it.

CHAPTER 9

On Relationships

King Hezekiah reigned in Jerusalem from 716 to 687 B.C. Jerusalem was facing an Assyrian siege, incredible danger. The armies of Sennacherib were marching against Jerusalem with many warnings that the battle must be given up unto the Assyrian armies.

King Hezekiah was one of the few good kings in the history of Judah. He consulted the Prophet Isaiah. He did not listen to threats. He knew the meaning of repentance. One of his great building feats is called, today, Hezekiah's tunnel. He stopped the upper outlet of the waters of Gihon, and directed them down to the west side of the Citadel of David. This removed the waters from outside the city, and moved the waters inside the city, thus, making it difficult for the army of his enemy, but safer for the people of Jerusalem.

Hezekiah's Tunnel is still in Jerusalem. It is still intact. We know, for sure, it was Hezekiah's Tunnel because a number of years ago, an excavation team, in searching through the tunnel, found the inscription stone of the dedication of the tunnel during the time of Hezekiah. I have seen the inscription stone with my own eyes. It is in a museum in Istanbul.

Believing it is important to know Jerusalem through faith, and by experience, I have led many tour groups on a walk through Hezekiah's Tunnel. The Tunnel starts at the Spring of Gihon, where Saul was crowned King, and ends at the Pool of Siloam, where the blind man was sent by Jesus to wash the mud from his eyes. The tunnel is a third of a mile long, narrow, filled with water. There are no lights in the tunnel. Sometimes the water is high. Sometimes the water is low. Sometimes the ceiling is so low that every bone has to bend over to get through. The tunnel remains one of the great testimonies of God's work amongst the ancients.

My own story of relationships will begin, as we're coming out of Hezekiah's Tunnel, and close to the Pool of Siloam. You might say, "Well, how can that be?" This is how it was.

Sam Bar-El, my dearest Israeli friend, was leading the group through the tunnel. I was behind him. The tour group was behind me. We are talking about a long line of people, single-file, walking through with great difficulty and care. As we were coming out of the tunnel, the Lord Himself spoke to me. He said, "I want you to love all others in the world the way you have loved this man. I want you to love your neighbor as yourself." I marveled at such a lesson. But, indeed, when God speaks, it becomes so.

Surprisingly, at that moment, Sam Bar-El began to sing the Lord's Prayer as we were coming out of the tunnel. It was the only time in 42 years I have heard him sing it. The walk was finished, but the story of genuine relationships was just beginning. In Acts 10, verses 34 and 35, Peter says, "The truth I have now come to realize is that God does not have favorites, but that anybody of any nationality who fears God and does what is right is acceptable to Him." These words were fulfilled in my spirit in Hezekiah's Tunnel, a word that cannot be changed. A word that is eternal.

All my life I struggled with relationships. Part of the struggle was that my mother did not encourage or allow friendships, and my circumstances of where I lived as a child and having no siblings until I was nearly eleven, were not ripe for the development of relationship skills. My mother claimed towards the end of her life, that I was her only friend. I suddenly understood that was the truth. She had needed an only friend as a child, and it had become me.

I definitely was not popular. Going to Grant High School, where they had sororities and fraternities, it was deemed important to be popular. I always knew I wasn't. It was a great blessing for me to find out, before I left Grant High School, that being popular would not be good at all. A new friend took me to a fraternity party. I saw everyone lying around drinking and smoking. The couples looked completely disconnected from everyone else. I then understood that God made sure I would never be popular.

In the earlier years of my adult life, I struggled hard to understand the meaning of friendship, the definition of my actions, and the actions of others. How can the developing and ripening of true friendship take place?

I thought in my mind that everyone was normal, although I never defined "normal," and probably never considered myself normal. Normal was normal.

It was a shock to find out everyone was different, and sometimes those differences were radically difficult. It was good to learn this, as then I could begin to bridge the distance between acquaintance and true friendship.

When I began to counsel in the house in 1977, I discovered one day, that I looked forward to seeing some people more than others, and I pondered that. Then it was clear to me, I was to have no favorites. I began to equally anticipate the visit of each person. It was amazing. It worked, and this was deeply satisfying.

One day, 10 years later, I got a severe fixation in my mind that Jesus had a close and trusted friend named John, and I wanted a close and trusted friend too. I searched, longed for, hoped for, and struggled for, the location of that one special friend.

The Lord never gives a short education. It starts with a long introduction, and He finishes the story.

After several years, He spoke profoundly into my life, "Everyone is your John. I don't want to hear any more about it!" It was finished.

Relationships for me involved mental struggle. In the early years of leading tours, I found it was extremely difficult to conquer the mental anguish we faced day after day, traveling in close proximity with a diverse group of people. One day, at Beersheba, in 1983, my mind was so disturbed, and so filled with arguments and anger, that I became absolutely desperate to conquer this mind and be healed immediately. In desperation, in my brain, I began to say these words, "You shall love the Lord your God with all your heart, with all your mind, with all your soul, and with all your strength." I said it over and over and over again, to conquer every other thought going on in my brain. Shockingly, after a few minutes, my brain was quiet, stable, and able to deal with all situations as needed. Later that evening, I was asked to pray with a Jewish woman who was in the hospital dying. The Lord spoke to me again, "If you had not obeyed this law; if you had not come to me with this, you could never have prayed with anyone in My Spirit."

This event had a profound effect on my life. God was moving from God to my Father, from law to intimacy. GOD IS MY FATHER. The realization of that, the totality of that statement, the completion of that, on both sides, the Father's and mine: this is our true challenge to live a life of faith in Him.

In the Ancient Mediterranean World, there were 3,200 gods. There were several temples to different gods in every city. The Jews were peculiar. They had only one temple to their god, and they had no image of him. They were the only people in the Mediterranean World who had no image of their god. They had one god. Jesus brought One Father into each of our lives. Indeed, He said in Matthew 23:9, "You must call no one on earth your father, since you have only one Father, and he is in heaven."

At the end of the Gospel of John, when Mary Magdalene and Jesus are talking outside the tomb, in Chapter 20, verse 17, Jesus said to Mary, "Do not cling to me, because I have not yet ascended to the Father. But go to the brothers, and tell them, "I am ascending to my Father and your Father, to My God and your God." She was to give the first sermon, the message from Jesus Himself.

Over the years in counseling, I found it very difficult to get people interested in a connection with God. Their minds were distracted by their problems, and God only came occasionally to their minds. Their problems were huge distractions and their problems had been very successful in preventing them from an intimate relationship with the living Father. They also had issues with their human fathers and they, therefore, thought that God created their human fathers to bring them pain.

When Jesus said to the apostles, "You may have only one Father, and that is God," it is a profound statement. We must not let this get mixed up with anything else.

Often I have said, looking deep into the eyes of a person, "God is your Father." They stare at me in some kind of a blank, dead faith, moving on to their next point. The whole point is that God is our Father. God is my father, God is your father.

Forgiveness is a tough assignment given to us by the Lord Himself. It is especially tough if we take it case by case. We need to respond to the help the Lord gives to forgive. *"So always treat others as you would like them to treat you."* (Matthew 7:12) It puts responsibility for our own action on each of us. This says to an individual taking this action, "You will make a huge difference in the whole world."

I struggled for years with issues that would trouble me, especially over my parents. It was a constant harassment of my mind sent by Satan to accuse, to belittle, and to make me sick.

Deliverance finally came. Powerfully, I began to see my parents as human beings, with their own life story – not just a story with me. I began to see them as my neighbor, not just my mother and father. I began to love my neighbor as myself. And then, in their humanity, I began to find my own sanity and balance.

Relationships can only be healed when we can see the bigger picture. It also must be that we see ourselves, and how we fit into our bigger picture and theirs. What can we do to make a difference?

Gradually, I learned that everyone was my neighbor. I didn't think this way until I saw so many people for counseling, and my picture was enlarged to include a broader spectrum of humanity. By the time Good Samaritan Ministries was in thirty-eight countries, and by the time my husband and I had four children, nine grandchildren, and two great-grandchildren, I could experience and live in the bigger picture. I began to see and know Jesus, and what He was driving home to us. His words were like a drill at the dentist, painful, but the only healing possible, *"You must love your neighbor as yourself."* (Matthew 22:39) Suddenly, my husband was my neighbor. My mother was my neighbor. Each of my children was my neighbor. My neighborhood expanded, and it became large; yet, shockingly, it was always manageable. It was astonishing how such a large neighborhood could be so absolutely manageable. You would think it would burn me out, but it set me free.

We often think of a neighbor as someone we need to do special favors for; someone we need to ply with gifts, someone we need to have over for dinner, someone we need to send a card, or make a comment that heals them. This is all true, but it is not the core value of neighbor. The core value is our neighborhood is the Kingdom of God. If God is the Father of all mankind, we had better look at our neighborhood with new eyes!

As I saw people overseas in a much more destitute situation than I was, or that any of us have experienced here, I began to see with compassionate eyes what their needs were. I began to balance my needs with their needs. Every night, when I went to bed, I knew who was hungry. I knew that in our large school of 1,200 Ugandan children, porridge was given for breakfast. Aside from that, they had only two meals per week. I knew our people did not want to know this. Here we make a list of our own needs. We want to make our own priorities. We want to keep our neighborhood small. Only occasionally did someone want to know the hunger of those children. Knowing this hunger causes great suffering to us, but it is meant to cause great deliverance of our greed. It is the Lord Himself that brings us this shared meal with our neighbor.

The word love, I learned, was not apprehensive. It was not trusting. It did not have great expectations. The word love, I learned, was all encompassing. Rather than choosing anger, I continued to choose freedom, both for my neighbor and for myself.

There is a big war in the Bible between exclusivism and inclusivism. Some of you may know about this war, but others may not even know about it. Is Christianity an exclusive religion, or an inclusive one? Can all people in the whole world come to Christ, and be welcomed? What would this mean? How would that come to pass? Would we treat them as we would want to be treated? Would we stay by each other? Would we remember so many all the days of our lives?

Large ministries are often focused on large numbers of people. Good Samaritan Ministries was to focus forever upon the individual. It is profound that Jesus said, "And you shall love your neighbor as yourself," not, your neighbors as yourself. How profoundly He knew it was easy to gather crowds. Yes, He knew that for sure. The apostles had to learn also to come to the individual and stay among them.

I found competition to be a very serious issue. 1 Co. 12:24 says, *"God has composed the body so that greater dignity is given to the parts which were without it, and so that there may not be disagreements inside the body but each part may be equally concerned for all the others. If one part is hurt, all the parts share its pain. And if one part is honoured, all the parts share its joy."*

Competition is when we're running a race against someone else.

We are running our own race, and we will receive our own reward.

Often people around me wanted to vie for special position, or try to imitate me as a person, or feel that their work was not as significant as mine was.

Thankfully, the Lord gave me the gift of never thinking I was very important. The fact is, remember, I was a failure at sports and a failure at music! I was also a failure at machines and computers. I was a failure at art, and I lost my teaching job, so I experienced being a failure as a teacher.

Each of us has our own gifts, and if we would just use them, and not look around to see if our gifts are just as important as someone else's gifts, wow!

I love the words of Jesus. I truly love them: *"In truth I tell you, in so far as you did this to one of the least of these brothers of mine, you did it to me."* (Matthew 25:40).

Who would you put on your own relationship list? Would you order them in terms of significance, or marvel at them as human beings you met along the road? Who would you put on your relationship list?

CHAPTER 10

On Marriage and Family

Part 1 – On Marriage

Marriage and family were born in the Garden of Eden. They were together. They were not separate, they were each a part of the whole.

Marriage is a covenant. It is a covenant between God, a man, and a woman. It is a permanent agreement that must never be lightly broken. In breaking the covenant, great amounts of suffering can be unleashed without ever expecting it to be so.

It has been my experience with the many couples I have married over the years that there is a great deal more time spent in planning the wedding than there is in planning the life they will live together. Good marriage counseling, prior to marriage, insists toward the planning of the life, but in secret, has the wedding itself become too powerful? This is a celebration that does not foreshadow the cross that must be born by each for the marriage to be whole.

It is interesting that the first miracle recorded in the Gospel of John was the miracle of the wine at the wedding in Cana. There was a great celebration going on, but they had run out of wine. Jesus' mother wanted Jesus to make the celebration successful, and asked him to do something about the need for more wine. Jesus was very hesitant about this, and yet he created out of water, a wine that was better than any they had tasted. He honored the celebration, but Jesus said, "My time has not yet come." Was it only the time of his public ministry, or was it the time of the cross, the sacrifice for forgiveness of our sins?

Just yesterday, I was meeting with a young couple who are spending several months planning their wedding, talking about their dreams and their ideal life together, but perhaps not realistically, as the "ideal" very seldom takes place.

In the conversation we had, they mentioned he was going to be fitted for a tuxedo to wear at the wedding. I looked at them, and said, "My husband was married in a suit that he bought at the Goodwill for $5." Our marriage has lasted 59 years. We were together less than three weeks before we were married, and then we were separated the first two years of our marriage, by the Korean War.

Do you know what they said? "Maybe we should look at the Goodwill tomorrow, to see if something would be good from there?" Often, I'm asked if I believe in divorce. It is a hard question, because if you work with troubled marriages, one or both of them often believe in it powerfully, and they are trying to manipulate you, as a counselor, to agree with them for divorce. Do I believe in divorce that is manipulated, and satisfies the emotions at the time, but does not look at the bigger time that lies ahead? Absolutely not! I do not believe in that divorce at all!

We hear words like, "I just want to be happy." Is being happy about being married, or is being happy about a choice to be made? Deep inside each of us we are called to embrace whatever state I am in, I will be content. This contentment is so powerful in the spiritual realm that nothing, absolutely nothing, can make a person unhappy.

Gradually, I discovered that unhappiness is a mood disorder. It puts everything in the perspective of what I wanted vs. what I got. It does not allow the hardship of the experience to become growth and blessing. Each of us is responsible for our own happiness. The road to happiness is to give up the right to be unhappy.

One day, I was meeting with a client, and I said, "I want you to sit in this chair. This is the chair of Mrs. John Lee. It is a position Mrs. Lee holds. She is a wife. It is a very wonderful and powerful position. Never let anyone diminish or take away from the position that you hold. It is your chair. It is your God-given blessing."

She had always looked at her marriage in terms of the two of them. I made her look at the marriage in terms of how she saw herself in her own chair.

In the Garden of Eden, the blame game began almost immediately, and it heavily extended into the lives of the children.

St. Paul explains in 1 Corinthians 4:3, "*It is of no importance to me how you or any other human court may judge me: I will not even be the judge of my own self. It is true that my conscience does not reproach me, but that is not enough to justify me: it is the Lord who is my judge.*"

I'm sure we all know that finger-pointing is not good; but, it is so much of a pattern to be anxious to justify ourselves, that we often use it far more than we may know or recognize. Use good judgment and leave the judgments to God.

My whole brain was dedicated, for many years, to who was to blame. I would try to take it to God, but I would get lost in the inner arguments between Satan and Christ. There was always a trial going on in my mind, and it would take a long time for the judge to interrupt and conclude the trial. "It is finished!" was my only hope.

I've always believed that it is harder for men to be married and get in bed with a woman for life, than it is for women. I may be way off in this belief, but men are giving up an independence that is important to them. Women are seeking the love and depth of someone they need; a kind and saintly lover and provider.

Sometimes I have told the story of the marriage bed. I think I'll tell it here. When Jerry and I got married, we slept in a double bed. We could not agree whether to keep the top sheet tucked in or out. So, we began to sleep in twin beds. One day, after several years, we began to have serious marital problems, and I recognized our beds needed to be moved together. So, we put the twin beds close to each other. Finally, we chose a marriage bed. It was king-sized. But the question remains, will we sleep with our backs towards one another? Will we have communion together in the spiritual realm in that bed? Is that bed holy and sacred? Does that bed stand on the forgiveness of sin?

There are two sacred pieces of furniture in a marital household. One is the marriage bed. The second one is the dining room table.

In our house, where we have lived for 52 years, we have a bedroom set that belonged to my mother's parents. It was their marriage bedroom set from 1900. When I was in high school, my mother and I took eight coats of paint off, and she had the set refinished. The mattress and springs left on the bed dated from about 1930. This bed was a marriage bed. My mother was conceived in this bed. Over the years, this bed has become a place where people are welcomed. It is our hospitality bed. People from nineteen countries and from all different walks of life have slept in this bed, even the Minister of State of Uganda.

What is my point here? My point is that a bed is not just a place for sleep and having sex, it is a place of marriage. It is a place of deep and powerful community between a man and his wife.

No one taught me this. It was not in anybody's curriculum or on anyone's list, but I want to say very loud and clear, how you conceive your marriage bed to be, and how it is used, will affect, not only your generation, but generations to come.

Too often children are placed in the marriage bed. I don't recommend this at all, for it ceases to be a marriage bed, and it becomes something different that it is not to be. Children can visit the bed in the morning. They can come by, and they can be in the bed if they're sick, but to make a habit of the children being in the marriage bed, blocks the profound sacredness of the marriage bed itself.

The dining room table is a powerful meeting place of family and community. According to Jewish belief, the family dining table is the highest altar of their faith in God.

The dining room is a place to gather together, a place of family prayer, a holy place of welcome to each one called to the table. It must be a place without distractions of what is next, like television or a game. It is uniquely to stand alone as a holy place – never a grabbing place for food or power.

The greatest meal I ever had at a dining table was at Ashdod, Israel with an Orthodox, Yemenite Jewish family. It was Shabat, the Jewish Sabbath, a Friday evening. We all stayed together, at the table, for two hours, sharing, talking of scripture, and singing sacred songs. This table was an altar because it was used as an altar.

If the table is sacred, family meetings held at the dining table became sacred events for sharing and planning. It is a place of every voice being "heard." It is the table of great decisions.

When our youngest daughter, Jennie, was five years old, we were having a final family dinner. My husband, Jerry, was moving out right after dinner.

There were five of us at the table. Everyone has a voice at our table; but the greatest voice that night was Jennie's. Speaking through that sacred Holy Spirit, she said, "Daddy, don't you know we need you?"

When Jerry left the table, he unpacked, and never considered leaving again!

I have never liked to do marriage counseling. People usually come in during advanced stages of blame and anger. They want to stay in a problem mode, and they want to continue the negativity as long as it is allowed. It is astonishing how hard people will fight to get their own way, and how little they know about the blessings of marriage.

I finally hit upon a really good idea and it was called "Agreement Counseling." The Holy Scriptures say that when two or more agree, then it is so. Now Agreement Counseling works on a whole different picture.

One day, my husband and I were in a car coming home from a camping trip. Our children were asleep in the back of the car, and I dared to open a conversation. I had been reading a book on prayer. I said to my husband, "May I say something?" He responded, "Shoot." I told him, very briefly, about the book, and how the book recommended that a couple pray together every day, but they only pray about those things they agreed upon. I asked him if he would be willing to try this and see if we could do it?

Immediately, a war broke out, for we had trouble agreeing to the prayer suggestions of one another. The resentment suggestions were made: "If you get off the phone, I'll agree to that prayer." We did this back and forth, two or three times, and then realized we were not being productive. By God's grace, we found our three agreements.

The next problem of significance was that it was extremely hard for us to remember to pray together, and if there was some tension or anger, my husband often did not want the prayer to take place. I had a lot of fear about this. I would humble myself, absolutely, and beg for the prayer to take place. But what about forgetting? That was really hard! We found that if the prayer time was forgotten for two or three days, we were back to the blame game and nothing was going well. Finally, I would say, "Look at me! Look at how bad I am! We have forgotten to pray. We must go back to prayer." It took us seven years to establish a pattern of consistent daily prayer together.

Often, I called my husband to come into the counseling office just to teach a couple this agreement-prayer. We decided on the morning for prayer. Our prayer lasted a maximum of three minutes. Whoever prayed first, prayed for the other, and for any family members who needed prayer. Then, the other one of us prayed, again following the same pattern. We learned the word, "amen" meant, "so be it." We had successful agreement prayer.

We made a new agreement. The agreement was that if either of us called for prayer, no matter what was going on, even if it was in the middle of a horrific fight, everything would stop, and we would pray an agreement prayer. It was amazing that never once, after that agreement prayer, did the fight resume for even three seconds! The negativity was gone. The darkness was gone, and the agreement stayed in the house.

Why such a short prayer? Isn't a long prayer better? I want to say to you, that my husband likes a short prayer, and that we agreed that this was the best prayer for us. If you want a longer prayer time, that's not a problem. The important thing is, there must be an agreement, and that agreement should meet the deeper needs of each of you.

I taught a Bible class of 100 women for 10 weeks. We were studying their relationships with God, others and themselves.

At the first class, I asked how many of the women prayed with their husbands. Only seven women said they did. I challenged all of them to begin to do this regularly, and taught them how to create agreement. Many women said, "My husband will never agree to this."

I persisted the whole 10 weeks, to create fertile ground for positive results. By the end of the ten weeks, every woman was praying with her husband daily.

Jerry and I made an agreement never to go to bed angry. The

scripture says, "Never let the sun set on your anger or else you will give the devil a foothold." Ephesians 4:26-27

This is exceedingly important, for if we go to bed and go to sleep angry, the anger and resentment go down into the storage of the subconscious mind, and this slowly creates a mountain of anger that will eventually explode, sometimes without any warning at all.

We could always tell if there was anger in us, because we didn't want to get close, or say "goodnight." We agreed to each take the responsibility for correcting ourselves. We have been 100% successful, because this has been a powerful agreement. We like agreements. It will defeat conflicts on any battlefield.

I can be mad at my husband all day long, and he can be mad at me, but when the light fades, it's gone, and the peace and the laughter come. Keep a good sense of humor. Keep it available at all times. Don't use tears to manipulate one another – ever! Use confession of your own sin, each of you, for your own healing, and for the rebirth of the marriage covenant.

One of the causes of the ruination of a marriage is game-playing. We could always say, "Well, my mate is just playing games." But, we must take personal responsibility to know individually the games we are playing ourselves.

Let's suppose the husband is terrifically out of order, and out of control. Does that give the wife the right to play a game, or can she stay free of games, and, therefore intercede for him? Can she agree with God for his peace of mind and healing?

Every marriage will have crisis periods. We've had three or four periods of major crises. It would have been easy to give up. The best thing in the whole of our lives, was that we kept the family together. We did not submit to be controlled by our flesh. It was a war and a struggle for each of us.

The best marriage counseling we ever had was by our pastor. He met first with my husband, and really got my husband to open up and tell the things he had done to undermine our marriage. Then, in the second session, I was brought in. My husband spoke to me, and told me he was fully responsible for all that had happened in our marriage. The pastor then turned to me and said, "What have you done?" I went down deep inside, and out came these words, "I gave up." Then, I had an overwhelming experience of the power of the love I had for this man. My love was hidden, and deeper than anything I could ever have dreamed. I could have confessed 1,000 sins, but it all came to one point. When I confessed I gave up, the love burst forth.

"I gave up." These are very powerful words. Remember these words. Keep them always. Giving up or giving in are destructive forces to our lives as individuals, let alone to the marriage itself.

What do I mean by "giving in?" It's when you pretend to agree, and you don't really agree. It's when you do not reveal what is true inside of yourself, always trying to please the other person, but not ever liking the fact that you are doing this. It is deep-rooted selfishness. You think, "In secret, I will give in." But you do not say in secret, "I will give."

My favorite scripture about marriage is found in Ephesians 5:21-28. In the Jerusalem Bible it starts: *"Give way to one another in obedience to Christ."*

Here is the perfect balance of mutual submission. The whole section is about submitting to God and submitting to one another. I love the words, *"Wives should regard their husbands as they regard the Lord."* Now is this always true? What if your husband just swore at you, and tore your whole personhood apart? Could you continue to regard your husband as you would the Lord, or does he have to earn it? It's a powerful question; a very powerful question. How, then, will you answer it?

To stay married is to maintain the generations of the family. We live in a season of divorces: broken generation, broken generation, broken generation. We must move to a new generation of holy marriage, great covenant, and profound friendship with God and one another.

Will you remember anything of what has been said here, or will you just maintain yourself in the status quo? Do not settle for a weak marriage. Do not wish you were married to someone else.

One day, about ten years ago, the Lord asked me a question. He said, "Do you think you deserve someone better?" I started to answer, "You're damn right I do!" All of a sudden, I put my hand over my mouth and I said, "Oh Lord, oh my God, my husband deserves someone better."

Part 2 – On Family

As a counselor, I found one over-riding consistent diagnosis of all clients and families: imbalance of power.

Often, in families, the imbalances of power show up clearly. One child may have a lot of power, another child feels powerless, a father is behaving as if he's powerless, and a mother is being domineering. We can remember, throughout our lifetime, all of the imbalances of power that we have seen and felt. We've experienced it in friendships, in schools, in churches; and, indeed, we have experienced imbalance of power in most parts of our lives.

Jesus is all about balance of power. When we look at a family, He did not teach on the roles of mothers, the roles of fathers, or the roles of children, He taught about "balance of power" that must permeate the lives of everyone.

If we are really going to live in the Kingdom of God, and know the dynamics of power in family life, we will have to know the words of Jesus that keep the family holy, respectful, and well-positioned with one another.

The greatest call to families is the Word, *"and you shall love the Lord your God with all your heart, soul, strength, and mind, and your neighbor as yourself."* (Luke 10:27) When I knew that my husband was my neighbor, my daughter was my neighbor, that all relationships outside of me were "my neighbor", and they were all defined by balance of power, it rearranged and changed everything inside of me. I became a new and consistent person with all people.

Internalized in the very core of our being, this becomes the "Kingdom of God within us." I love the scripture: *"Put yourselves to the test to make sure you are in the faith. Examine yourselves. Do you not recognize yourselves as people in whom Jesus Christ is present?"* (2 Corinthians 13:5)

I leave this challenge with you. You will have to discover for yourself the meanings and corrections that are hidden within this question.

We have become obsessed with disciplining children and yet, we as parents, have often been far more undisciplined than they are. We have become obsessed with children's behavior, but they often reflect the weaknesses in our own behavior. Do you agree? When are we going to check our own behavior and deal with it?

In 1979, I began a significant new journey, and developed Family Therapy Camp as part of Good Samaritan Ministries. The twice annual camps were always held at Christian Renewal Center, and they always involved several families. There was a special definition, however, that if you were a single adult living alone, you could come as you, too, were considered a family.

The goal of the weekend was to develop a single concept that every member of the family would learn together. This concept would be put into children's wording so that no one could miss the point.

On Friday evenings, in order to bring about the first balance of power, each person in the family had to stand on top of a fireplace hearth, face the whole camp, use a microphone, and introduce themselves. They were each to tell how old they were, and answer a simple question that brought individuality and individual viewpoints into the common understanding of each family. The goal of the camp, and the introductions, was that each family member had to speak for themselves, each one had to climb the hearth, and each one was responsible for their own words, and their own actions. It was astonishing to see that even the babies could participate. It might be a smile, it might be holding up one finger because they were one year old, but there was something that baby could do to balance the power of the camp. Occasionally, we had shy or difficult children that did not want to participate. They did! We consistently saw the families that played the most games were usually the participants in camp. We made sure the games began to end on that hearth, and that every person would understand what it would mean to love their neighbor as themselves, to show respect in order to gain respect.

Some of the families raised their children by the concepts of those camps. They built their family life and their family history around the concepts we learned together.

I particularly remember a boy named Steve. His mother first brought him to camp when he was about seven. Along the way, I baptized him. He had never met his father. His mother had addiction struggles. His life was tough. When the First Gulf War occurred, Steve was in the military in Kuwait and Iraq. He was living in a tank with the members of his team. He wrote to me and told me he was teaching all the members of his team, in that tank, the concepts he learned at Family Therapy Camp.

As the years have passed, I have become a stronger and stronger believer that families need to study together, worship together, play together, learn together, and experience together. Families can build upon agreed-upon concepts that they like and will use, not only in the nuclear family, but in the new families that lie ahead as the next generation grows into the next generation.

I want to pause at this point and ask you a point blank question: what are the concepts of your family? What determines a common standard of behavior in your family? Is it agreed upon? Is everyone participating? Does everyone believe that it is vitally important?

Some of the most memorable family therapy camp concepts have been:

1) You need to start from scratch with family money. Put all of it in one large jar, cashing the paychecks, and allowing the children to see what money is and what the family has. When you are going to pay a bill, let the children see you take the money for that bill out of the jar so that when the father

or the mother says, "we have no money," they understand that to be true. Never use "we have no money" as a control, a game, or a spiritual attitude towards money itself. Never, under any circumstances, play with the gifts that God has given the family to work together and to survive. When the family is low on money, or even has no money, children will gladly help. They will offer to get a part-time job. They will offer to help meet a deadline that the family could not do without their help. You draw the whole family into the role of economics, personal development and understanding. Teach them the truth about family provision!

2) Another concept that has been tremendously important is: *"All you need say is "Yes" if you mean yes, "No" if you mean no; anything more than this comes from the Evil One."* (Matthew 5:37) This means no double mindedness, and absolutely no mixed messages. It does not allow manipulation to control family decision-making. Parental answers or children's answers must be clear and well received. It means that you cannot mean one thing and say something else just to provide a temporary solution. A clear "yes" and "no" brings healthy balance in the family as a whole.

There is a core question, "Is it all right for children to say "no?" I believe it is. If you ask a child to do something and they say "no," the question can be redirected, "Would you be willing to do it tomorrow morning?" Almost always, the child that has a choice will then make the choice to say "yes."

3) *"Give, and there will be gifts for you: a full measure, pressed down, shaken together, and overflowing, will be poured into*

your lap; because the standard you use will be the standard used for you." (Luke 6:38)

We use a teeter-totter to understand this principle. People can go up and down, but they must keep a balance of power. If one person is holding another person hostage, there is no balance of power. The greatest balance of power is expressed in these words, *"As you give, so shall you receive."*

We find it very common that people might love to give, but feel embarrassed, or hate to receive. We find it common that they don't want to ask for help, so there is a scripture that goes with this: *"Until now you have not asked anything in my name. Ask and you will receive, and so your joy will be complete."* (John 16:24) We usually apply this scripture to God alone, but God applies it to all of our transactions with Him and with our neighbor.

Giving and receiving does not imply buying, loaning or selling. The Kingdom has a freedom in it, and a great and holy spontaneity.

When our daughter, Laura, was 16, she went with her father to look at a car he was considering buying. He didn't buy it. She went back the next day, and on her own, bought it for herself. She came home with the car. We accepted the fact that she had made a decision to buy the car, and we let the decision rest as part of her experiences.

About three months later, the car had a significant breakdown and the repair bill was $600. Now, if we operated on an imbalance of power, without a kind and generous heart, we would say, "Well, these are the consequences of you buying a car that Dad might have bought, and you'll have to learn to pay for your own repairs." Instead, I said, "Our gift is from God to encourage you. We will pay for the repair. We will give it to you by the Father's hand."

This child has gone on to be generous in heart and spirit. She has lived a life of giving and receiving.

Now, some people might say, isn't this enabling our child, and don't they have to take responsibility? This would not be a repeated pattern. It was one lesson, set aside in her lifetime. The lesson did not come from us, but from the Lord Himself.

I want to speak of chores. We made a list of all chores. The first day of school, we passed the chore list around and each of us signed up for chores until all the chores had been divided among us. We chose one chore at a time. The children saw the balance of power. They saved the easiest jobs for the youngest. We never had chore wars when this became our annual action step.

Some scriptures must be internalized and operational for a balance of power in family relational interactions:

"Never pay back evil with evil, but bear in mind the ideals that all regard with respect. As much as possible, and to the utmost of your ability, be at peace with everyone." (Romans 12:17)

"Do not be mastered by evil, but master evil with good." (Romans 12:21)

"So always treat others as you would like them to treat you; that is the Law and the Prophets." (Matthew 7:12)

"Be generous to one another, sympathetic, forgiving each other as readily as God forgave you in Christ." (Ephesians 4:32)

"Give, and there will be gifts for you: a full measure, pressed down, shaken together, and overflowing, will be poured into your lap; because the standard you use will be the standard used for you." (Luke 6:38)

"Be compassionate just as your Father is compassionate." (Luke 6:36)

This is only the beginning of the list. You yourself must seek and find the definitions that create your families' lifetime patterns. It is imperative that we act upon what we believe.

When I was a child, my mother taught me not to start sentences with "I," and not to put "I" at the center of my life. It was very hard to learn. She was teaching me this at three and four years of age. I don't believe I ever really passed the lesson, and I did not fully understand it for years. When I began to listen and believe the Lord's Prayer, I began to understand my mother's words,

> *"Our Father in heaven, may your name be held holy, your kingdom come, your will be done, on earth as in heaven. Give us today our daily bread. And forgive us our debts, as we have forgiven those who are in debt to us. And do not put us to the test, but save us from the Evil One."* (Matthew 6:9)

It has come to me often that in corporate worship, we continue to emphasize "I" words. "I love you Lord." Jesus emphasized inclusive words. "We" love you Lord.

When we pray the Lord's Prayer, we can bring the entire world into balance with us. Being aware that we pray with all of the generations, and with all of the nations, we are on the road to wholeness. Remember the words, *"And when I am lifted up from the earth, I shall draw all people to myself."* (John 12:32) The reality of ourselves is "Our Father."

Families need themes. The themes need to suit who you are and how you want to be noted. The themes are sometimes developed in the beginning of marriage, but usually they develop gradually as we learn to live together for definite purpose.

Does your family have a theme? Does everyone in the family know the theme? Has the family developed the theme as a family unit?

Themes may be one word, such as "trust," action words, such as "We live for Christ," playful words, such as "adventure;" or an ethical word, such as "courage." Themes have endless possibilities, but no theme will be worth very much unless every family member grasps the theme.

CHAPTER 11

My Father

When a baby is born, it is presented to the father. The baby is a gift from God. It is a great moment in a man's life to receive his new child.

You have learned that my father had distant priorities. It was hard for me to communicate with him, because he could not communicate back. He lived in his own world.

I want to talk about the breakthrough.

First, and foremost, we must never give up. I fought for my father. I fought hard for his life. I fought for him to know God, and for his heart needs to be met.

I received wounds in the spirit. The disappointments usually involved money, or the spirit of banality. As I did not know the definition of this word when the Lord first revealed this as a core problem on my father's side of the family, I give you the definition: banality is a hackneyed or trite expression that is used frequently. You've seen it in this book. My grandfather always responded he wanted "beans and eggs."

I admired many things about my father. Once he was out of work for a year, and he had to look for a common sales job. Rather than seeking pity, or a handout, he sought that common job and held it willingly for a year while he developed a very significant part of his life's work.

When my father was 65, he was hospitalized with severe and life-threatening health issues. He had two embolisms and nearly died. The doctors decided they would operate on him. During the operation, he did die. Since he was on an operating table, it was a well-documented truth.

From that moment of his death, he described an experience with heaven. This experience had such a powerful lasting impact on his life, that he spoke of it the rest of his life. The banality was gone.

First, my father described he was met by his earthly father, who put his arms around him and told him he loved him. He said the colors and the intensity of hues in heaven were unbelievable. It is a place that has no equal. He said he saw Jesus at a distance, and the Lord sent him back, waving him back to this life.

It took my father over a year to recover his health. He was a man physically broken, but spiritually healed.

My father talked about this experience all the time, which annoyed my mother because she felt like he was talking too much about himself. In 1978, my father and mother joined a 27-day tour I led. The tour included a journey into Syria and Turkey, where we visited Antioch, on the Orontes River. There is a cave on a cliff near the city. This cave became the early church, the place from where Paul and Barnabas were sent forth on their first missionary journey. While we were in the cave, which contained a wall facing outward and an altar table within, my father was slain in the spirit. Unbeknownst to us, he had been asking the Lord, "Why didn't you receive me? Why was I sent back?"

When my father came around, he had seen the Lord. The Lord had spoken to him and told him why he had been sent back. He had also instructed my father never to tell anyone what He had told him.

My father was again a transformed man. The spirit of God rested upon him. It was a remarkable event, culminating my many years of being for him, not against him. True to the Lord's word, he never told anyone what the Lord had said.

In 1983, my father was still alive. I took another tour group of fifty people. We made a journey that included the stop at Antioch on the Orontes River in Turkey. When I entered the altar room, I too was slain in the spirit. Some in the group picked me up and laid me on top of the altar. Some considerable time passed, and I knew what the Lord had said to my dad. My dad was not to talk about his experience, but show it through his actions. He would reveal the Lord by his actions. I then understood the years that preceded 1983. I understood that the Lord was sustaining my father to keep his assignment, and to fulfill his revelation of the Kingdom of God by his common actions in the Spirit!

In 1983, my father and mother made a trip around the United States visiting my father's relatives. It was a very exhausting journey, as it even included going to Florida. When they came home, I met them at their car. My father got out of the car and said these words, "They are all saved."

In the early 80's, my father unexpectedly knocked on our door one morning. He had never, in his lifetime, come alone to see me or to have a conversation. He had rarely been willing to talk on the phone for more than a few moments before he handed the phone to mother. He came in and said, "I want to talk to you." This was one of the greatest shocks of my life; a shock that brought me absolute joy. We sat down at our dining room table and my father said the following words, "When I was a young man, I had all of the spiritual gifts you have and even more. Then I began to compromise, and I lost them all." He looked me in the eye, in my full face, and said, "NEVER COMPROMISE!" As suddenly as he came, he got up and left.

In January 1984, my father had a major stroke. He died six months later.

I want to comment on one other story. It is important for you to understand the whole.

After my father had his stroke, he was in a state of great confusion. My mother had Alzheimer's disease, and she was very fragile. I took her into his hospital room at 8:00 the following morning. As we walked in the room, he had grabbed the nurse and was trying to kiss her. This upset me so badly, I said these words, "Lord, I want you to take him to hell."

Five days passed, and the Lord gave me an assignment. He said, "If you can think of five good things that your father has done for you in his lifetime, I will save him."

My wrath was so advanced that it was very hard for me. One of the memories I remembered was when my father, mother, and I decided, on a Friday night, we would go to a movie. There was so much snow outside, that it was up to my knees, but they called the movie theatre, and the movie was running. Although it was almost two miles away, my dad pulled me on the sled all the way there and all the way home. After a few days, five great memories brought closure and permanency in my profound love for my father.

My father was in a nursing home close to our house. I could go to visit him frequently. My mother could get there. I was scheduled to go to the Holy Land. It was 1984. I was radically exhausted from what happened during the eight years of my life as a Samaritan. The work had exploded, and I saw tremendous needs everywhere I looked and listened. My Israeli brother, Sam Bar-El, offered to pay part of my way if I would come with another tour group, not run by myself. I decided to go.

Before I left home, I went to see my father to say goodbye. We had a very intimate talk, and then I said, "Perhaps you will not be here when I get back. Would you give me your blessing?" Then, he asked me for my blessing. Those were our last moments together.

I was baptizing people in the Jordan River when I suddenly became aware that my father had started to die. It was just a "knowing." Three days later, I was at a hotel in Tel-Aviv. The tour group had left and I was remaining behind to rest and visit the Bar-El family. Alone, I awakened from my sleep, and said aloud, "My father has just died." I called home. He had just died.

I learned more about my Father in Heaven from my father on earth than I did from anyone else. No organized training could give greater clarity than the steady comfort of God's own house.

Again and again, I have come back to my father's words, "never compromise." Many clients have needed those words. Many people have been healed by my father's faithful testimony to tell me the truth.

CHAPTER 12

Leading Tours

I have been to 55 countries, and 24 times to the Middle East. Leading tours has been a significant part of the call on my life. By taking people away from their families and environment, God heals, challenging and encouraging each to reach their own effectiveness. During the tour the evil often comes out in heavy doses.

In this chapter, I am going to give you the stories that stand out in my recollection of events and people we met along the way. This will allow you to see highlights and the incredible opportunity for each person to be along the road of learning to live and work together as a team, in the Kingdom of God.

The tours that I led number at least 16. The following countries were involved: The Netherlands, Israel (Palestinian territories and Gaza), Syria, Jordan, Egypt, Lebanon, Cyprus, Greece, Turkey, Poland, Italy, China, and Japan.

At the end of these stories, I will give a summary of the most important concepts I learned about leadership. This will give you a chance to consider leading tours. I share the essentials I learned the hard way from a lot of experience.

Monk Alexander

In 1976, when we were on the way to Mt. Sinai, after being held on the border in Jordan, we stopped for the night at a town called Dahab. During the evening, two or three of our people met a monk who was sleeping on the beach of the Gulf of Aquaba at Dahab. His name was Monk Alexander. He was attempting to get back to St. Catherine's Monastery, where he served as the monk in charge of the Charnal Room, where the bones of all of the deceased monks were kept on display for people who wanted to see them.

We offered to take Monk Alexander to St. Catherine's, which he gladly accepted. He talked to us a lot on the way up, but when we arrived, he said, "I cannot talk to you anymore because I must be silent, and just available when I'm called to be available."

As we were leaving Mt. Sinai, I met briefly with Monk Alexander, got his address, and learned significantly more about his life. He gave me some of his poetry. We became friends.

"We became friends" could be the seam of this whole chapter. I'm going to put it in bold black for you: **We became friends**. Much of being on the road, and the purpose of going, is developing lifetime friendships. How deep will the friendships go, and how long will they last?

1978 Tour

In 1978, I led a tour of 38 people, which crossed all of Israel, Syria, most of Turkey, and included going to Haran in Eastern Turkey. Then, from Istanbul, we flew to Thessaloniki per our world map, to finish the journey of Biblical sites, including Thessalonica, Athens, Philippi and Corinth.

This was a terribly difficult tour experience. Our guide in Turkey was a woman who was hysterical. Her mother was in Beirut, where bombings occurred daily. In addition, the woman confided in me that she had been married 25 years and her marriage had never been consummated. She was an emotional wreck, and I spent most of the time sitting next to her in front of the bus just keeping her calm and able to focus. She spoke no Turkish. Our bus driver spoke no language but Turkish, so a Turkish translator had to be added to the staff taking us on the 10-day journey across Turkey. Often, for hours and hours we had no stops. But I can still say to you that Turkey is a very great country, and I love the experiences we had.

By the time we reached Istanbul, I was pretty much a wreck. When you are the person leading a tour, you have to keep a lot of personal, emotional control. You can't just say what you think all the time. You can't fly off. You have to be patient, longsuffering, and probably a better person than you are in the usual sense of the word.

By the time we reached Istanbul, I was ready to explode. In fact, I got on an empty elevator at floor three, and as I went down to floor one, I kicked the wall of the elevator all the way down. Needless to say, by the next morning, I was dreadfully sick, as an emotional explosion produces sickness in your body. I had a full case of diarrhea and vomiting, and we had to get on the plane and fly to Thessalonica.

When we got off the plane, there was a huge surprise. There was Monk Alexander, meeting the plane with a bouquet of flowers. He told me a very special story of how this came to pass. He was staying in a monastery in Greece, and under the vow of silence. He was not to leave. Three nights in a row, the Lord spoke to him and told him to go meet me in Thessalonica at the airport. The Lord gave specific instructions, and after the fourth night, he talked to his confessor. His confessor said, "You must go," and thus, he was there! Again, he met with the people and gave them encouragement, which they badly needed. But most of all, I was healed by the instant recognition that God's grace covered me. For the sake of the whole group, His grace covered us all.

1981 Tour

In 1981, two other women and I put together a tour group of 43 people. The whole tour was one of the most unusual experiences of my life.

First of all, who would go? Some members of the homosexual community had contacted me and asked if they could go. I said, "Yes." As the tour group came together, there were two couples whose marriages were in the final stages of death, seven people who were drug addicts or alcoholics, three homosexuals, two lesbians, my Aunt Audrey from Denton, Kansas, and an assortment of business and family people.

Before we left the United States, our flights to the Middle East were changed. Instead of going across the U.S., as originally scheduled, we were suddenly scheduled to fly across Canada, and stop in Munich, Germany.

On the entire flight across Canada, we were served free alcohol. Two teens on the trip were drinking heavily. I believed their father should stop them. When the father didn't, I stood up, looked at the young men, and said, "If you have one more drink I am sending you both home on the next plane." My Aunt Audrey from Kansas stood and announced to the whole plane, "And I will help her!"

I knew my friend, Monk Alexander, was in the Black Forest near Munich, Germany. I was able to make contact with him before we left. I said in the letter I sent, "If you can come with us to Athens, go to the Munich Airport." I told him what time we were to arrive, and that I would come out the gate and look for him. If he were there, we would pay for his ticket to go with us to Athens. Sure enough, he was in Munich, and we sat next to each other on the plane to Athens! During our visit on that plane, I learned that Monk Alexander had been a hippie teen. One day, he got a cheap ticket on a boat to tour the Greek Islands, and found himself on the Island of Patmos (where St. John wrote the book of Revelation). When he went up to visit the Greek monastery, they would not let him go in because he was not properly attired. Lo and behold, standing outside the monastery, he received Christ, which led him to train to become a Greek Orthodox Monk. He told me it is common to live in highs and lows, but it is important to live a consistent life in the Spirit. We must not be driven by experience, but guided by the faithfulness of the Lord. I found out Monk Alexander had spent nearly seven years living in a cave on the Mt. of Temptation near Jericho, interceding for the world, before being assigned to Mt. Sinai.

When we got to Athens, I put him in charge of spiritual matters with the group. We were there two full days and three evenings. When our time with him was coming to end, he and I had a very profound conversation. He said, "I have never seen a worse group of people! How can you take these people to the Holy Land?" I said, "Surely these are the people that need to go more than any." Surprisingly, we became closer friends. He remembered his own story at Patmos.

I have not heard from Monk Alexander for many years. We used to write letters. Once in awhile he would send an icon. But then the mail stopped, and I know he is in the silent monastery for life. I remain with the gift of some of his poems. Here is a bit of what he has written:

"In the home of the crippled children. A shattering sight; the sad-apathetic eyes. But speak a few kind words, give a small toy and stroke their little heads and this is to them like sun-rays on Easter morning. But don't come only once but as often as there are Sundays in the year, because one single good deed is only a whim, a rain, then draught."

The 1983 Tour

The 1983 tour impacted all of us, and this journey has brought fruit up to now.

First of all, we were 45 people flying from Oregon to Damascus, Syria on the first lap of the journey. When we arrived in St. Louis, there was plane trouble. We were delayed five hours. We spent much of that time on the hot plane, before we were able to fly to

New York City. When we arrived in New York City, of course, our plane to Damascus had left. Now some of the people, who were on this tour, had severe financial problems; in fact, some of them were given scholarships to go. One of the girls had $25, and another girl had $75 to spend on the whole trip. Here we were in New York needing to catch a plane to Damascus, Syria. How does one get 45 seats on a plane to Damascus, Syria in a reasonable length of time?

By God's grace, the airlines sent the group to a hotel. I stayed at the airport until 2:00 a.m. to assure us of a plane to get to Syria. They finally found a way to get us to Damascus, Syria, but we would not be leaving New York until 8:00 p.m. the following night.

Since the following day was Sunday, I decided to see if we could get a tour of New York City. Amazingly, that was arranged. I believe it cost $20 per person. To me, it was a miracle! Since I had been to New York City before, I took them to places I found important and interesting. An example would be the first U.S. Capitol where George Washington became the first president of the United States. That small building is still quietly standing near the Stock Exchange, with the financial towers of the world around it. There is a plaque of George Washington in the front facade, kneeling in prayer.

Excited that we were visiting St. Patrick's Cathedral, a woman named Margaret began to gush with enthusiasm. She had been in the Bible classes I taught for many years. She wanted to go on this tour! Every week, Margaret stood up in Bible class and said, "I know I'm going to go! I know the Lord is going to provide for it!" Eventually, a man with a serious mental disorder, who was in the Bible class, came up to me, and said, "I'm going to pay for Margaret to go. Don't tell her." The provision was also for her passport, all visas, and expense money. Tour paid in full! The man also went on the tour!

As we were coming into St. Patrick's Cathedral, and Margaret was still gushing with her enthusiasm, she suddenly, brightly announced, "I haven't been here since my wedding day. My husband and I were married at St. Patrick's Cathedral by Cardinal Spellman. I must go down to the altar where we were married." Suddenly, I knew our delay was part of God's grace over Margaret's life. I can't say that it made me terrifically happy at the time, but I tell you, the joy in that woman was profound for the rest of the journey. God had many surprises for those on this journey!

When we arrived at Damascus, we met our final tour members, a family of five: three children and their parents. They had waited three days and they had been worried about us because we had not arrived. They had come from Saudi Arabia. Paul, the father, had been writing the Food and Drug Laws for Saudi Arabia. They had been there almost three years. They had been doing some quiet witnessing. They were given 48 hours to leave the country. Here, they met us and joined the tour. We now numbered fifty.

A tragedy for me, personally, was my suitcase was lost. It contained many gifts and special awards. All the suitcases arrived in Damascus except two, another woman's and mine. Within two days, her suitcase arrived. At the end of our time in Syria, my suitcase had not arrived, and we were leaving by bus for Jordan.

I made an emergency trip, in a taxi alone, to the airport to see if possibly the missing suitcase was somewhere in the airport. It was nowhere and I had to make peace with the fact that everything in that suitcase was gone.

As I returned from the airport without the suitcase, it was about 10:00 at night and I hadn't had any dinner. I went into the dining room, when I saw there was a light on in the corner, to see if I could get some food. In the corner, the waiters were sitting having their dinner together. They invited me to sit with them and eat. I was telling them my problem about my lost suitcase, and I was on the verge of crying. We all began to reveal our problems. All four of them were Palestinians. All four of them had to leave their families, and all four of them were trying to make enough money to support their families at home. I began to have something different to cry about. It was the dawn, the beginning of a relationship with the Palestinians that would last through the rest of my life.

As if we didn't have enough problems in New York, one of our tour members, Becky, a girl in her mid-20s, had advanced Cystic Fibrosis. She required a minimum of four hours of lung treatments daily. These treatments had to be given twice a day.

In New York, we went to the airport in the late afternoon. We had to find a place to give Becky her treatments. She needed to lie on a slanted bed or board; one man, Pastor Ted Baker, agreed to give the treatments to her, but where? I went downstairs, found an empty room with a door lying on the floor. This door could be propped up for the treatment.

When we got to Frankfurt, Germany, Becky needed another treatment in the airport. Fortunately, they had an in-airport medical facility, and they volunteered to give the treatments.

After three days in Syria, we were in the northern Syrian city of Aleppo. We took Becky's temperature. It was almost 104 degrees. I could have panicked, but this would have helped nothing. We laid her down and gave her a treatment. The next day, we left her to rest while we went to Antioch, Turkey.

When we returned to Allepo, Becky was better. She had received a scholarship for her whole tour to the Middle East. She had to make it!

She made it, and it made all of the difference in her life!

There is one more story about the Syria tour of 1983. This story took place at the hotel in Allepo, Syria. Again, I was alone in the dining room and the lights were dim. There was a group of Russian Advisors to Syria (KGB men), about ten or more of them eating and drinking at a table. They obviously wanted to be alone.

Having the Holy Boldness, which often defines my character, I walked over to their table and asked them if I could sit down and have a beer with them. They were hospitable and I could talk with them. Every eye was riveted to me, wondering what this could be about. I began to tell them that I knew about the suffering of Russia. I personally knew that 20 million Russians were killed during World War II. I knew of the pain and suffering of Mother Russia. I told them I knew that they each prayed. Deep inside, none of us can stop praying. It is part of who we are. God made it to be so. Slowly, I got up, left the table, and went to the tour group. I invited them over because we were going to dance. They marched out of the dining room in formation.

The Syrian advisor to the Russians returned after they left. "That was a miracle, greater than you know." He said.

The highlight of the whole tour for all of us was the Syrians. They were so excited to see us. We were the first Americans to come to Syria in two years. We celebrated, with all of them, along the road, and every one of us fell in love with Syria.

Once we came to Israel, there would be an event of that 1983 tour; a prayer that was prayed that has borne fruit ever since that hour.

I had a Muslim friend named, Yassin, who was a student at Bethlehem University. I had asked him if we could come to his house for lunch. (All 50 of us!) He had agreed. I said afterwards, "Can you go down the road with us to the Inn of the Good Samaritan?" It was only about six miles from Bethany, and then we would bring him back to Bethany, leave and go on. He said, "Yes."

We came to the Inn of the Good Samaritan, which was, at that time, a pretty primitive place. It consisted of a small building and a courtyard. I suddenly said, "Yassin, what if we all laid hands on you, prayed, and asked for you to do the Lord's work, to do the kind of work that I do? Would you be willing for us to lay hands on you and pray?" He said, "Yes I am willing." All 50 of us said that prayer over his life.

Later in the book, I'm going to write a whole chapter about Yassin. It suffices to say, on that day, Yassin went into the Kingdom of God. When he got out of the bus in Bethany, he said, "What do you want me to do?" I said, "The Lord will tell you. I'll be back next year to see what you did." At the time, I had no plans to be back in 1984, but the Lord being faithful to who He is, I was back in 1984. The Israeli guide helped pay for my trip, and I didn't have to lead a tour. It was a miracle. When I went to Yassin's house to stay for several days, I asked him to show me what he had done. He took me to Bethlehem University. We went into a classroom where there were five other young men, all students at Bethlehem University (five Muslims and one Christian.) I opened the conversation saying I was 50 years old, and I had come to talk to them about the Parable of the Good Samaritan. I had come to ask them what they were going to do to help their people. I came to talk to them about counseling and the kinds of work they could do to make a difference. Immediately they responded, "We don't need counselors. Our family elders are our counselors. What does this parable have to do with us?" Nevertheless, we continued the conversation for two hours and then I said, "Go home, get your things. You'll go with us up to the Galilee." Although it was not a place they could legally go, the Israelis in charge of the tour agreed to take them. For two days we were together. I said, "If you like us, if we like you, if it is important to both of us, then we'll go on. If not, then you've had two days in the Galilee, and we've had an opportunity to learn more about each other." They agreed. This would begin a very significant journey with the Palestinians. This journey still continues. In 1989, one of those Palestinians became our legally adopted son, Mohammad Bader.

Journey in 1985

In 1985, my husband and I came to the Holy Land twice. The first time, we came in March for a wedding. Our great Israeli friend's only daughter was being married, and we decided to go to the wedding. There was a large reception in Tel Aviv with more than 200 people present. Because we were the only Christians at the wedding, and because we were very special friends of the family, Sam Bar El, the father, said I will invite whomever you want to come from the West Bank. Two tables of people from the West Bank came to the wedding. Again, Tel Aviv was off the list for the Palestinians to visit, but the Lord arranged that this would take place. It was truly a miracle.

At that time, we had already made a decision to legalize an organization called Al Sadiq Al Taieb Association (ASTA). Yassin, Mohammad Bader and I went to see an Israeli attorney, Joseph Azram, in Tel Aviv. He was glad he could help us. We legalized ASTA as a non-profit in Israel. We had offices in Jerusalem. We were the last Palestinian non-profit organization ever legalized by the Israelis.

Later, Joseph Azram took the legalization papers to the Palestinians in Jerusalem. It was Ramadan. Together, they sat outside the ancient walls of Jerusalem, on ancient stones, and the papers were signed. ASTA is our oldest international non-profit organization in the history of Good Samaritan Ministries. Our director has been Majed Alloush since 1985

.

The 1985 Tour

In June of 1985, a Jewish woman and I led a tour to study inter-faith relations. We went first to Poland and visited many of the holocaust and concentration camp sites, as well as the old Jewish cemetery in Warsaw. It was an incredible experience to go to Poland. As we went to Auschwitz and spent half a day there (note: I had been to Auschwitz before with our daughter, Jennie, and my husband in 1983), we visited the original buildings, the crematorium, now crumbling with age, and saw the films that were captured by the Russians when they liberated the camp. On the way back to Krakow, I asked each on the tour to write a poem or essay. I can remember so clearly one man said, "Well, I know I'm supposed to feel something, but I don't feel anything." He couldn't write. Everyone crosses a bridge, and some have a hard time processing what is unspeakable and unknown.

As the tour group went on into the Holy Land, we picked up seven Palestinians along the road that were at a prearranged location. All of these Palestinians were Muslims. We picked up three Druse. The Druse are the fourth monotheistic religion in the Middle East. With the Muslims and Druse, three Jewish people, and 32 Christians we began our inter-faith journey. We made a 10-day journey throughout the Holy Land. Each of us was to see for ourselves what God had done in this land. Our visit to the Jordan River was memorable.

I had written to Abuna Elias Chacour, asking if he would meet with this group up at Ibillin in the Galilee. He wrote back and said he would make an exception and meet with us. He was in fasting and prayer that week and he was seeing no one. Because we were traveling together in a powerful interfaith experience, he would make the exception. Thus, for the first time, I personally met Abuna Elias Chacour, who went on to become a good friend. He is a man of significance in Christianity, and interreligious peacemaking. He developed the possibility of a healthy relationship between the Palestinians and the Israelis. Twice he was nominated for the Nobel Peace Prize. When Shimon Peres received the Nobel Peace Prize instead, as soon as Peres returned to Israel, he made a special trip up to that small village of Ibillin to share the prize with his friend, Abuna Elias Chacour.

Today, Abuna Elias Chacour is the Archbishop of the Marionite Catholic Church. They are the largest Christian denomination present today in the Holy Land.

It was at the final banquet of that tour that Fadel Bader, a part of the birth of ASTA, did a final closing speech to all of us. Abuna Chacour brought us close to the real Christ of salvation.

1988 International GSM Convention, Jerusalem

The first International Convention of Good Samaritan Ministries took place in Jerusalem in 1988. We had two internationals with us, our National Director from Kenya, James Opiyo, and Sadiq Masih from Karachi, Pakistan. In addition, we had 30 members of Good Samaritan from the United States. All members of ASTA joined us! This was a very significant journey because we were not coming just to look at holy sites or to have personal religious experiences, we were coming together for the Lord to work on us, to open our eyes, to develop our conscience, and to develop a spirit that would unify Good Samaritan Ministries with the needs of others. In this journey, there were two significant stories.

Sadiq was a pastor from Pakistan. Pakistani people were not allowed to get visas for Israel or come into the Holy Land. God would change this for Sadiq by a miracle. I had suggested to Sadiq that he fly to Cairo and take a bus to Mt. Sinai. He was to climb Mt. Sinai the night before, stay there, and meet us the next morning on top of Mt. Sinai. He, being very eager to do this, made the journey, and followed the instructions. He was wearing white patent leather shoes. When he came to Mt. Sinai, he discovered this was an enormous task, taking hours and hours to climb while carrying his suitcase. His white patent leather shoes wore his feet into a bad condition. Sadiq was diabetic. When we reached the top, there he was. There we were. James Opiyo of Kenya put his arms around Sadiq of Pakistan on top of Mt. Sinai. The relationship between the

Kenyans, the Pakistanis, and GSM has been very powerful since that hour.

Now, of course, we had to come into Israel and we did not know if we could get Sadiq in without a visa, a visa he would never be allowed to receive. Here he was with no visa and not allowed to come in because he was Pakistani. Nevertheless, our Israeli guide, who had gotten us to the top of Mt. Sinai on that journey, agreed to meet him at the Israeli border and try. When we came to the crossing, the border police said absolutely no. Sam Bar-El talked to them for awhile, and he talked them into calling Jerusalem to see if they could get special permission. They did, and they got the permission. The only hitch was that Sadiq had to leave his passport at the border, and he would have to pick it up when he went back to Egypt to go back to Pakistan. This took place, and Sadiq was the first Pakistani to ever be allowed into the Holy Land of Israel.

During the International Conference, which included many Palestinians, we visited several refugee camps, and made a journey into Gaza Strip. This was not just for the purpose of knowing the story of the Palestinians. It was for the purpose of bonding Israelis and Palestinians in a permanent way that could influence both sides. The journey developed and matured the members of Good Samaritan Ministries. We were developing strength as permanent peacemakers. The journey helped to strengthen ASTA.

At the end of the International Conference, the tour group went home. I stayed on in the Holy Land with James Opiyo and others from the United States who were willing to stay. It was the 25th anniversary of my healing in the Jordan River. We were staying at Yassin's house in Bethany.

I asked Sam Bar-El, who lived near Tel Aviv, to drive to Bethany, West Bank, and pick us up. I asked him to take us to the Jordan River. I wanted to celebrate the 25th anniversary of that day with all of us together! Sam Bar-El is a very unique individual.

He is hard to describe. All I can say is that he remains one of my greatest teachers.

It was a strike day, and all of the Palestinian businesses and shops were shut down. As we drove near Ramallah, a boy came running to throw a stone at us. Here we were, in an Israeli marked tourist car, several Christians, breaking the rules of the strike. I yelled, "duck!" Sam Bar-El chided me for this. He said, "Do you think I would drive through the West Bank on a strike day if I did not know God is with us?"

As we rode farther north, toward the Jordan River, Sam stopped us in a Palestinian Village and said, "I want you to meet someone while we are here." Lo and behold, he took us in to meet a necromancer, a woman who was hired to spin fortunes. The room was full of Israeli soldiers wanting their fortunes told. Needless to say, we did not ask for any help from her; but the experience was a strange balance to the sacred visit to the Jordan River. It gave us a unique look at the strange events that happened as Jesus travelled along the road, one day delivering the Gerasene demoniac, and another day, worshipping and teaching on the Mount of the Beatitudes. I believe the combination of these two visits that day were a significant lesson for Christianity; a lesson Jesus gave which could so easily be ignored. Would we know Jesus? Would we really know Him?

When we arrived at the Jordan River it was late in the afternoon. It was in October because that was the anniversary time. We sat down at the Jordan. We didn't get in the water, we just sat down to be together. I was thinking, "What is it that brought us here today?" Sam Bar-El and I had a conversation. During the conversation at the Jordan, he said, "My son, Avi, has serious psychological problems. I would like for you to do for Avi what I have done for you in the last 25 years. Whatever happens to Avi, even if he would become a Christian, I will bless it." Finally, I just simply spoke out loud to all who were near us at the Jordan River. I gave my testimony. We quietly left and drove at night back to Bethany. Sam went home.

I choose to close this chapter by developing the wisdom I gained from the years I spent on the road with tour groups. I challenge you to consider, could you be a tour leader? Are you one who will make a difference on the road you will take?

Each tour must have its own theme. The theme is very important because it helps you to develop the training you will give to the people going, before the tour leaves. I suggest at least two or three meetings before the tour takes place to give specific training, not only in where they are going and what they are going to see, but how this will unfold, and what is expected of them. Being well prepared will make a huge difference in their journey.

Responsibilities of a Tour Leader

A tour leader is responsible to work in compatibility and confidence with agents and tour guides in each country. Together, they must present a positive, encouraging relationship, as it will make a great difference in the quality of the tour that is given. The tour guides receive a list of sites that tourists want to see. They don't receive anything else. Without this relationship between the tour guide and the tour leader, without the development of the theme of the tour, and the development of the relationship between the guides and the people, then you'll just see a site, hear the history of the site, take a few pictures, take a few notes and go on. This is not an effective tour. This is not a journey of growth. The purpose of a spiritual journey is to bring together an encounter with God, and the people with one another. If you are looking for the definition of a tour, it is this: the group is to love the Lord their God with all their heart, soul, strength and mind, and their neighbor as themselves. Without this working and growing in you, as the leader, it will seldom work in most of the people on the tour. What you are interested in, what you can add to the tour, what encouragement you can give, what personal relationship you can develop with each person on the tour, brings about a season of great miracles and life-changing experiences, the Kingdom of God in our midst.

Airplane Instructions
• Be on time and don't wander off.
• You are not to carry over-weight luggage.
• Drink no coffee, tea, or pop, and no alcohol on the plane as this will cause dehydration.
• You are to drink water or juice every hour you are awake, and you are to stand or walk on the plane once an hour.

I learned that if these instructions were not followed, most of the group would have sickness, usually within two or three days. This can only be prevented by ample hydration.

You are responsible. Take this responsibility to heart. On a larger tour, you must share the leadership. As the key leader, you are responsible for the clarity of each person's assignment. The assignments must be agreed upon.

Jerry and I did well leading tours together. He handled the back of the bus and the tail of all stops. I handled the front, and all the instructions.

If you become ill, or you are not able to be responsible, you must immediately appoint someone else to be responsible. You are responsible for how people relate to one another, how well they listen and respect the guides, and the timing of the journey. You are responsible to make good decisions in facing times of danger. You are responsible to take a leadership role and be a person of deep prayer and living faith. You are to encourage this in the people. You are responsible, in God's eyes, and He is responsible over all. You are responsible if there is some acting out, which always happens. It is easy to blame the people who act out. On one tour, a woman stole drugs from a drug store. She wasn't caught, but I was informed that she did do it. Now, it would have been easy for me to get mad at the woman, blame the woman, and become hyper-vigilant. But, I had to remember that I was responsible for what she did and how I handled this. That's a hard call, for most people want to push the responsibility on others and keep their own space for themselves. You may not believe this, but I want you to ponder it and see if it is true.

There are three kinds of travelers that stand out over the years. Some will be kind and courteous. They will be interested in what the guide is saying, they will show interest in the sites, and they will be interested in everything they experience, including the people on the bus with them. They will be miracles for the sake of many.

A different kind of traveler is more interested in themselves than they are their neighbors. They get bored, restless and fussy. Their irritability can destabilize a tour group if it cannot be dealt with diplomatically. I learned that it could always be dealt with, and the person could always grow in the spirit.

The third kind of traveler is, perhaps, the hardest for me. After every meal they fall asleep on the bus. They are not looking at the wild flowers, or the rocks they go by, or places where God significantly did miracles. They are just "comfortable" and they are on a journey to experience a few things, but to basically not be inconvenienced by the whole experience. Now, these last two types of travelers may sound very negative; as if the miracle traveler is "always good," and the others are "always bad." But, I think there is a little of each of those three travelers in each one of us. I'm not making a list of those who were one way, and those who were another way, but I'm saying that these things you will see for yourselves. One must ponder and pray for the integration of everyone into the whole group and full experience.

Evaluating Yourself Daily

Processing is important to each individual on the tour. There are things that you must process, and, as a leader, you must evaluate yourself each day. How did I do today? What do I need to do tomorrow that I did not do today? Were my directions clear and followed? Self examination led by the Holy Spirit can produce remarkable growth in you as a leader. You will find you drastically need this growth!

Significant Assignments

The "Hot Seat" is the microphone being used on the bus by the tour people, as well as the guide and yourself. Many can share using the "Hot Seat" and the microphone on long drives!

I have found it very important to give everyone on the tour significant assignments. An example of this: "When we go to the Jordan, you are each to plan. Who do you want to baptize you? Do you want any scripture? Do you want a song?" When 32 people are going to be baptized, this is a long baptism experience. All baptisms are individualized. We've always stayed at least two hours at the Jordan, sometimes longer. When people go home, this experience is something they will keep deep inside. This depth will produce change in them day by day. With every baptism, raising their arms up to God, praying for the infilling of the Holy Spirit, and anointing them with oil completes the baptism. Usually, about half of the people want to be baptized. Watching the baptisms is a powerful experience. The Israelis and Muslims have been deeply moved by what they saw.

Share the responsibility for prayer with all of the people. Share the responsibility of worship with all of the people. Share the responsibility of intercession with all of the people. In all of this, the list could be endless, but this is what you must remember: give everyone significant assignments.

Prepare Them to Go Home

On any tour I organized, we were almost gone three weeks, and visited two to three countries. With a tour group, the first week is the honeymoon period, where everyone is very excited. The second week, people are getting very tired and crabby, and the relationship difficulties burst out at about this time. Traveler sickness is common at this time. The third week, the group is beginning to integrate. They are getting along better, and they are thinking a lot about going home. It is in the third week that you begin to develop them to go home prepared to lead significant lives from this experience. What did you learn on this journey? What are you going to share when you get home? Who are you going to share it with? I teach the people that someone may come up to you and ask, "How was your trip?" You may start to say something, and then they may start talking about their last three weeks. They must expect this to happen. They must not be turned off or disappointed when it happens, but they must expect it will occur. It is normal that most people center more on what they've experienced; much more than what someone else has experienced.

I suggest they be more specific about sharing, and more specific about choosing with whom they will share this experience. Set a time that is convenient for both of you. Ask for the time you need, "Can I spend two hours with you and share with you what happened?" When those agreements are made, great breakthroughs can happen in your life as well as in the lives of your family and neighbors at home.

In all of the years we went on tour, the two greatest spiritual moments seemed consistently to be the climb of Mt. Sinai, and being washed in the Jordan River.

It has been quite remarkable that on almost every journey, almost everyone climbed Mt. Sinai. Most reached the top and safely descended.

The Story of a Successful Climb

Lyla Swafford was born with Cerebral Palsy. We gave her a scholarship to go on this tour. She always had a perilous time walking, but a fabulous, plucky spirit.

At Mt. Sinai, she and my husband, Jerry, stayed behind. He had severe hip problems.

Now, they spent a significant amount of time climbing at the foot of Mt. Sinai. They were successful. This was their top of Mt. Sinai.

I have never seen greater growth than the growth produced through the climb of Mt. Sinai. First of all, you have to instruct people, "This is God's holy mountain. On the way up, and on the way down, you will be silent before the Lord." The climb is very dangerous: five miles up and five miles down. There are many uneven steps to navigate, and no railings. Teach them to take each step in the Name of Jesus Christ. "I take this step in the Name of the Lord Jesus." Ultimately, after several hours, an imprinting of this upon the mind develops, and later, in all steps of life, they begin to realize they are taking these steps in the Name of Jesus.

Give people clear instructions. Be very specific. Don't presume they know the logical things to do, because they really need clarity. Give the instructions slowly. Practice them. We practice taking our steps in the Name of Jesus the night before. At 1:00 a.m., they're ready.

It is important to give people detailed instructions. For example: You are to wear a hat. You are to carry a full water bottle. You must have your sunglasses with you. You are not to share your water bottle. Everyone is responsible for his or her own belongings.

On the climb of the mountain, I've always emphasized keeping the group together. As the years have passed, and the mountain is more crowded, that has become more difficult, but in the early years there were hardly any people on the mountain except us. By staying together, we did not leave the slowest behind, but kept them with us. One year I chose Louisa Pasquesi to lead the climb up Mt. Sinai. In previous months she had broken her foot and injured her ankle. She was very unsteady. She, of course, was recovered enough to walk, but surely, having her lead the group five miles up Mt. Sinai? This was the greatest miracle in Louisa's whole life. God gave her His grace to do it.

I have witnessed great miracles on Mt. Sinai. I choose to tell you two. Brenda was very heavy. She was panting after ½ a mile, sitting down resting and overwhelmed, she was way beyond her capabilities. I looked at her, and I said to her, "Brenda, are you going to go to the top of Mt. Sinai?" She said, "Yes I am." I said, "You may not sit down again." She didn't. She made it to the top, and it changed her entire life!

Nancy, her husband, and his mother made a journey together to Mt. Sinai in 1980. They loved the journey. It was life changing. When we are at the top of Mt. Sinai, one person is chosen to read the Ten Commandments. It is important that this person be the chosen person to read, not a volunteer, not just looking over the group and picking someone, but the right person to read the Commandments, the chosen one.

Five years later, in 1985, Nancy had gone through great tragedy. Her husband committed adultery with their neighbor's wife. The neighbor murdered Nancy's husband, stabbing him many times in the body. In fact, before he died, I was with her husband, Chet, in the hospital. I was asked to do his funeral.

Nancy then married Doug, a man she could trust and count on. They decided to make the journey together to the Middle East and joined the 1985 tour. When we came to Mt. Sinai, I said, "Nancy, you must read the Ten Commandments, for you know the suffering of God for us. "Will we keep His word?"

My Own Climb of Mt. Sinai

I climbed Mt. Sinai eight times. The fool climbs it twice. It was enormously difficult for me as I'm not athletic, and seldom, at any time, did I ever train. My life was tied up with the ministry, sitting in a counseling office eight to ten hours a day. On one particular tour, I was particularly tired. We were climbing Mt. Sinai early in the tour, so we were still suffering from jet lag. Also, since the Volcano of Mt. St. Helen's had gone off the night before we left, (which is a whole different story of our group being the only ones to fly out of the Portland Airport the next morning), I did not sleep for almost a week. I tried so hard to get a few hours of rest before the climb, but I was unable to do so.

Several weeks before the tour, a man gave me a T-shirt, and on the back of the T-shirt it read, "Powered by God." At midnight, I put on the T-shirt and I was the fourth one up the mountain. To this day, there is no accounting this to anything except I was powered by God.

Cana to Nazareth

I love the journey to Cana, where the first miracle Jesus performed took place. We usually stopped there when we were on tour.

One particular time at Cana was significant. Sam Bar-El was giving me a bad time because I run a tour to meet the needs of the people, and the time schedule cannot control the tour until those personal needs are met. God has always worked it out that the needs are met, and the time schedule works itself out.

CHAPTER 13

Yassin Awad Ali Hamdan

By 1978, I had read major archaeological and historical background material on Bethany as a result of hearing the Lord say to me in Lazarus' tomb, "Go and find out."

Jerry and I were leading a tour group. As we had a day off in Jerusalem, I invited six others to go with me for a special visit to Bethany. I needed to find a way to understand and experience all I had studied. I sought to know Bethany and the tomb of Lazarus, not just as a holy site, but as primary evidence to the Gospel of John.

When we arrived by taxi in Bethany, we went to the Tomb. There was a young man standing at the entrance of the Tomb. I asked if he would be willing to spend the afternoon with us and take us around. I asked him to teach us all he knew about Bethany's history, and the story of the ancient ruins.

As we walked up and down the streets of Bethany, the Lord suddenly, without warning or my request, said, "Ask Yassin if there are any handicapped children we could pray over!"

I asked Yassin the question. Later, he told me how difficult and shocking this request was. He had to plan fast, but he determined to make the request bear fruit.

In a few minutes, Yassin had arranged for his Uncle Ibrahim, to receive us, and the call had been sent out for the children to come.

What happened next? We were on Uncle Ibrahim's porch, confronted with three boys, all of whom had severe handicaps.

One boy had his feet on backwards, one boy had a congenital hip defect, and one boy, Uncle Ibrahim's son, was nearly brain dead, totally out of function and control. He normally laid on the floor in a room by himself.

I said to God, "I know my prayers won't create miracles here." It was terrifying for us to pray. When we finished our prayers, no miracles had occurred. The only miracle was some pregnant women and their children showed up to receive prayer. I was amazed at their trust and willingness to receive our ministry.

It was in this way that I met Uncle Ibrahim and we became friends. A couple of years later, he sent me a letter requesting rags for his son. I willingly sent him a box of rags.

There was only one problem. He meant clothes, and when he received the box of rags, he was angry and humiliated. Later, I explained what happened, and we remained respectful of one another.

Finally, we were ready to go back to Jerusalem. We left Yassin at the Tomb, and I handed him five dollars as we left. He took my address, and when we returned home, a letter was waiting for me. This was the beginning of our lifetime relationship!

I have related to you that I have known Yassin since he was 16 years old. Today he is a mature man of 49 years.

Yassin and I had a great influence on one another's lives. Through all seasons of our storms and discoveries, I have found him to be one of my most significant and consistent friends. He is a Muslim. I am a Christian.

As you will remember, we laid hands on him at The Inn of the Good Samaritan—fifty Christians prayed that he would come into the Kingdom of God and do the work. This had a profound effect on his life.

There were special reasons Yassin was chosen; reasons that I would later gradually learn. Yassin was one of 23 birth children to his two mothers. He was the second son of the first marriage;

his mother, Sarah, and his father, Awad. Awad chose to send Yassin to Christian schools from the beginning all the way through University. None of the other children went to a Christian school. It was as if from the very beginning, something special was going to happen to Yassin. His father gave Yassin to the Christian world.

His experience in Christian schools was brutal. Since he was the only Muslim in most of the classes, he was tormented a great deal. He was made fun of. He became insecure and doubtful. This insecurity grew over many years. It produced in Yassin a tendency to later be his own abuser, his own persecutor.

Yassin had been beaten a great deal as a child, not only by the other Christian children, but also by his father, who had a problem with impatience and did not have any skill at rearing children, especially so many of them.

From very early in the relationship between Yassin and myself, there was a complete surrender to the friendship that God had made possible for each of us. It was not a friendship that was one-sided. It was a friendship that was complete. I learned many things from Yassin, and he gives testimony that he learned much from me.

One of our learning experiences took us to Bethlehem for him to see the life of Jesus in a film. Much of our learning was centered around, "Love your neighbor as yourself," "Love your enemies," "Repay evil with kindness," and "The Kingdom of God."

Yassin had a tendency to go into long periods of depression. During those periods he would nearly give up. But, there was always this thread in our relationship that made it possible for him to hang on.

I've always enjoyed friendships that required much fighting. The fighting would never be against a person, but for a person. My fight with Yassin was for him to accept that I was for him, and for him to become for himself. It was a long fight.

In one season, when I was in the Holy Land and able to spend several days at Yassin's house, we were in this period of fighting; me fighting for him, and him fighting against himself. This had to break. He said, "Let's go down to the Inn of the Good Samaritan very early in the morning. We'll take bread and salt and we'll make a covenant." We sat in the bare courtyard around 7:00 a.m. At some distance, an old toothless Bedouin sat staring at us. We broke the bread, we dipped it in salt, and we made the covenant. Between God and us, there would be peace.

Yassin was bold at times. I want to tell you the story of a very significant visit he made to Oregon. He had just married Huwaida, who was a very devout Muslim. She was a beautiful young woman. She was newly pregnant. Jerry and I invited them to come to our house to stay for a month. It was a big, large decision, and it gives you a measure of the depths of our friendship.

Just before they arrived in Oregon, my husband Jerry and I had been helping with a tour to China and Japan. We had been gone a month. It had been a grueling journey, and I was very weary and deeply troubled when I returned home.

The day we came home from the tour was an awkward and difficult day. We had no food in the house and our children were gathered around us. We had to make some decisions. My husband and I were not in a good place, and on this day, there was a breakdown. This breakdown was profound. I had a complete breakdown, which lasted three years, and he had a complete breakdown too. The Lord would insist His way that we would be grateful for small things.

When Yassin and Huwaida arrived in 1986, we also had just received, two months before, three Palestinians from the West Bank: Mohammed Abu Zayed, Fadel Bader, and Mohammad Bader. They were all to be sponsored for Master's Degrees at Portland State, as they were not able to obtain Master's programs in the Palestinian territories. To compound this whole story, my mother died of Alzheimer's in July of 1986. The students came in August. We went to China and Japan in September, and almost immediately, upon our return, Yassin and Huwaida arrived.

I expected to have my energy, my sense of humor, a certain sense of joy and purpose. Instead, I had eyes that were blank, and powerful overwhelming grief that could hardly be expressed. It was not the kind of depression that a pill would take care of, for it was a spiritual training ground, and God would begin to have me all the way, with nothing left out.

I talked to the Board and the staff at the ministry and said I was not well. I told them I was struggling deeply. I would do the best I could, but don't expect me to be as I usually was.

To compound the difficulties of that whole situation, Huwaida was terrified of me. She felt she was in the house of an infidel. She was early in her pregnancy, very sick, and had no ability to cope with or sort out what had happened to her. Therefore, for three weeks, she would not speak to me. In the meantime, every night, she and Yassin would go to their bedroom. He would smoke out the window, and the days passed.

In the middle of one night, Huwaida, pounded on our bedroom door, screaming, "Give me milk!" Of course, I came out to give her milk immediately. Suddenly and unexpectedly, she fell into my arms sobbing!

One day I came in from work and sat down at the kitchen table. Yassin was sitting there, and Huwaida was over in another part of the room. I put my head down; I was so sorrowful and broken. I said, "I just can't make it." Suddenly Yassin spoke up in a way that was vastly significant. I am still in that same room with him today, hearing the same words, " Mitchell, you know what to do, now do it!" Then, he said, "Huwaida, Huwaida," (waving her over to me.) "You come and lay hands on her and pray right now." This event had a lifetime impact for my strength and healing.

This was not Yassin's first trip to Oregon. He came once in 1982, before he was married. On that visit, I will never forget one event that happened. It was his birthday, and we decided to have a surprise birthday party for him at the Good Samaritan office. I bought him a lovely watch as a gift. When he came in and saw the cake and all the people, he hid in the corner of the room, covered his face, and sobbed.

Yes, Yassin and I know each other well!

I loved to visit the Hamdan's! Whoever was with me, whether it was my husband, Jerry, our daughter, Laura, or others, we would go out to Bethany and stay at their homes. Since it was usually summer, it was hot. The windows were open. You could hear sounds from all over: Israeli gunfire, calls to prayer, and the sounds of many animals. It was a living atmosphere, and it drew me into a relationship with Yassin's entire family.

After several years, Yassin's father, Awad, decided to come to Oregon. For the following four years, he came once a year, for one month. He said, "I want you to train me to be a good father." Each year he went with us for one week to the Christian Renewal Center Family Camp.

I love all of Yassin's family. His uncles and I are very close friends. His family and our family have always helped each other. I love going into the souvenir store across from Lazarus' tomb, and remembering the summer my husband spent five days working in the souvenir store to help the Hamdan family.

Lazarus Saturday is the most sacred day of the year in Bethany. It is just before Palm Sunday. Elderly pilgrims come from all over the Greek world to remember the resurrection of Lazarus. They descend the 24 very uneven stone steps into the open tomb with great difficulty. Our daughter, Laura, and I were in Bethany working at the souvenir shop. Laura worked all day helping elderly people up and down the steps, many very crippled. We lived as part of the

Hamdan family in Bethany.

Although Yassin was the founder and the builder of the base structure of ASTA, our non-profit organization to help drug addicts and alcoholics in prevention and treatment in the West Bank, he never presumed that he was more than just a Board member. He was very faithful in this. He was encouraging. He was wise.

One day, in 1985, Yassin and I were having one of our usual fights. We were at Bethlehem University where I had been sitting for several days talking to Palestinian students about Good Samaritan Ministries, and again asking them what they were going to do to help their people. Yassin came to me and he said, "There are three Palestinians that I want you to take to the U.S. to get Master's degrees." I said, "Three? Three? Three? Out of the question!" Thus, began a conversation that went back and forth for several hours, and for my remaining days in Bethany. It came to pass that I said I would take only one. Yassin said, "Three!"

By God's grace, and the Holy Spirit working through this young man, it was supposed to be three for my third choice was Mohammad Bader, who later became our son.

Because of my mother's death, the funds were provided; the three could gain their Master's Degrees at Portland State University. They were housed by the ministry.

It might be good to note here that all three have done great things. They have done great things in the United States, and they have done great things at home. Mohammed Abu Zayed has a PhD and is currently a professor and head of a department at Birzeit University in the Ramallah Palestinian area. Fadel Bader went home to Hebron and took care of his mother and father for nine years. As his Master's training was in ESL, he taught English at the University in Hebron. He is now back and continues to work as an ESL teacher. He has an incredible gift for bringing the best out of people who have come with fear from other countries. In fact, he is so spiritually gifted that I asked him to be my permanent prayer partner. He is always there if he is needed.

Mohammad Bader lived with us. Now, that's another story, but it shows that the fight between Yassin and myself about three students was significant, because now Yassin was fighting for me.

Christians shook their heads at Good Samaritan Ministries when they saw Muslims move in. There was a lot of antagonism over our openness. How could we be so open to receive those who were not of the same faith? As the flack continued, I weathered the storm. The Board weathered it with me. We made a decision that what God had done, man could not tear asunder. There are some things that are beyond our understanding, and they are from a Hand above. He profoundly understands what we do not know.

For many years, Yassin tried to figure out ways to make a living. He and Huwaida had eight children. It was very difficult for him. He struggled, and struggled and struggled. For a short while, he worked for ASTA at the treatment center. He and Huwaida each worked as teachers in the Palestinian territories. Because of the Intefadah and the terrific problems with strikes, the children became so rebellious and out of control, that one day Yassin walked out and said, "I am a teacher. I will not do this." He put his hand to many things, but inside he was struggling, really struggling with the call on his life to teach nothing but the Kingdom of God. In 2000, he founded an organization called Rose of Jerusalem. It is a legal non-profit, and we are sponsors of that organization. He and Huwaida had struggled, struggled, struggled to build a two-story house. He said, "We'll live in the second story, and Rose of Jerusalem will be on the first level. There were some foreign diplomats that helped fund Rose of Jerusalem. There were small miracles and bigger ones. Rose of Jerusalem is a living testimony of the life of Yassin Hamdan in the eyes of Our Father.

Rose of Jerusalem takes in very handicapped children: crippled,

160

lame, or mentally marred by birth defects. They mainstream these children with other children. They develop rapport with and the self-esteem of each of these children. Rose of Jerusalem provides physical therapy, and trains the mothers to do the physical therapy on their profoundly handicapped children. Physically handicapped adults are welcome. Exercise and competition programs have been developed for all of the children in the larger community of several towns.

From 1978, when we asked Yassin if we could pray for some handicapped children, the call on Yassin's life was fulfilled.

Perhaps the most significant decision that Yassin made for Rose of Jerusalem was to build the first Playground for Peace—a playground for all who would come. Whether they were in Rose of Jerusalem or not, they could come to the playground to play. People from six countries touched the playground building process. It is a miracle!

Now, why was this so significant? Because several years before, the Lord had spoken into me, "Playgrounds for Peace," "Playgrounds for Peace," "Playgrounds for Peace." So, over the years, even up to today when an envelope or newsletter is mailed, it is usually stamped with a stamp that says "Playgrounds for Peace." Yassin Hamdan built The Rose of Jerusalem, and fulfilled his lifetime dream of making a difference. Children would receive the grace of God, and a love that could never be defeated. He is one of the most loving men I have ever met. Of course, he's conflictual, but oh my, the love pours out from every corner of his heart.

I could tell you a hundred Hamdan stories. If you want to hear any, ask me one day. Yassin and I are both storytellers.

It is significant that Yassin and Majed Alloush, who developed ASTA, became very close friends of our Israeli guide, Sam Bar-El, and the bus driver, Shevach Winberg, who was with us for many years. We formed a team that literally could not be defeated by the circumstances. In fact, we worked out a system for leading our tours. The Israelis and the Palestinians met in East Jerusalem and exchanged us. The Israelis finished with their part at that time, and the Palestinians took over the tour, doing their part.

When the wall was built in Jerusalem separating the West Bank from Jerusalem, this wall entirely shut Jerusalem off from West Bank access. It satisfied the need for less casualties, but did it satisfy the need to love our neighbor as ourselves, and to pray for those who persecute us?

We were all deeply immersed, as a team of peacemakers; Christians, Muslims, and Jews we acted upon peacemaking in all that we did. In all we experienced, we kept the faith in our God and our neighbors.

AND WE HAVE LEARNED MORE ABOUT
GOD AND EACH OTHER!!

To this very day, Yassin remains our first and senior international called to be a Samaritan. He keeps in touch with directors in all Good Samaritan countries. He and Sam Bar-El came to the 2002 International Conference held in Beaverton. They were honored guests of the whole ministry.

Yassin prays from the depth of his heart for all of us. He knows the cost.

CHAPTER 14

The Spirit of Hospitality

From the very beginning of Good Samaritan Ministries, there was urgency in my spirit to train the people in the spirit of hospitality.

The spirit of hospitality would begin in our house. We opened our house for five years, welcoming any and all that came, providing for them, and often feeding them at noon. It was a huge assignment, as so many came. It was the beginning of the spirit of hospitality that would greatly influence the ministry.

For a whole year, all of those who had become part of Good Samaritan Ministries, including myself, trained hard in the spirit of hospitality. This had to be a shocking story, a shocking life of hospitality.

How is the spirit of hospitality different from the culture of hospitality? All I can say is cultural hospitality is "form," and the spirit of hospitality is "substance." 1 Corinthians 14:1 says, "Make love your aim." Love embraces, draws people, and pulls us together.

We opened our house to visitors, and in the early years, the ministry began to not only feed people out of our house, but it also housed people in our house. Now this was a difficult assignment, as we live in a small house. Nevertheless, it is an assignment we have kept even unto this day. Until I retired from Good Samaritan Ministries, four to six months each year, we were housing visitors. Since retirement, we house occasional visitors. The visitors came from many nations. They spoke many languages. Some were easier, and some were more difficult, but while it was the guest who was sometimes difficult, it was our spirit learning not to be difficult; our spirit learning to truly share the fullness of the gospel of love.

In that whole year of training Samaritans, we experienced and learned the spirit of welcoming. In the office of Good Samaritan Ministries, the spirit of welcoming grew up. It was for us who said we were Samaritans, to truly be Samaritans, not just on easy days, or when convenient, but from the depths of our beings, submitted to Christ and fully open to this spirit. If we were inconvenienced, it was God's training ground for the Spirit of Hospitality.

Our house has always welcomed people from other religions, particularly Jewish people, and Muslims. In fact, in the center of our mantle, is a picture of Jesus praying in the garden, on the right of this picture is a picture of a Muslim praying in Hebron, and on the left, a picture of Moses. It was part of our hospitality to say, "You are welcome." This Kingdom is given unto you. It is the Lord who spoke, *"There is no need to be afraid, little flock, for it has pleased your Father to give you the kingdom."* (Luke 12:32)

This had enormous effect on the lives of the people who came, and there were many adventures with the people who stayed. There were visitors who stayed six months. There were some who stayed two weeks. Currently, we have Perry here from Singapore for three weeks. We are still learning to say, "We're so glad you are here. Your life is very important to us. Blessings upon you. Peace be upon your life. We give this in the Name of the Lord." This is the Spirit of Hospitality.

The spirit of hospitality is not perfection. It is an unusual open hand. In different ways, different people feel welcome. Perhaps one of our most remarkable visitors was the Minister of State of Uganda, B.K. Kirya. B.K. and I were friends since 1990. We were close friends at his house in 1990, in those first hours I was ever in Uganda. B.K. asked to be my father in Africa. As a father, he was loyal to me as a daughter. He made himself available at all times to the ministry of Good Samaritan in Uganda. Four days after our first meeting, B.K. took Jerry and myself to a personal meeting with the President of Uganda, President Museveni.

When B.K. Kirya was coming to the United States to attend the Presidential Prayer Breakfast in Washington D.C., I asked him to make a special trip to Oregon to visit us. He did. When he came, I said, "How long can you stay?" He said, "Three days." I said, "We need you for a week." He stayed for a week. This kind of hospitality is unusual. B.K. insisted on us seeing President Museveni in a private meeting. We insisted upon him, a profound welcome which kept him through the heart.

Now, the first night B.K. was at our home for dinner, I served leftovers. I am sure that is a shocking faux pas in cultural hospitality, but in the Spirit of Hospitality, the leftover meal was a feast. It still makes me laugh.

I might add that when B.K. Kirya died a couple of years later, on the day of his death, his wife called me and notified me that my father had just died. Our hospitality was profound for one another.

I might also add, for the record, that B.K. was noted for his Spirit of Hospitality in his own country. The first meal and first night we ever spent in Uganda, our team spent visiting his house.

Among the many foreign visitors, Osborn and Louise Mdutjana of Uganda stayed in the guest bed in our house. This antique was the bed in which my mother was conceived. It is a shorter-than-usual bed, and the mattress and springs were profoundly old. I did not know how old the mattress really was until the bed collapsed during the night. When we got up the next morning, Osborn and Louise were lying on the floor. The mattress and springs had fallen through. They said it happened during the night, but they didn't want to awaken us. Out of that event, we had major repairs done to the bed, and purchased a wonderful new mattress and springs. We discovered the mattress was probably from 1930. It is still the bed of hospitality!

I must confess, my husband struggled with our hospitality being so extensive. He struggled with our lack of privacy, and the need to continue to make people feel welcome, even after they had been with us for a time. I must say, in this book, that the Spirit of Hospitality conquered my husband's spirit of hesitancy, and changed his life dramatically by the remarkable people who visited us.

Another special guest was David Bhatti. David was our field director in Pakistan, and he spent seven months living with us, training full time to become a Samaritan.

David was a total orphan from the time he was four years old. He was raised by a much older brother, but seriously lacked the depth of parental love. On a visit to Pakistan, I had so impacted his life, he fell to the floor. David was called of God in our house, and nurtured in our house.

There is a funny story about David that I like to tell. During the process of his training, he had to study the Bible. He decided to study first the book of Genesis. He spent at least six months just studying Genesis. It was life-changing for him.

Another assignment David had was to complete the writing of his autobiography. It took him weeks to write ten pages. This too, was life-changing for him, for he began to regain the wholeness of himself. His story, for the first time, was a story he could see, experience, and appreciate as part of God's glory over his life.

When David returned to Pakistan, he asked many of the people he met with, and even the children, to begin to work on their life stories. Over the years, we found if someone learned something they didn't know before and it was deeply and powerfully healing for them, they then began to give this healing training to others. The autobiography was a life-changing opportunity for Good

Samaritan Ministries in Pakistan.

We have never been afraid to ask guests to participate in our family life, and there is a great story behind this which took place in Bethany, East Jerusalem, on the road between Jerusalem and Jericho.

As I often visited Bethany and stayed in the Hamdan house, Awad, Yassin's father, taught me the most valuable part of the definition of hospitality. He said, "For three days you are a guest, and on the fourth day, you are a family member." During the time we were guests, he himself came in and changed our bed everyday. On the fourth day, we relaxed, participated, and laughed together as family. We played games together, told stories, sat on one another's beds, and fully, fully, fully became family members. Later, we realized we were always family members.

I am going to repeat this because it is so important. If you just use the word "hospitality," it is easy to think of cultural hospitality. But there is hospitality that remains greater than the cultural norms. For the first three days you are a guest, and on the fourth day you have stayed with us, you are a family member for life.

CHAPTER 15

A Time of Sorrow, A Time of Joy

In August of 1986, Mohammad Bader arrived from Jerusalem to live with us as a sponsored foreign student.

Without warning, I broke down in early October, and a spirit of grief, a spirit of mourning became a part of the next three years of my life.

In the beginning, and for several months, I would be doubled over without warning in torrential grief. I am not speaking of crying, I am speaking of grief; a kind of mourning I had never experienced. I was not grieving over personal issues. I came to know these words, *"He had no form or charm to attract us, no beauty to win our hearts; he was despised, the lowest of men, a man of sorrows, familiar with suffering, one from whom, as it were, we averted our gaze, despised, for whom we had no regard."* (Isaiah 53:3)

In September, Jerry and I led a tour to China and Japan. In a church we attended in Shanghai, most of the Chinese attending were asleep. The Lord spoke to me through a small upper window where I could see pigeons. He said, "Learn to be grateful for small things." At the time, this was a hard assignment. I wanted bigger things. He insisted, and slowly gave me the gift of gratitude for small things.

The day Jerry and I returned from Japan, my breakdown

occurred without warning.

Mohammad Bader was part of our household, a family member. Yes, he lived with us. Upon our return, the first news we had was that his father died in Jerusalem while we were gone. Mohammad was devastated by this loss. Although his father was 86, his father was a man that he admired greatly. When he was a young boy, Suleiman, as an orphan, had walked from Hebron to Jerusalem. He lived in the streets of Jerusalem, making his way as best he could. When Mohammad was born, Suleiman was 65 years old. Mohammad was the last born of seven children in his family.

Mourning increased. I kept looking for everything to be all right, and it wasn't. In December, toward Christmas time, I received a call that Mohammad's mother, Yusra, had died in Jerusalem. She died as her daughter, Aida, was carrying her out of the city to get medical help. They were coming down the stairs facing the Western Wall.

At the time of Yusra's death, Mohammad was hurrying as fast as possible to get through the Master's of Counseling Major at Portland State University. He was worried and rushing to get home to take care of his mother. He was broken. He was devastated. He hit bottom. I was already there.

I had met Mohammad's mother and father in Jerusalem before we knew he would be coming to live at our house. His mother was deaf all of Mohammad's life. She was 47 when he was born. He had a special love for her. I saw that. Love given freely can be painful. "I'm a child, and I want my freedom too."

At the time I met with Suleiman and Yusra in 1985, I asked them how they would feel if Mohammad came to the United States, and if it was all right for him to live with us. They agreed that it would be a blessing. In that meeting, I felt a close bonding to Mohammad's parents.

The painful grieving months passed, our household was in a time between times. Mohammad began a second Master's degree, working more slowly this time, and really learning. He chose to focus on the handicapped and seniors for his life's work.

As a family, Jerry, Mohammad and I had many adventures. We went swimming often. We went on trips across the State of Oregon. I will never forget when we went roller-skating. Mohammad's legs were going in all directions. He was always game for conquering anything. He had some unstable parts, but on a whole, at 21, he had a pleasing personality. It was our first experience of having a son, a boy, a male staying in our house in a more permanent way. After some adjustments, it worked out well. Mohammad, Jerry and I took organ lessons together. None of us did very well, but it was a diversion from the pain of that time.

Over the next few years, Jerry and I met all of Mohammad's brothers and sisters. It was good to know them as a family.

All three of the Palestinians I sponsored had been founders of our work, Al Sadiq Al Taieb Association, in Jerusalem, and; therefore, I required them to go to the Bible classes at Portland Community College Adult Education, and to participate fully in the ministry. This was quite a challenge for them, but they were young men of integrity, and they appreciated our struggle to give them life. They appreciated that my mother had died, and it was my inheritance that was giving them an education. There was a bonding among us that is still there today—a permanent calling that knit us together as family and friends.

We were quite tough on the students, not allowing them to work under the table to earn extra money. They were each given $100 each month to meet their expenses, and they made due with that amount.

We had many Palestinian dinners, and I learned the importance of their food in their culture. It was a strange experience to sit at our table. Arabic was spoken as often as English. It required an adjustment to understand that a foreign land was living in our land. It was very good.

At one point in my depression and sorrow, I reached bottom. Mohammad came out to the kitchen to talk to me. He stood me up, grabbed my hands, and began to dance with me back and forth, back and forth. He said, "Mornings are for dancing." I cannot tell you how profound that statement was, for it changed all of my mornings, even up to this day. Yes, mornings are for dancing, for praise, for the glory of God to be among us.

Mohammad was a man of sensitivity and compassion, a man with a heart, and a man who slowly found his way to bond very deeply with Jerry. It was a long journey, but a completed journey. It was very good.

I travelled often. Jerry was often with me on long trips to foreign countries. The travel was hard, exceedingly difficult. Each journey required me to go to many countries, live with the people, learn the culture, challenge the systems, urge the call for Samaritans to come forth to help their people, and change lives from desperate to effective. Good Samaritan was a ministry that was shocking. Most of the countries had never heard of counseling. They didn't know anything about it, and only teaching them the value of profound listening could bring our neighbors to true and lasting development.

There was this tension in our lives: continual work I had to do--work, labor, long, hard days at home and in the counseling office, listening, listening!

Once, when we were out of the U.S., Mohammad had to meet a plane from China. Chen Chen was arriving from Mainland China to also work on a degree at Portland State University. We were to house Chen Chen. It would mean that we had two foreign students living with us. Our home remained the same—small. It was quite a time!

Chen Chen was one of our most difficult guests. When he came, he had little ability in conversational English. He set a goal for himself to learn 100 English words each day. I believe he daily met the goal. Adjusting to two cultures, the Chinese and the Arabic, stretched us. We had to develop a sense of humor to survive the things that would happen day by day.

After six months Chen Chen left. I learned the hard way that many foreign students come to take advantage. They were getting for themselves, but they were giving little to others. With the 13 foreign students Good Samaritan Ministries sponsored, I saw this to be a continuing problem. The students did not know how to show deeper levels of integrity. The exception, among the 13, were the three Palestinians.

During their time here, I made several trips to Israel and Palestine. I visited their families. I came to know them well. I saw the horrific situation going on in Palestine. In the West Bank, the people were really suffering. There were strikes, violence, and unbelievable tensions. I lived in the midst of this in the West Bank. It was not something I read in the papers, but something I lived. When I came back, I told the young men that they must not go home, as it would add too great a burden to their families. They must succeed here, and they must do much here. I kept thinking the West Bank would get better; but no, it got worse and worse.

I have an Israeli heart and a Palestinian soul. It is a strange marriage. As a Christian, I was embracing the Muslims and the Jews. I was learning their stories, their thoughts, their passions, and their disappointments. I was inspiring them to be men of God and to be men of integrity. In my brokenness, they were very kind.

Always, the picture on our mantle of Jesus in the Garden was the central focus in our home and in our relationships.

Most days, during the three years of my sorrow, I wore a shawl around my shoulders. I found wearing a shawl was very comforting. It brought protection, a woman being comforted by

God Himself. (Note: I would highly recommend this to anyone who is experiencing deep levels of grief.)

As a child, I had lived through the years of my mother's mental illness: her joy, and her violence. Her death changed my life dramatically. I gained a freedom in my spirit. I gained the years that had been lost. I was set free. The healing was profound, deep inside me, and yet, as I look back, my mother influenced me more than any other for the tasks I would have in my lifetime. It was she that made me travel. It was she that took me to Iraq to the Walls of Nineveh.

Mohammad Bader lived with us for almost three years. When he moved out, he and Jerry made a trip to New Jersey. They crossed the U.S. together, seeing, experiencing, and bonding in this shared experience. Mohammad stayed with his family for several months.

Jerry and I were close to Mohammad. We felt a deep sense of permanent connection, and there came a day that a decision was made for us to adopt Mohammad Bader as our son.

It is something Mohammad asked of us. It had nothing to do with him staying in the U.S., or getting a green card. Adoption would only give him a family.

The adoption of Mohammad was one of the most significant events in the history of our family. Jerry and I made special trips to see our daughters. Individually, we voted "yes" for the adoption, or "no" against it. Each daughter, after careful personal consideration, voted yes. At the last of this, my husband said, "Well it means a lot to you, so I'll vote yes." I said, "Then I'll vote no, because Mohammad needs a father more than a mother." At that moment, there was a change in my husband, and we both voted a strong "yes."

Over the years of meeting his family members, there was unity in our agreement.

The adoption of Mohammad Bader took place on the 24th of March, Good Friday, 1989. We signed the papers before the judge in the morning. At noon, we came to Good Samaritan for the three hours of Christ's passion.

For all the years of the ministry, since 1977, up to the present time, we have always kept Good Friday from 12:00 to 3:00, as a set aside time, not to be violated by other times. Over the years we came to understand that from 12:00 to 3:00 is a time between times. The time is entirely outside of our time.

At noon, we ended our year, and at 3:00 p.m., we began our new year. It was at that Good Friday event that Mohammad, Jerry and I would eat our first meal together as a permanent family.

After 3:00, we drove to the cemetery, which is approximately 20 miles from our house. We took flowers and placed them on the graves of each of our family members. We prayed together at each of the graves, and brought Mohammad into a realization that he was part of the whole family, and would always be part of our bigger family picture.

I have always believed in the honoring of a mother and father as a God-given call. In my heart and spirit, I honored Suleiman, Mohammad's father, and Yusra, his mother. I always told Mohammad that he must honor them. We were another family, but they were deeply important in his life. This was so much a part of me, that when I went to Jerusalem, and found that his mother had no marking on her grave near St. Stephen's Gate, I did something about it. She was my friend. I made sure that the grave was marked, and a fine stone put upon it. Yusra was a woman to honor. Suleiman was a man of integrity. They produced the finest of sons. It was God who granted us their son, our first and only son.

After Mohammad completed his second Master's, he worked for Good Samaritan Ministries. It was a significant part of the history of the ministry that a Christian counseling agency suddenly had a counselor named Mohammad. When he had a client, often they said, "Are you a Christian?" He said, with great integrity and passion, "The issue is not my religion; the issue is yours." It always satisfied the people that he was more interested in them than he was in himself. He did great work. As years passed, he became a great therapist, teacher, and leader.

Today, Mohammad works for Multnomah County in Oregon, as a Director for Senior Program and Disability Services. He has two children, Sarah and Gabriel. He has a wonderful wife, Diane. He is a man who is whole, and we are a family that has become whole.

Who are our mothers, brothers and sisters? This is a question that Jesus asked when His family came to see him.

"He was still speaking to the crowds when suddenly his mother and his brothers were standing outside and were anxious to have a word with him. But to the man who told him this Jesus replied, 'Who is my mother? Who are my brothers?' And stretching out his hand towards his disciples he said, 'Here are my mother and my brothers. Anyone who does the will of my Father in heaven is my brother and sister and mother." (Matthew 12:46-50)

And our family grew in inclusivism. Love was being written on each of our hearts, and we learned to express it, not only in our family, but to the entire world. Jesus' arms were outstretched; they were inclusive, each arm pointing in the direction of a thief. Inclusively he embraced us, that we would do the will of the Father in heaven.

CHAPTER 16

Bearing Burdens

The Story of Dennis

I met Dennis at the Christian Renewal Center in late 1970. I was teaching and focusing on inner healing. There were 150 people at camp each week. Dennis was one of so many. They had heard I did inner healing. They came in desperation to, perhaps, receive understanding and release.

That second week, the far more serious case was Dennis. He was almost catatonic, not able to get up, not able to function.

Since I was burdened that week with the lives of many, I went to Dennis and said, "If you come to see me in Oregon, I will see what I can do to help you."

Three months passed, and one night at 11:00 p.m., Dennis rang our doorbell. He had come to get the help. He had also come to move in with us. We had no prior warning of this, but there was Dennis.

Being a Samaritan is not a convenient ministry. It doesn't have any set hours. It does not have a certain event that is going to happen that is always predictable. The arrival of Dennis was certainly an unpredictable event in our lives. He moved in with us that night, and lived with us for the next six months.

Dennis was tragically mentally ill. His deceased mother had been mentally ill. His deceased father had been in the CIA. He was gone most of the time during Dennis' childhood, (This fact was confirmed by Dennis' brother after Dennis' death).

When he was 18, Dennis shot his father in the head. For this reason, my husband was very worried about having Dennis with us. His father was not killed, but died eight years later from complications caused by the shooting. After the shooting, Dennis was in a mental hospital. He was in jail, under treatment. Unusually, Dennis was befriended by the man who was the prosecuting attorney in his case. This man did not befriend Dennis for a week or a month, but for the rest of Dennis' life. He and I would be the greatest influence on Dennis, throughout the years ahead that Dennis would be with us.

I'm not much of one to allow diagnosis to control my relationship with any client. I knew the problems Dennis had, and what his diagnosis might be; but, I'm always one who looks at the person, and I look at the potential in the person. I always like the person. If I do this, then one day, the true person starts to come out. No matter how long it takes, it is worth the wait.

To show you how sick Dennis was, the first week, I took Dennis to the store to buy a suit of clothes. He went into the dressing room and was gone an hour. I sent a clerk in to bring him out, or to find out what was the matter. When Dennis came out, he explained that he had been examining all the seams to determine if they were perfect, and he couldn't make up his mind if they were.

My husband was able to find Dennis a job. This, in itself, was a miracle. The job was at an azalea nursery. Dennis loved the job. He particularly loved that they gave him all of the dying azaleas free of charge to take home. He became obsessed with azaleas. Over a number of weeks, he filled the apartment, where he eventually lived, with more and more azaleas.

There was a special day in the relationship between Dennis and myself. I could see he was getting more and more obsessed with me, and he was becoming angrier with my husband. It was like he was competing with Jerry for my attention and my love.

He brought home a beautiful azalea tree to give me as a gift. He gave it to me in the morning. I said, "Dennis, I don't want an azalea tree." He picked up the tree, wound up his arm, and threw it all over the living room. The soil was hanging from the ceiling. He ran for the door, broke his watch, and finally heard me say, "I don't want the azalea tree, Dennis. I want you." This was the turning point. His obsession with me was over. I had shown him the love he never received as a child.

After six months, Dennis got his own apartment. It was very challenging for him, as after azaleas, his new obsession became boxes. He literally kept every box he ever found or saw, and he made aisles of them throughout his whole living area. If he had a hamburger box, it was kept as part of the box aisles in his apartment.

We invited Dennis for Christmas. He came two days after Christmas. He brought a gift, beautiful ceramic glasses engraved with Christian markings. I still have those glasses today. There are twelve of them. Every time we have ever had company, they have been used at our table. God used Dennis' provision for our ministry of hospitality to others.

Another Christmas Eve, we had several guests. Dennis came, and he got very upset during dinner. I'm not sure why, but suddenly, he began to yank the tablecloth off the table with the food and dishes still on the table. Fortunately, it did not end in a disaster, but Dennis was not stable. He was not able to stop a rage.

A girl moved into the apartment next door to Dennis. Her name was Melissa. Dennis and Melissa became friends. Melissa was a runaway from a Florida prison. She had stolen a car. She was never very stable either, and had been a severe childhood diabetic. As a little girl, her father had removed her from her mother into a trailer on another area of their property. He kept Melissa beside him to be his wife. This was from her very young childhood. It left Melissa in a desperate state. Childhood diabetes was on top of this profound tragedy of Melissa's young life.

Dennis and Melissa liked each other. They did not prepare to marry. It was not a romantic relationship. It was a deep and permanent relationship that greatly influenced each of their lives. They worked together for what was best for each of them.

I will never forget the day Melissa stole some magazines at a doctor's office. She finally came and told me. I turned her over my lap and paddled her gently in the Name of the Father, the Son, and the Holy Spirit, and said these words, "Thou shall not steal!" She never did again.

I also remember when Melissa was at our house for a Christmas Eve dinner. It was our custom for a few years to have 12 to 15 people for Christmas Eve dinner, people who generally had no other place to go. After dinner, we went into the living room, and I read the Christmas Story aloud. Melissa said, "Why, I have never heard that. I didn't know anything about that."

One day I received an emergency phone call. Melissa had been burned, badly injured. They lived about six blocks from our house. I arrived there in three minutes. As I walked in, she lay on the floor, her arm still steaming from the fire. Their neighbor had been cooking something on his stove. The pan was filled with grease. He got angry when flames burst out, and threw the grease fire on Melissa. I got down on my knees, laid hands on Melissa, looked into her eyes, and absolutely admonished the spirit of fear, and the spirit of permanent injury, to come out of her. God would sustain her and heal her. When the medics came they took over.

Melissa weathered the burns and did heal up well. This event brought Dennis and Melissa closer together, and he became more and more aware that he could be a good influence on her health problems. He really helped her receive the medical attention she needed.

Gradually, as the years went by, Melissa became more and more ill. Dennis was largely overwhelmed by her physical problems. Eventually her mother came and took her to Florida. She was put in a nursing home. Two years later, before she died, Jerry and I visited Melissa in Florida.

When Dennis lost Melissa, he went into depression. It was a profound slump. He sought psychiatric help in a psychiatric facility, and he was there for a number of weeks. When he was released, and a few days passed, Dennis shot himself in the head, just as he had long ago shot his father in the head.

His brother came. He confirmed the story of Dennis' life, and said we had done more for Dennis than anyone had ever done. He was very grateful to the ministry, and gave all of the belongings of Dennis to Good Samaritan Ministries. It was a big job to clean out the apartment. The one thing I saw that was significant, Dennis had largely outgrown all of his obsessions. He could not recover from depression and loss. We all helped with Dennis' burial. It was at the burial site that I first met Dean Pontius, the prosecuting attorney; Dennis' sole other friend. Dean said he had heard about me for years from Dennis. They had often played chess together. I had heard about Dean. He joined Good Samaritan Ministries.

We will never forget that Dennis Fortuna was a permanent part of our family. Blessed be the Name of the Lord, who gives us the burdens we will carry.

The Story of Dianna

Dianna came into my office with a look I had never seen. She had a face full of pain, carefully masked so it wouldn't ever show. She said her pastor had sent her to see me. She saw me weekly. The first six months, she never sat down, but spent the whole time pacing back and forth in my office.

The only voice coming out of her mouth was Satan's. Only Satan would speak to me. His favorite sentence, "She's mine, and you can't have her." It was a growl: a deep penetrating voice, meant to continually disturb any calm waters.

Deliverance is the normal approach for a case like Dianna's, but it's not the road I took. The Lord led me on another journey.

I eventually found out she was initiated into a satanic cult when she was three years old. Her father and grandmother brought her into the cult, and, as far as she knew, she was raised to be a high priestess for Satan.

This was important information because it told me there was a child of three that had been lost, and it was that early childhood I had to find. We can't deliver people if we don't develop them. I found the development of that young child was a life and death issue for Dianna. The growling voice of Satan continued.

I would not talk to Satan, argue with him, or engage him at all. I engaged the lost child. It took a long time for small pieces of her real life to come to the surface. The longest wait was for her voice to be free and clear, that she might truly be Dianna.

Love conquers all. It isn't a lukewarm love that fades when success doesn't follow, but a flaming fire of love that never gives up. This passion, this flaming fire, is the greater part of my life. It is the greater part of the ministry.

Dianna wouldn't let me touch her. If I tried, a burning rage broke out in her. "Dianna" was being blocked from being touched, and it was Satan holding her tight. Gradually, I learned that she had been forced to sacrifice her dog when she was a young child. She was forced to choose children for human sacrifices, to drink blood, and to do things that were unspeakable and little known by the outside world. I came to know her lost baby, impregnated in her too young. There were many parts to Dianna, but the greatest part was unspeakable horror. Trust came slowly. We went to Lebanon,

Oregon, and saw her grandmother in a care facility. We looked at her childhood house. When we drove by the woods where the cult had met, near the road on the way to Lebanon, she freaked out.

Twice in her teen years, Dianna was committed to the State Mental Hospital, once for six months at 13, and again for seven months when she was 20. The hospitalizations destroyed her trust. Her voice was gone. In her memory, she had never opened a Christmas present, although she always received some gifts.

Inside Dianna was a gentle and wonderful child, absolutely forced into silence, and absolutely controlled by the powers holding and surrounding her. Gradually, she became one of those powers. She never knew her greater power was that small child. In 1988, I took Dianna on our tour to the Holy Land. She wasn't ready to be taken from the viewpoint of any sane person, but the little girl needed to grow, and the new environment would create growth.

Once, and only once, Satan trapped me. It was in Jerusalem. He convinced me that we had to hold her down and do deliverance. She broke loose from four people holding her, picked up a large tray with sharp edges, and threw it across the room at my head. It was the only personal violence she ever committed. It taught me, "Be careful. Do not allow Satan to trick you!" His voice could get warm and seem friendly and modified, but it was the same actor programming that little girl and controlling her life.

Dianna moved, and for several years, she and her husband lived in Kent, Washington. Her health was precarious. I made sure she got some health care. Her husband did not know or understand anything that was going on in his wife's life. Her children only sometimes saw the rage. She kept herself under tight control so they would be safe.

One day, Jerry, myself, and our son, Mohammad, were on our way to Juneau, Alaska, for a Good Samaritan U.S. Conference. We stopped to visit Dianna for the day. We all went together to the park and played a baseball game. We had no baseball, no bat, and no mitts. We had an imaginative creative ball game. We acted out the game. I always wondered what the kids thought when they took a look at us from afar. It must have been strange, but it was so beautiful. It was one of those beautiful and perfect days when the play is real.

It took many years for Dianna to grieve openly. If she would cry even a tiny bit, she would shut it off immediately and apologize. Gradually, the opening of that grief occurred. The beauty of the Lord is that it occurred in safe amounts, so the little child would not be frightened once again by the power of this grief, a power over which she had no control.

She gradually told me she had been sent up to Oregon to cause problems in a church. She was to be a destructive force. The pastor, who sent her to me, did not know what to do with her. It was a miracle and a blessing that he sent her to Good Samaritan Ministries. Dianna had lost all of her developmental stages of life. She was boxed in by a personality of Satan that would completely control every move she made. She had completely lost her freedom of life, thought, tenderness, and creativity. Over many years, all of these attributes came to life, and she was developed. Dianna's greatest fear was that she might suddenly physically hurt me, or that she would hurt someone else. Once, when she was supposed to take Holy Communion, she got so violent, that we had to contain her until the violence passed. No one who has not been in this war could understand the cost to the survivor. After 17 years, Dianna was able to tell her story, help teach counselors, teach the Bible, and release herself to be touched by the tenderness of a true mom. She reconnected with her family, and she has found healthy ways to cope with them.

Dianna received divorce papers, served to her on Christmas

Day. She was devastated, but I can truly say she was also released.

Her children have done well. They know only a little. She has kept them away from the power of evil that could have devastated their lives.

Dianna had a new granddaughter, Sarah. At six months, she began an illness, which led to her death at ten and a half months. Dianna and I flew to San Antonio, Texas, to visit Dianna's son, his wife, and that precious little girl. She was tremendously ill, able to do almost nothing, yet, she was one of the most beautiful babies I have ever seen in my life. Her beauty was greater than the illness. Other healthy children followed Sarah, but this child had a special assignment, another place of healing in Dianna's heart.

In 2005, Jerry and I helped a group of women find bonding with others. They are called, "The Sisters." Jerry and I serve as mentors, a spiritual mother and father; but, it is, as sisters, they must gain their ability to relate. Each of them had traumatic childhoods, tremendous losses, and great fragility. As we have met together twice a year, the sisters have grown stronger. They can call upon one another, and no rejection is here, not among the sisters.

The whole story of Dianna's healing can be summed up, "DELIVER US FROM EVIL." If you try to deliver evil from a person, it is going to spill all over. It can be very dangerous. But Jesus said you hang on to that person. You deliver that person from the evil. I have found this harder road of recovery brings the greatest fruit of the ministry.

The Story of Cinnamon

We had our dog, Cinnamon, for eleven years. She died on my birthday in 2010 at Good Samaritan Ministries during the International Day of Prayer.

She was a dog who bore the burdens of many, particularly, of Papa Jerry. When he had a major fracture of his ribs, I got the doctor's permission to bring Cinnamon into the hospital to comfort him.

Cinnamon was a small poodle, weighing about seven pounds at the most, with cinnamon coloring, bright eyes, and passionate pride and determination that made her a champion of the heart. She was a great healer of our marriage. We had many communication problems. When we got Cinnamon, we would talk through Cinnamon, "Cinnamon, would you go tell Grandpa..." "Cinnamon, would you go tell Grandma..." She stood between us as a marriage counselor, healing our communication struggles.

When we had to be gone, Dianna took care of Cinnamon. They had a special relationship. Cinnamon had three favorite sisters: Laurie, Jan, and Dianna. When one of them came, she went hysterical with joy.

Cinnamon had a heart murmur from birth. She had some health struggles, but not anything too drastic until the middle of her tenth year. She then developed a valve problem in the heart. She began to suffer.

Papa Jerry was not ready to give up Cinnamon, and Cinnamon was not ready to leave. It was terribly difficult for us to watch her suffering. She would look at us for hours. Her communication was profound. She never licked my face; she gave me hugs. She tried to talk, and sometimes, when the pain was bad, she screamed.

Jerry finally determined it would be good to have her put to sleep. We set a date, June 8th.

Good Samaritan has always had something we call The International Day of Prayer. On that day, all the nations where we are as a ministry, and all the Samaritans in the United States gather where they are, and pray in a time-coordinated agreement. We have set the time zones to match with Oregon time. This is a time of total fasting: no food--no water. It is a time of intentional praying with one another. Is is our greatest call to faith in action.

On June 6, at 6:00 a.m., we had to be at Good Samaritan

Ministries. Jerry said we had better take Cinnamon with us. He took her bed and a little dish for water. He laid her by his feet. She was in a room with many people praying. It is a day of quiet prayer. We don't make loud, noisy prayers, we pray very silently during the International Day of Prayer. It's not the kind of praying you do when you are "talking" to God. We pray "being" with God, closeness and agreement, something much beyond the world of noise.

Cinnamon took two sips of water during the four hours. Papa Jerry took her out to go potty. She lay, obviously in a really broken way among us. Several Samaritans came up to her bed and prayed, laying their gentle hands upon her. There was another special dog in the room named Taco. Taco was not anything like Cinnamon in looks, but he is little like Cinnamon. He, too, attended the International Day of Prayer. When he saw that Cinnamon was in trouble, suffering in her bed, he walked across the room and came beside her. He comforted her.

After four hours, Jerry put Cinnamon in his arms, to carry her to the car, to take her home. She died in his arms on the way to the car. We took her home and came back to finish the time of prayer with our fellow Samaritans. We buried Cinnamon in our back yard and put a miniature rose bush on top of her grave. It was raining. Then we could say, "Amen."

Now, Cinnamon was a pioneer dog. She was the first dog we ever let into the International Headquarters of Good Samaritan Ministries. Yes, we let her come through the door, sniff, and run around the office all she wanted. As we had let one in, we let all the dogs come in. One day, I wrote an article for the Good Samaritan Newsletter, "The Whole Ministry Has Gone to the Dogs."

One time, a woman came in with four small dogs on leashes. She brought them to my office and asked me to do therapy with them. Sometimes we have other pets come to visit: a snake, mice. Everyone is welcome!

For, you see, the animals were created on the same day as man.

Cinnamon was seen at Dianna's, after she died, by her grown son, who did not know Cinnamon had died. She made a couple of appearances to Jerry. The Lord let her reassure Jerry that she was still with him.

I learned the great value of the animals. Great teachings come from them. Each of them has something to say to us. We have dominion over them, but they have a part of us inside them. They, indeed, carry our burdens.

CHAPTER 17

Don't Come, It's Too Dangerous

We were all shocked to watch 9/11/2001 on T.V. In October 2001, I was scheduled to go to Jordan, Iraq, and Pakistan. Would I go?

A few days later, Pakistan GSM called me and said, "It's too dangerous, don't come!" I said in return, "That is why I will come! We will never submit to a Spirit of Fear!" They were shocked.

Pakistan made plans for how to keep us safe. We would keep our mission with all the Samaritans in Pakistan.

We did not go to Iraq. Not because I was afraid to go to Iraq, but because I knew the American government would not appreciate us going, and it was a good decision not to go.

At the exact moment Kathy Lane and I landed in Amman, Jordan, the U.S. began the war in Afghanistan. Three days later, we were in Karachi, Pakistan.

Why Pakistan? How did Good Samaritan Ministries, a Christian organization, come to be in Pakistan, a country that had been founded to be a Muslim nation, a country of 97% Muslims?

I first went to Pakistan in 1989 with a small team. It was a huge adjustment to a culture that seemed strange and difficult for me. I'm sure as I met with the Pakistani Christians, they felt the same about us.

After three weeks, we decided to found Good Samaritan Ministries in Pakistan. I met with a Board of Directors that we instituted, and we selected a National Director. The National

Director was Maqbool Kamal Masih. He was the treasurer of the Philadelphia Pentecostal Church. He had been raised in the Sikh religion as a child. His parents sent him to a school outside his village, as there was no school available where he lived. He had a Christian teacher at that school, and she had a vast influence on his life. He became a Christian. His whole family became Christians. By 1989, Maqbool and his wife, Gul, had five children. They were all young children.

How Maqbool became National Director of Pakistan is an interesting story. Pastor George of the Philadelphia Pentecostal Church in Karachi recommended to me that there were three possible men who could receive this position.

I had a meeting with several people, and called out the three men. I asked them to leave the room, pray together, and ask the Holy Spirit to select the person who was called.

I sensed, in my spirit, that the men went out, talked it over, two of them not wanting the position; therefore, Maqbool was chosen. This did not cause me difficulty as Maqbool is a man of God, but I believe it caused them difficulty as the Holy Spirit choosing a person is different than talking it over. From that day, Maqbool Kamal was responsible for Good Samaritan Ministries in Pakistan.

I went to Pakistan with small teams seven times. In 1994, Maqbool came to the United States for a six-week Good Samaritan Ministries conference. He became closely connected to the whole ministry, and Pakistan became a very significant country in Samaritan development. Their need for this ministry was overwhelming!

As I traveled all over Pakistan, everywhere I went the Christians cried out in frustration. They were a minority, less than two percent of the country's population. They were suffering in their education. If their children went to school, they were only one or two Christian children in a Muslim class of 100. The Christians were suffering inferiority complexes because they were always treated as less than, never the same as. One day I looked at the people who were crying out. I looked at the men who were crying out, and I said, "Don't you understand? It is the Lord who has put you in this country." You are the tithe of God for Pakistan!" From that day forward, I never heard that complaint again. Mindsets changed, and attitudes became open to new learning. A new spirit developed.

Several hundred people became involved in Good Samaritan Ministries in Pakistan, and more than ten local centers were developed throughout the country. The seven trips to Pakistan were to examine, encourage, strengthen, and continue to train and inspire. Each journey was a God event.

In Pakistan, in 1989, less than 25% of the girls in the country had ever gone to school, Illiteracy was at an unbelievable rate.

The passion of Pakistan's Good Samaritan Ministries was the need for educating the Christian children in a safe environment. They had an anointing upon them to develop Christian/Muslim private schools that would be available to elementary aged children. In each school they would have one Muslim teacher and one Christian teacher. As it turned out, in most of our schools, 60% of the children were Muslims, and forty percent of the children were Christians. Good Samaritan Ministries built and developed eight schools and provided the freedom for God to build a bridge between the two cultures. This gave each child the chance to feel accepted. All teachers were exceptional, and they were in open agreement to have each child taught from the Bible. There is a phenomenal giftedness that runs through these schools. I am still amazed today. I am sure the children from our schools will be a real tithe, from a living God, to their nation and to the world.

I met David Bhatti on our second trip to Pakistan. He was orphaned when he was a very small boy, a young child with only older brothers and sisters. He had a very hard childhood, and suffered great losses. I will never forget the last day we were in Pakistan in 1991. When I was praying with David, he fell sobbing on the floor. It was at this moment that a special anointing came upon him and upon our family. Our families would cover each other for life. We would be the Samaritans that stopped for each other.

At my request, David wrote his own story for this book. He wrote for a full night as follows:

Since 1978 I worked in Oman in the (Middle East) with the Ministry of Defence where I met people who came from Pakistan, India, Bangladesh, Britain, Sri-Lanka, Philippine, the United States and other parts of the world. Here the Lord brought me to receive my basic training to know about Him and the needs of His people in the wilderness.

I learned English and began to translate to other languages including Urdu, English, Arabic and Punjabi.

The Lord trained and used me to help people in many different ways. For example, when individuals were away from their families, I helped them to read and write. I wrote letters to their families on behalf of them and also read letters for them from their families. Sometimes they received bad news, which they did not like to share with others, which led to fear and feelings of shame and depression. Sometimes they cried. I listened and counseled them, trying to uplift and offer prayers with them.

I was also involved in leading and conducting weekly Bible study and prayer.

In August 1990 I got an opportunity to attend Advanced Christian Leadership Training at Haggai Institute in Singapore. This was a great opportunity for me as I met Christian leaders from around fifty-five different countries. I stayed there for a month. During my stay I experienced the touch of God and many great miracles.

In February 1991 I resigned from my job in Oman and went back to Pakistan where I began to work for the community development in my hometown to help poor and needy people. I also formed various groups to empower, develop and uplift the community. These individuals were pressed down by poverty, ignorance, hatred and anger and had many questions about their existence in this world.

We started teaching about forgiveness, unity, love, and hope and also helping their fellowman. Some people were angry and hopeless about sending their children to school, because as a Christian they would not be able to gain employment. We counseled people and brought awareness to the fact that education is the only weapon against poverty, and hopelessness.

I cleaned the sewage and swept the streets in many villages and also engaged youth to serve their community. We opened sewing schools for women to learn new skills and to earn money.

We opened catering service where young men served the community and also raised their funds. People were depressed and looking for sincere leadership. We listened to them and helped them. I worked day and night for my Father's business.

In March 1991 I went Karachi to visit Maqbool Kamal, where he gave me the Mama Bettie P Mitchell GSM booklet, Training Handbook.

He was asking some people to translate. In return they were asking for money.

When he showed me the book I read it and promised to translate it without any charges, which I did in 20 days. The book was very unique. By completing the translation I came to know Mama Bettie very well and was attached to her in my spirit. I was so blessed that I wanted to meet her.

In 1991 Mama Bettie, Papa Jerry, Nancy Paul and James Opiyo visited Pakistan.

I attended the GSM training in Faisalabad, where I met Mama Bettie and Team. I interpreted the speeches during the seminars.

After the training in Faisalabad, I continued to travel with the team and went to Karachi where we had more training seminars. I attended all of the training and got the chance to interpret from English to Urdu.

When the tour was coming to an end, the GSM team was staying at a YMCA building in Karachi. They had a board meeting. At the end of the National board meeting, Mama Bettie and the team were ready to leave. Mama Bettie came to me, and she took me in her arms and put me on her lap.

As soon as she touched me I felt an electric current in my body, which was very powerful (I think it was the anointing of the Holy Spirit). It was so powerful that I almost fainted. As she was praying, touching and moving her hand gently on my chest, I cried and cried. Afterward, I felt that a big burden was removed from my body; I was released and felt at peace.

After that, Mama Bettie and the team went to the US. She continually wrote me and I continued to faithfully pray for the ministry. I transferred all my ministry work to GSM.

In April 1994 I went to Beaverton in US for GSM training, and stayed with Papa Jerry and Mama Bettie for seven months. I learned a lot from Mama Bettie and other teachers.

My life was totally changed and I received a new outlook on life.

In October 1994 I went back to Pakistan as a field director, and expanded and developed the GSM work in many local centers in Karachi and other parts of Pakistan.

We legalized GSM, bought property for centers for Faisalabad, and built schools with orphan children, land for Fateh pur; land for Francis Abad; land for Rawalpindi; and land for Karachi. We registered the schools with Government.

We opened counseling centers and libraries, helped widows and orphans, built a continental training center, putting in water supply, electricity, natural gas connection, and Internet hook up. Each life which is transformed and each brick which is laid and each person which is trained I remember, each thing, in these centers:
Rawalpindi, Islamabad, Talwandi Musa Khan, Francisabad, Sheikhupura, Manawala / Nai wala, Faisalabad, Sialkot, Mehmood Town, Fatehpur, Quetta, Azam Basti, and the Kashmir colony GSM head office in Karachi.

I am always focusing on schools and education. Still 50% of the population is illiterate, and among Christians and women the number is also very high.

Education is the key to bring peace in Afghanistan and other parts of the world; we should focus on education of Pakistani and Afghani children. Lack of the mercy of education leads to a lack of respect, tolerance and love.

People need good leaders, and teachers, who are passionate. They cannot be greedy, selfish or full of anger, because this crushes souls and teaches about killing and hatred.

I always remember the call to Mama Bettie on wall of Nineveh.

"Here are the children, where are the teachers?"
Jesus said, "Harvest is plentiful but workers are few".

David Bhatti, as Field Director, traveled all over the country, delivering the school fees, checking on the children, and gradually developing the quality needed in each of the centers. Maqbool had a full-time job. He had a small company that annually built a section of the oil pipeline being developed in Pakistan.

I want to tell two stories about David Bhatti because they are very significant. They show something in the way God puts together His anointed ones.

When David went to Faisalabad, at the edge of the city of several million, there was an area where none of the children were going to school. It was an undeveloped area, and there was great abuse and neglect of the children. It was here that Good Samaritan Pakistan decided to build a school.

Did they hire builders? No. David Bhatti gathered the children who were nearby in an orphanage, and asked the children if they would be willing to help build the school. It was in the hottest part of the year. The temperatures were often 120 degrees. The building work started very early in the morning, and continued through the morning. The children who would go to that school and David built the school together. With much secondhand material, and the making of brick, the school was finished. It is used seven days a week, not just as a school, but also as a community center. Special classes are offered for adults. The building has two stories. This is one of the truly important and remarkable Samaritan stories. I love to tell this story. I would love to see children involved in building all schools around the world. I believe it would change the children, and they would feel a part of the development of their education. Their names would be written as builders, not just attendees.

We sent the money for David's salary and for the needs of Good Samaritan Ministries Pakistan every two months. Aside from his salary, and the money to help run the schools, that was all we sent. It was not enough. With David's salary, he made all his trips around Pakistan. His family did without much, for he knew the anointing from God was to give himself to the Lord's work. His wife is Maqbool's sister. David and Nasreen have three children.

One day David called me. He had gone to the bank, and taken out the money we sent. He was in a rickshaw when four robbers with guns came in two directions. They aimed guns on him and on the driver. They took all of the money.

The funding of Good Samaritan Ministries has been very difficult. When I look at the needs of the people, and they are genuine and serious, and I look at the givers, it doesn't always meet to give enough help. Miraculously, however, God has always provided, according to His purposes.

This time there was no money to send. The income of the two months was lost. It was grievous to me, but all of us were giving almost all that we had day by day, that others far needier than we would be sustained.

David continued to get more education. Eventually he got a Master's Degree in counseling. He had health issues that became more serious. Somewhere, deep inside, he burned out. He knew that his time had come to leave Pakistan. He moved his family to Kingston, Ontario, Canada, where we have Good Samaritan Ministries. His two oldest daughters are now going, on full scholarships, to Queen's University, the Harvard of Canada.

These are miracles. The price paid to begin the work in Pakistan was enough. The call of the work continues today.

Over the years there was a price to be paid at home. One night, I was in the village of Talwandi Musa Khan sound asleep.

It was 3:00 in the morning, when I sat bolt upright in bed and said out loud, in the empty room where I was sleeping, "My husband has just been in an accident."

Very early in the morning, we located a telephone in Gujranwala and I called home. It was confirmed that Jerry had just been in an accident. He had been on his way to the coast to visit our daughter, Laura, and her family. When I talked to him, he was quite disoriented, and planning to take a bus home. I said, "You are not to take a bus. You are to have someone drive you home." The car was totaled. The last thing I said to him was "Be sure to have a newer car in our garage when I get home." When I returned home, there was a beautiful red Pontiac. He had paid $2,000 more than I ever would have thought to pay. It was the greatest gift I had ever received from my husband.

Yes, there is a price to be paid, but the price is worth it.

As Kathy Lane and I landed in Karachi, Pakistan, in October 2001, we really did not know what to expect. Immediately, we dressed at the airport in Pakistani clothes. We were put in a vehicle and taken to Maqbool's house. We spent eleven days in Pakistan. They kept us covered from head to toe every time we went anywhere in the vehicle. They had armed members of Good Samaritan Ministries covering us as we drove in the transport. They never told us this. We found out later.

The whole time we were in Pakistan, Pakistani Taliban were running to fight in the Afghanistan war. The wounded were sent back to Pakistan where there was great grieving. There were churches burned. It was absolute chaos outside; but, we Samaritans stood without fear. We would not submit to a Spirit of Fear. None of us did. We had a conference for several days in Karachi. Samaritans came from all over Pakistan to attend. It was one of the most significant events in the history of Good Samaritan Ministries, and one of the most significant events in my own lifetime. We must never submit to a Spirit of Fear. If we do, we are already conquered.

On the tenth day, Kathy Lane and I were taken to the airport to leave. The fog was so heavy that the planes did not fly that day. After spending several hours at the airport, Maqbool came to get us and take us back to his house for another day. While we were sitting at the airport, we were not covered from head to toe. We felt naked and exposed. Nobody seemed to notice us. Remember, almost all of the Internationals had left Pakistan before we arrived. I would remember Pakistan as a tortured country, meaning well, but easily destroyed by factions.

On one visit to Pakistan, there were general strikes almost daily. A political group of men would go through the stores in Karachi, and if the businesses did not shut their store down immediately, they would torch them. During that year, the stores were closed 50% of the time. There was always a sense of violence in the streets. Although the evil part might be smaller, the power to create fear makes it larger.

As the founder and director of Good Samaritan Ministries, I made myself available to the Samaritans of each country 24 hours a day, seven days a week. I would listen to them. They could reach out with a touch. We paid enough, giving a far different amount than money. We gave respect to one another.

One day, by God's grace, we had enough funds to buy property in Karachi. This was really a miracle. Gradually, after a considerable wait, we began to build a Continental School. The Continental work is just developing now in Pakistan. Christian evangelism is allowed in Pakistan and there is good response to the healing power of Jesus.

Recently, and for the second time, Maqbool went to Kenya to be at our Continental Headquarters in Uranga. He met with our National Directors from 17 countries. In an earlier season, Maqbool and David Bhatti came to Egypt and we climbed Mt. Sinai together. There was this knowing in my spirit that if you are going to develop anything, you have to develop the people. When you develop the people, they will develop many.

Every year Pakistan keeps the International Day of Prayer. They pray holding hands in a circle. "This is the way we pray as Samaritans; they say, "We pray in unity; we pray willingly."

In 2003, out of the blue, my husband and I were invited by the Oregon delegation to go to the Presidential Prayer Breakfast in Washington D.C. We were thrilled. It was a strange experience. We had much to learn. It had never happened in our lifetime that we had gone to breakfast with 4,000 people.

Jerry and I are very patriotic. We were children during World War II. I was in Washington D.C. when I was seven years old. This event was a great God gift to us. Out of the 9/11 ashes, God's glory will be revealed.

The prayer breakfast lasts three days. Of course, it is not all breakfast. The President of the United States and a significant speaker spoke to us at the breakfast, but other events and other meals follow. People were present from at least 168 countries, Heads of State, significant dignitaries. It is the most universal event on the planet, with more people groups represented than even in the United Nations. It was one of those surreal events in your life where you can hardly believe that you are there.

At the 2003 prayer breakfast, one of the members of Good Samaritan Ministries, Mike Taylor, met Benazir Bhutto, the former Prime Minister of Pakistan. During a special meeting with her people, it was arranged for her to be in Oregon with some of the Oregon delegation. I had read her autobiography in the 1990's. I knew she had been Prime Minister of Pakistan twice. In one of those times, she was pregnant. I knew how unusual it was for a woman to be a leader in a Muslim country. Her autobiography was deeply moving, revealing the terrors and challenges of a life dedicated to the needs of her people. I felt bonded to Benazir from the time that I read her book. Little did I dream Benazir Bhutto would come to the United States and visit Oregon.

Benazir Bhutto had much contact with American Christians. She was very open to Christianity. She was a woman of deep personal faith. At the time of our meeting, her husband was in prison, and the National Prayer Breakfast leaders were working to get him out.

Jerry and I were invited to a small breakfast given to honor her in a Portland home. We were each allowed a very significant time for personal relationship. Since my experience with Pakistan was more than any of the others, the conversation at the table largely extended between Benazir and myself.

I was surprised at how ordinary she was. She wore a wrinkled, cotton, Pakistani dress. Later that day, she was a speaker at Willamette University. She was casual and profoundly relational with us. There was something in the spiritual realm that I have rarely found in this world. It's not something Christian, Muslim, Jewish, or Buddhist. It was the Holy Spirit! That, I do know!

Eight of us sat at this breakfast, Benazir at the head, and we talked. Later we all talked in another room. There was a connection made, a bridge between us that was put there by the Father's hand. I shared with her that Good Samaritan Ministries' purpose was to break victim mentality, and to develop the real people that want so much to be free. She was enormously attracted to this idea, and she asked me to send her everything I knew about this. She kept asking me, "How do you break the victim mentality? How do you do it? How do you break people out of thinking as victims?" Before the breakfast was over, we were all kneeling around her and praying over her life.

After this time, Benazir and I had some contact in that I sent her all the materials I could put my hands on, and wrote her letters of encouragement, letters emphasizing the breaking of victim mentality.

Mike and Debbie Taylor were present at the small Portland breakfast. They had been interceding in prayer for Benazir and for Pakistan. Mike and Debbie Taylor, along with others, agreed to be a satellite to help with the Samaritan work in Pakistan.

In November 2005, the Taylors, Kathy Lane, and I were together in Pakistan. Before we left the United States, I had a letter inviting us to attend a dinner in Karachi with the leaders of the People's Party of Pakistan. This was a huge surprise! Benazir could not come into Pakistan at that time. She seemed to send us in her place. It was an intimate dinner with all key political leaders. There was a stream of conversation between the Muslims and us. They really sought to understand, I believe in a sincere way, why the separation between the Christians and Muslims was so profound. It was a night to ponder!

I was asked to speak after dinner. I remember that I looked at each person. I talked about their constituents, the people of Pakistan. The true constituents, the true people they must seek and find were not the adult voters, but the children. I talked much about the lives of children. Do not just legislate for children, but create for children a place of safety, and a homeland of rest. I was seeking to speak to the conscience of all of us present. It is so easy in politics to get lost on the issues, but forget the people. I found some present to be outstanding people, others perhaps cynical from the years of strife in Pakistan, and the struggle of the People's Party, without Benazir being present in Pakistan.

There was one more connection in the United States, between Benazir Bhutto and Good Samaritan Ministries. She was in Washington D.C. before she made the journey to Pakistan. She spent a week at a house dedicated to ministering to world leaders, to comforting the weary, and to giving them a safe place. The week that Benazir was there, one of the members of Good Samaritan Ministries, Karen Otis, was serving at that refuge, comforting and encouraging, not only Benazir, but the many weary travelers who must leave the crowd to find spiritual retreat.

When Benazir returned to Pakistan and made her parade through Karachi, the people were profoundly touched by this woman of much suffering who had come home to her people. The

Christian community had succeeded in obtaining the release of her husband from house arrest. He did not come with her. They needed to protect the children, and they both knew that it was not a safe trip.

When dozens of young people in the parade were shot and killed in the late night streets of Karachi, I was heart-broken. A few days later, Benazir was murdered during a rally in Rawlpindi. One could say it was about the politics of Pakistan. I would say it is about the power of Satan to destroy any hope that would bring greater unity in a foundational relationship with all the people. It was a time of great hardship. Afghanistan was raging in war. The Taliban were everywhere, and the government was not pleased with her return. Was it a conspiracy? There is no doubt of this. Was it the time of Satan, or the time of the coming of the Kingdom of God? Let us not divide over these issues. I am not a political person. I stand with the Spirit of Jesus Christ, the Son of God, that He would call all men unto Himself.

Pakistani people do not understand the value God placed on the animals He created.

In 2005, we were walking twice a day from the orphanage to the school in Faisalabad. On my route, a donkey was tied up and his excrement kept piling up behind him more every day. I always stopped and talked to the donkey. I always said, "I love you, Mr. Donkey, and I am so proud of you."

I began to wake up in the Spirit and this was the teaching I was to give:

God created animals the same day He created man, and He saw it was good. Bless the animals, name them, talk to them. As you treat others, God will treat you.

The people's hearts began to awaken and they noticed animal abuse everywhere.

The Gospel of honor and kindness must conquer the gospel of

neglect and abuse.

In 2010, we had education offered in several regions of Pakistan: 11 daily schools in Pakistan, and 1200 Students.

Our work continues in Pakistan. The schools have grown. The children are quietly being developed. May the fruit of these labors bring genuine peacemakers, no longer manipulating doctrines, but children living a life of grace and a fruitful life of peace.

We must commend the laborers, and remain one ourselves! Most of all, where will we stand with the children?

CHAPTER 18

My Fellow Samaritans

When Jesus told the Parable of the Good Samaritan, He told a story.

This chapter, my Fellow Samaritans, is to tell the story of some of those who came into the ministry and made a difference, a deep and profound difference in the lives of many. It reminds me of a scripture, *"I have called you by your name, you are mine."* (Isaiah 43:1)

Jerry Mitchell

Jerry Mitchell did not plan to be a full-time Christian worker. When we married, he agreed to become a Christian and go to church. He had no vision for this assignment, but he had a good heart, and he was committed to travel to better understand the world around us.

There are two great moments in Jerry Mitchell's life that affected thousands of people around the world. The first moment was when I came home from Iraq and told him what the Lord had spoken to me. I asked him if he agreed for me to obey the Call. In this first great moment, he said, "Yes, you must do what the Lord has asked you to do."

The second moment was years later when both of us were pretty badly broken down; me, from exhaustion and grief, and Jerry from tons of pain from his childhood, and the suffering he saw in children during his years of teaching school. I asked him if he wanted me to quit the ministry, stay home, and help him. He said these words, "No matter what I do or say to you, you must never leave the work."

Once, I was at the Christian Renewal Center teaching a summer camp. A couple came up to me and said, "We can see that you are Christian, but we don't know if your husband is." I spoke the following words to them, "I don't know if he is or not, but I know he has greater faith than I do." It was the end of their doubts.

Jerry paid all of his way on every ministry trip he took with me. He was always interested in the children. He took books and hand puppets with him. He played with the children wherever we went. I can remember when he was playing with the children on top of the ancient city of Irbil in Iraq. That day he handed out plastic puppets to many of them.

Those who like to witness a lot may play with the children, and they may like children, but sometimes they like to witness more than they like the children. I believe it is very important that children know we like them, that we "suffer the little children to come unto Him, for of such is the Kingdom of God." It was his gentle play and his great passion for children that made Jerry visible as a lifetime Samaritan.

When Jerry was in the Army, he was trained to be a Medic. When he went to a village in Uranga, Kenya, he found the health conditions to be shockingly severe. Every place we looked, people were terrifically sick or dying. One boy had a severe burn. There had been a wound, and they poured boiling water over it to sterilize it. From that day, Jerry became Dr. Jerry in Africa. It wasn't the medical treatment he gave, which was primitive and little, as he is not a doctor. It was the compassion he had. When he touched a person who was terrified with the darkness of their illness, he brought love and light to them.

From the time my mother prophesied that I was to marry this man, when she had only met him at the front door. From that point until today, it is the Lord who has revealed the great Samaritan life of Papa Jerry.

Pastor Allan Hansen

Allan Hansen had a great influence on the development of Good Samaritan Ministries. When I first came home from Iraq in 1976, he had scheduled me to come to the Christian Renewal Center and teach the whole Thanksgiving weekend. I had made a trip up to the Renewal Center area, and visited them over the prior summer. He, at that time before the Call, decided to invite me to teach. Thus, he gave me the opportunity to do the first public teaching, when obedience to God's call of the ministry began.

Allan was a man of great faith and vision. He and his wife, Eunice, were profoundly influenced by the Baptism of the Holy Spirit. In 1960, Allan was the pastor of the largest Lutheran church in Los Angeles. When he received the Holy Spirit, the Lord changed his life so dramatically, that the church sent him away. He did not mind, for the assignment he had then was to go to the streets and be among the street kids to help them get their own vision through Christ Jesus.

After several years, Allan and his wife, Eunice, felt called to develop the Christian Renewal Center, a family owned and operated camp that would charge little and provide much. In the summer, teaching family camps were offered by donation only. I know one family came every summer with ten children. They had nothing to pay, and they stayed three weeks. In the state of Oregon, there is no other camp like the Christian Renewal Center.

Allan was a great minister and inspiration to me personally. When I watched him set the tables for meals, knowing he would have been waited on at most tables, I learned from Allan what a true Samaritan really is.

One of the greatest Christmas gifts I ever received, in my whole life, was from Allan Hansen. He beautifully hand-carved a pulpit. He saved the pulpit for me to be the first to use it. It was his permanent gift to me.

As Allan and Eunice aged, they never seemed to give out. One Christmas season, about a week before Christmas, we did not have enough people to come fold and prepare the newsletters for mailing. Allan and Eunice drove 60 miles to Beaverton and folded newsletters all day in a cold warehouse.

Whatever I am, whatever I have become, there were secret mentors who were lifetime Samaritans.

Pastor Orville Nilsen – "O"

I met the Nilsens at Bethel Congregational Church in Beaverton, Oregon. Jean was the organist and choir director. Orville was a member of the Methodist Church. We seemed to click and it was good. This was in the early 1960s.

Orville is a man with tremendous integrity. He has suffered much. He was seriously wounded twice in World War II.

When Orville was in his senior year at Yale Law School, he was one of 16 survivors in a plane crash during a Boeing Field take off. 14 had not survived. He had burns over most of his body. In the next ten years, he had 49 skin graft surgeries to try to repair his body.

After the crash, Orville tried twice to pass the Bar Exam. He could not, and as a result, he went into the title insurance business. He went on to work for the Portland Development Commission, but he secretly knew, inside himself, he was not doing the work he was called to do.

After the plane crash, Orville and Jean married and they had five children. Orville was the first Chairman of the Board of Good Samaritan Ministries. On the Board were Orville and his wife, Jean,

Laura Sheron, Jerry and myself. Orville was Chairman of the Board for five years, and we met regularly.

Orville and I led a six-week course called "The Workbook of Living Prayer." We divided the group, as so many had signed up for the class. He took one of the groups, and I took the other. It was an astonishing experience that began to speak to me deep inside, "Do we know how to pray, or do we just think we know how to pray?" The course consisted of a small reading, and answering a page or page and-a-half of questions each day. Each week we had a group meeting to share what we had learned during the week. Attendees were asked to agree to do the workbook daily throughout the six weeks.

One woman in our group never did it at all. I want to add she was elderly, but she came every week. Others were spotty. Since I was the group leader, it was my goal to do it every day; but, one day, I forgot. I was in bed asleep at 11:30 p.m. I suddenly remembered I had forgotten! I jumped out of bed and did the assignment, realizing at the same time, that my brain was saying, "Oh well, you can do two tomorrow." In that way I learned never to put off today's business. I knew, from deep within myself, that if I had gone the way my flesh wanted to go, my spirit would never have won the battle. This training was a time of life-changing experiences in living prayer for everyone.

In the early 70's, Orville received the call from God to go to seminary in Bangor, Maine. He became a Methodist pastor. Several of us did what we could to help with the expenses, but it was a terrifically difficult time, as they also had three children in college.

When Orville retired as a Methodist pastor, he came back into Good Samaritan Ministries. He served as a counselor, working with many clients. He connected with the training we were giving every week, and really enjoyed this time. When a need came up to have someone take responsibility for our work in India, he and his wife

Jean agreed to form the India Satellite.

We made a trip to India together, and they went several other times. They formed a very viable India satellite organization, and they have always met the financial responsibilities to back the work in India with consistency, and spiritual covering. They have brought many important events to our work in India.

Orville is a dreamer and a visionary, but he never pushes his ideas on others. He believes that we discover these things when we seek to find them ourselves. He is a fellow Samaritan for life.

Jean Nilsen

When Jean and I made the decision in 1979 to work as a team, we committed to being full-time Samaritans. Each of us took our own path. The great call on Jean's life was in the healing ministry. The great call on my life was to teach and encourage deeper reconciliations needed for wellness. I stood on the hard road for "development of the whole person." Jean worked in her house; I worked in ours. Each month, whatever came in that we could give, we kept for her support while Orville was in Seminary. These were times of passionate love and mutual sacrifice. We were exploring the frontiers of what it meant to be a healing ministry. As I saw the most profoundly disturbed, Jean worked with those who came to her through her ministry in music.

Jean graduated from Western Washington University, and went on for advanced work at Westminster Choir College, Princeton. She is enormously gifted, a giant in music. Her life of music brought her to the inner lives of others where the music might not be going well. The soul has its own music, and much distress creates much disharmony.

Jean and I coordinated our work. We were accountable to the Board, we did reports, and we shared our spiritual growth.

One day we were called to work together in prayer. We went

to the home of a man named Greg, who had Hodgkin's disease. He was terribly ill, and they were not sure he would live. I took his feet in my hands, and Jean took his head in her hands. We prayed his body would be healed for his life and freedom to come out of darkness. He recovered, and has never had a recurrence.

As the years went by, Jean went ahead with the healing ministry, and I became totally given over to the development of Good Samaritan Ministries. Not only did I work with clients every day, I had to teach, do lots of supervision, and develop the international work. There are no words to say how hard the journey was. Today, Jean and Orville are in their mid-80's. They are still each about the Father's business.

Joan Baker

There were many strange things that happened, and you always knew it was a God event. I was called one day, by a man I didn't know, who asked me to go out into an area that was 50 miles from our house, to lead a Bible study for two sessions. When I went to that house, I discovered the parents had 15 adopted children. Phil and Ann Scott were a most remarkable couple. The experience was a joy. What if I had said "No, I am too busy."?

One of the women attending this Bible study was Joan Baker. As I revealed to the group that I did see people for counseling at our home, she asked if she could come and see me. She and her husband had three children of their own. Her brother's wife had abandoned their four children, and her brother was in Viet Nam. Joan and her husband, Ted, agreed to keep the four children together and raise them.

Joan was concerned about two of the children, and somewhat feeling overwhelmed by the traumas that had so affected their lives. She came to the house to see me for counseling. She came several times.

I discovered in Joan Baker a remarkable inner strength. She had gifts and talents that were greatly needed in ministry. I desperately needed help. Joan had a Bible degree from San Jose Bible College.

One day I said to Joan, "I need you to be a counselor. I cannot handle the work alone." I read about this training called "Reality Therapy," and I said, "Maybe it could give you the tools to work with people while using your faith as a base to bring healing and reconciliation into their lives."

The course was fairly expensive, and we put it before the Lord. He proved His faithfulness to call Joan to the work by providing the exact amount that was needed. When Joan returned from the training, she began to counsel and help several days each week at our house. She sat on our king-size bed, as it was the only other available room with a closed door to give privacy. We shared our struggles to reach the hard-to-reach. We learned we were teachable. We knew that we knew little, and sometimes, we knew nothing. But, God revealed much for the sake of the people who came.

Neither Joan, nor I had a vision that the ministry would go so far. Each day, as we went into our offices later, we worked long hours, barely having time to talk to each other. Joan organized things and put the professional pieces of the ministry together. She continued to see clients. We worked together as a team for 25 years.

There are many hard parts to a Samaritan life, rough journeys to be made, long hours to be kept, and the Father's business pressing at our door day after day, after day. Joan paid that price of laying down her life. She gave hundreds of people the chance to be well, and to function to their highest calling.

Joan and Ted, her husband, continued to be pioneers in the work. Ted took over a lot of the ministry responsibilities. In the early years, he and I performed many weddings together. Ted was an ordained pastor.

Two things stood out in Joan Baker's time as Assistant Director of Good Samaritan Ministries. Her organizational skills were greatly needed, and she gave everything she had to those times when it had to be a sacrifice.

Perhaps, one of her hardest assignments was when we added on to Good Samaritan Ministries headquarters. In a warehouse, adjacent to our offices, we had to build several offices, a large group room, a kitchen, and a wheelchair bathroom. One of our members was a builder, and he agreed to take the responsibility of the job. He, with the team who worked together on this building project, worked every Saturday and Sunday for several months. I asked Joan to be there, and she took on that assignment and completed it. I have never been more proud of a person than I have been of Joan Baker.

The second story I need to tell is about our trip to Pakistan as "The Three Mamas." Joan and I were joined by Judith Sellangah, a board member from Kenya GSM, who lived in Nairobi, decided to do a three-week ministry trip throughout Pakistan. Since I was called "Mama Bettie," and Joan was called "Mama Joan," we decided we were the "Three Mamas." Throughout most of the journey in Pakistan, we slept in one large bed together, taking turns in the middle; but, I usually got the outside spot because I had to go to the bathroom more frequently. We had so much joy on that journey, and I believe it made a deep impression on our people in Pakistan. We left everything, came to them, and lived with them.

When Joan Baker retired in 2002, just before the G.S.M. International Conference, she was exhausted to the bone. Physical problems had begun to prevail over her life. It was time for Joan to go home and find the quiet days that would heal her in body, heart, and spirit.

There is a terrific cost to ministry. There are many blessings, but as St. Paul struggled and suffered to carry the Gospel, Joan struggled to live it. She is a woman to be highly honored in the memory of the generations of this ministry. She is my fellow Samaritan.

Lynda Donaca

Lynda Donaca joined Good Samaritan Ministries after an event that occurred at Lake Grove Presbyterian Church. I was teaching about the healing miracles of Jesus. Classes were five hours each, and I taught several of them. One day, in the middle of the class, Lynda Donaca stood up and said, "I am in such pain, I can hardly stand it. Will you please pray for my healing?" We immediately moved towards her. She lay on the floor, and the Lord touched her. When she cried out, He gave her the healing. In this class, many powerful events took place, and three people out of the class became full-time Samaritans. Full-time Samaritan means full-time availability. It does not mean a full-time worker. It means sensitive understanding that we must be wisely available to the needs of others.

I have chosen Lynda Donaca out of all the prayer support teams over the years to be one who has faithfully touched the ministry. She would come to the office every Friday and vacuum the whole office. At home, she had cleaning help. At the office, she was willing to be the cleaner.

Lynda Donaca went on, with Laura Fribbs and others, to develop the International Education Satellite. As the number of students we were sponsoring grew, as the need was so profound in several countries, we had to make enormous sacrifices. Our decisions were life and death to children.

People are interested in knowing the little child they are sponsoring. We were interested in that little child knowing that God took care of that sponsorship. If it did not come from God, but came from their sponsor, they would always want their sponsor to give them gifts and bring them to America. If it came from God, then it was to God that they would give their thanks. We didn't have individual sponsorships very long when we realized this could cause the children great harm. We realized there was a greater calling to widely speak of international education. We were to live a life calling for the education of children. We formed the International Education Satellite, and gave them the impossible task of raising funds to educate several thousand children, in 22 countries, annually.

When I was in Uganda the second time, and again met with President Museveni of Uganda, he and I spent the whole meeting talking about the urgency of education. He sent me on a long trip out into the bush to visit a school he had built for war orphans. He provided a driver, a vehicle, and an armed guard. I went. Lynda put her whole passion into the needs of children. She and Laura Fribbs have carried the responsibility of consistently keeping our international children in school, and schools open. This is a hard assignment.

Sheila Hair

People from other regions in the Northwest wanted Good Samaritan Ministries to develop in their areas. Gradually, the Lord allowed that to happen. It was not I who came to develop their area; it was they who developed their area. We were all part of Good Samaritan Ministries, but we all had autonomy. The development of each area of the ministry worldwide has been according to the talents, the passion and the call of those who would faithfully develop it.

Sheila and John Hair were brought to my office as they had a serious problem. Friends had driven them from Walla Walla, Washington, to Beaverton, and I met with them for several hours. Out of that meeting, John Hair had a great reconciliation with his father that was permanent and life-changing. Out of that meeting, I sensed great gifts and talents in Sheila Hair. She would become a life-time Samaritan.

Sheila had many struggles. They had adopted a boy from India named David. He weighed four pounds when they flew him from India. David had serious emotional and mental challenges. Sheila worked with him every day. I continued to see the Hairs from time to time. It was a round trip of 400 miles to come to Beaverton. Our relationship grew. Sheila was a college graduate, but if she would develop the work of Good Samaritan Ministries in Walla Walla, she would need to get a Master's Degree in counseling. I asked her husband if he would allow her to do that. He said, "Yes," and she did!

Sheila Hair continues to be very highly committed and gifted at working with Attachment Disorder children. She has clarity. She has simple childlike faith, and she has a depth of perception. Her confidence in the Spirit grew. There were great breakthroughs. Sheila, John, and their son, David, went to the Middle East with us. We climbed Mt. Sinai together. We experienced the full reality of what the Kingdom of God is, and what we are to be as servants of His Kingdom.

Pastor Willie Booysen

I met Willie Booysen in 1995 in South Africa. An African from Kenya, living in South Africa, had written me a letter of inquiry in 1994. That letter impressed me that he, perhaps, was called to develop Good Samaritan Ministries in South Africa. I decided to make a trip to South Africa to visit him, and see what was possible. It was a strange team that I found, but the beginning of great potential for Samaritan laborers. Two of the young men were from Uganda. They were both Mormons. The young man who felt the call to lead was a charismatic Christian from Kenya. They all had some relationship with a pastor, Willie Booysen.

As we spoke together in Pretoria, Pastor Willie Booysen agreed to become the Chairman of the Board for Good Samaritan Ministries in South Africa.

Willie Booysen was the pastor of a very large mixed race church in Pretoria named Elim Christian Church. He is a remarkable man and I liked him a lot. He liked the idea of Good Samaritan Ministries. He understood from the inside out that Christianity is not church attendance; it is living a life that bears fruit for the lives of many. We grew in our respect for one another. I made three trips to South Africa.

The most important Samaritan journey Willie made was a visit to Oregon Good Samaritan Ministries. He was coming for the first time to the United States to attend a meeting of his denomination in Tennessee; but first, he came to Oregon. The first words he spoke to me were these words, "I had to come home first, and then go to my church meeting."

Willie Booysen was only with us three days, but during that time, he attended group, took some training and learned a lot about the ministry and the call behind it. During one of the groups, he shared the following story:

"I was pastor of my church. It was during Apartheid. Pretoria had to be emptied in the early evening of all black people. There were many black orphans on the streets that had nowhere to go. I decided to take 30 of those black children into our church. We developed a space for them, beds for them, and the food they needed to survive.

One day, our church was burned to the ground. Someone had found out we were hiding black children at night. All of the children died. The news went into all the papers in South Africa. It was a big shame and scandal as we had broken the rules of Apartheid. I became a shame because I was a Dutch Afrikaaner. I went into the darkness of the pain of those children, the cost of Apartheid, and what it means to be a Christian. From that day on, and every day, I feared they would burn the new church again.

When Apartheid ended, our church became a home base for not only the black population, but for all the different people groups who have made South Africa their home."

When Willie had finished talking, there was profound silence. That silence moved into prayer. It moved into prayer reality. It moved into the place we often don't go in prayer because we go with words. This prayer was too deep for words.

When these moments were over, Willie Booysen looked up and said, "for the first time since the fire, I am free of the burden." When he left, he gave his word to continue to back the development of Good Samaritan Ministries.

When Willie earned his PhD, I asked him to send me a copy of his dissertation. I read all of it.

Relationships have a silent part, and the silent part is not judgment, but faith in the God of our relationship.

Don Miller

Pastor Don Miller retired from Rock Creek Church several years ago. He became interested in our work. One day he asked me to lunch, and during that lunch, he asked if he could join Good Samaritan Ministries and be trained. My reply was, "What you have asked for is very hard, for you would have to give up everything you know in order to learn what you don't know. You are a systems man, and there is no system, but only creative grace." He was really shocked. He asked, "How did you know my doctoral dissertation was in systematic theology?" I didn't know. It was the Holy Spirit.

Don Miller decided to receive the Samaritan call. The call touched the lives of everyone in his family. The passion of the Samaritan, and the Call to action, took he and his wife, Nancy, to live their lives for the greater purposes of God's will.

Don's family roots were in parents who came from Ukraine to Canada. In Canada, they were in a lot of poverty, but they saved a lot, grew a lot, and the family made it. They produced eight fine children.

Don was interested in his Ukrainian roots. He was interested in what happened to those family members who stayed behind when the Germans came in World War II, and when the Russians and the KGB nearly destroyed Ukraine. What happened to the German people? He decided to pursue research in the archives in Ukraine, and to get the testimonies of people in Western Ukraine. He decided to lead "Roots Tours," taking people with Ukrainian German backgrounds, and helping them find facts, artifacts, and memories of their family history.

Before Don made one of his trips, he asked me about bringing Good Samaritan to Ukraine. I said, "Well, if the Lord reveals a person to you, then go ahead. You will know."

When he was on the second floor of a hotel in Zhitomir, a maid was there who was a Christian. At the time he saw her, there was a Christian group acting out the Parable of the Good Samaritan. He felt this was a sign, and he called her to the work. She accepted the call.

Today, we have a very significant ministry in Ukraine because it has been built on a strong foundation of God's love. The ministry was not built with any kind of need to produce our fruit. It was built to produce God's fruit. Don and his wife, Nancy, have faithfully made at least one, or often, two trips to the Ukraine each year. Don has taken dozens of people on the Roots Tours. The people have found their history, and many have helped Don develop Ukraine Samaritan Ministry.

Recently, after a long faith struggle, the Ukraine Satellite from Oregon supervised and funded the building of a wonderful home for widows, who are called babushkas. Many of these widows have no one to take care of them, and no place to turn. They have also developed an addiction recovery center, and a vocational school, so that as the residents are coming out of addiction, they can find work and support themselves.

On my first trip to Ukraine, I bought land and several buildings. The whole cost was $8,000. The Lord had spoken to me and said, "Now is the time to purchase land. Later it will cost too much." This purchase later provided the treatment center and the vocational school.

Don and Nancy are Samaritans every day of their lives. Don is a gifted writer. He has published books that help clarify what happened to the Germans in Ukraine. He and his wife, Nancy, are very faithful to attend Monday morning prayer time at the Good Samaritan Ministries headquarters. They both have taken and given much training, and they influence all of our International Samaritan workers.

Rose Slavkovsky

Rose was a very young child when she became a Samaritan. She took this spirit of sacrifice to her heart. It was an assignment she has never ignored. Rose lives out this assignment.

The first incredibly important story I remember about Rose is when she asked her mother to allow her to stay home from school so she could do a project to raise money for Good Samaritan Ministries. She worked all day designing and creating Christmas paper and cards. At five years of age, she then took them out, sold them and turned in the money for African education.

Rose has grown up. She daily is an inspiration to others. Her parents have both suffered serious physical illnesses, but Rose, and her other two siblings, have graduated with great honors from Universities. Rose, today, is on a journey that will bear fruit in the next generation.

I have a burning desire that parents stop training their children in the superficial. They must start training their children to be fellow Samaritans, with a lifetime passion for others.

Jackie Wilhelm

Jackie Wilhelm came into Good Samaritan Ministries in its early development stage. She and her husband were members of the original prayer support team. They were two of the twenty people whose names I had been given by the Lord.

Jackie was always a gung-ho person. She lived a lifetime encouraging and inspiring others. She did not need to be the center of attention, and she knew how to be a full Samaritan.

In more than twenty years on the GSM Board, Jackie Wilhelm was Chairman of the Board of Good Samaritan Ministries for two years. It was a hard development time, and she did a wonderful job of pulling the Board and the ministry together.

Jackie and I were great friends. It was not in the usual sense of friends, it was deeper than that. It was a connectedness that was sent by the Father.

Jackie had health issues for many years. They got more serious as the years went by. She travelled with me on several significant journeys. There was struggle and victory in every journey.

I especially remember Jackie's time in the middle of the hottest part of the summer in Pakistan. We were having a conference for several days, and I asked her if she would lead the exercises every morning. Jackie, being who she was, did exactly that. There is a video to prove it! Although leading exercises was not her expertise, it was her grace to do something that would establish important steps of growth in the Pakistani families.

Jackie was never selfish. She was always willing to go the extra mile. She was willing to fit in where needed, and that is the core value of being a Samaritan for life.

For many years, Jackie was my permanent typist. I didn't have time to use a computer. I didn't learn to do that until I was 75 years old. I used a dictaphone, and Jackie typed and typed and typed, often, 30 to 40 hours each week. For example, we sent out personal letters. I said "we" because Jackie was sending them out also with her spirit and with her prayers, to every local center's director in the world. I remembered to write to children. Speaking into a dictaphone, I was speaking directly to those who would receive the letters. The Holy Spirit used that gift of Jackie's so people would hear the words. She put them down in writing, and we passed them along to the nations of the world.

Jackie asked for little and gave much. Sometimes that isn't good, for the scripture talks about balance. "As you give, so shall you receive." It was her delight and her joy to give. I believe when she received the fullness of God's grace, and she went home to be with Him, she received the fullness of His reward for her giving.

When Jackie Wilhelm died after a long illness, I was notified of her death when I was on a Civil War battlefield in Virginia, on a personal trip with my husband. I was so glad to know that her suffering was over, but I still today, several years later, miss her, dream about her, and feel that deep connection from His Kingdom to ours.

Sherrill Baker

When Jackie Wilhelm became too ill to type, Sherrill Baker took her place. Sherrill was a gifted pianist, an outdoor girl, strong in the humble gifts of true ministry. I really gained a lot from watching Sherrill. When things were difficult, she chose encouragement. I never saw her choose victimization. It was there at times, but she did not choose to stay in it.

I love Sherrill deeply. Today, she is struggling with Alzheimer's and I don't see her, but in my mind's eye, she will always be a lifetime Samaritan.

Kathy Lane

Kathy Lane came in as a client, and stayed to be a lifetime Samaritan. She had been an RN who was given many responsibilities of leadership.

Kathy has the gift of teaching, and she has the gift of professionalism from the heart, not just the doctrine of professionalism. She builds bridges when others tear them down. She has learned to look at things in more than one way. Perhaps, Kathy's greatest gift is her ability to see deeply when she is wrong; to take spiritual correction seriously; and to continue to pray for those that others would have given up on.

When Jackie could no longer travel with me, Kathy came to be my travel partner. We made two trips around the world. We made trips into hard and dark places. We shared the Pakistan trip after 9/11. We shared many beds. We did not encroach upon one another's lives. We were grateful to serve and uphold one another. Kathy did not seek for herself. She lived, and lives, for the Lord.

Kathy, too, was Chairman of the Board twice. She was very instrumental in drawing some of the poison out, and replacing it with healthy interaction and reality in seeing problems and dealing with them.

I have honored several people as lifetime Samaritans. This is only a small list of incredible people here, and in other countries around the world who "got it." They "used it," and they "kept "it."

There are many Samaritans who do not function through Good Samaritan Ministries. I have found them all over the world. You will notice them because they don't ask for anything for themselves.

They give full measure and running over to others. Many ministries in the world today are filled with Samaritan laborers. I want to remind the ministry, and I want to remind myself that we are not an exclusive organization, but we are an empowering organization of the ministries of others. This is a great truth that must not be lost in the unraveling of time. One of the profound purposes of Good Samaritan Ministries has been to cover the small laborers who had no one to help and support them, and to train the young to fulfill lifetime Calls as Samaritans.

You may be a Samaritan at times; would you consider becoming a full-time Samaritan? Do you hear the Call? Do you tremble? Do you weep? Do you thirst? Can you give your life to help?

CHAPTER 19

Pyramids and Egyptians

In 1968, when my mother and I travelled to the Middle East, we spent 36 hours in Egypt. To see Cairo in one day was a big stretch.

When we came to the great pyramids of Giza, built 4,500 years ago, it fed something into my spirit for which I hungered and thirsted. I needed to know ancient man. I needed to know what was important to him. I needed to see the ancients in historical perspective. Ruins that are well preserved are an awesome sight.

The base of the Great Pyramid of Cheops covers 13 acres. Each stone weighs two and-a-half tons, and there are over two million of these stones. The Great Pyramid of Giza is 450 feet high.

How did ancient man struggle to know God, to know eternal life, to search for what was good? What would it mean to govern? Who was qualified to govern? Was eternal life just for those who were rich and famous, or also for the poor, the lame, and the weak? These pyramids began for me a long study of archaeology that extended to many parts of the world.

The first trip I took to the Middle East, I took pictures. The second trip to the Middle East, I took notes. The third trip to the Middle East, I looked at what I was seeing. I paid attention to what my eyes were teaching me, and my ears were hearing. Gradually, I saw people. As I saw and met people along the road, I began to connect history with today. History can give us clues to where we are going. Ancient ruins teach what they teach. Around us, not only the ancients, but the everyday person on the street can continue to teach us to know and to understand.

In 1968, the buses in Cairo, Egypt were sites unto themselves. People were hanging all over on the outside of jammed full busses. The City of the Dead, a cemetery from more modern times, was filled with mausoleums. It was also full of people living among the tombs. Piles of garbage were everywhere. The eyes of poverty could not be missed, for several million people were living in the streets, homeless. Cairo was a hub for the people of the villages and towns to come and see if they could survive there and make more opportunity for their future and for their families. At night you could watch the men lie down on the streets, in parks or in corner places. With no blankets, they wrapped their galabiyas around their bodies and slept.

How do I sleep? A minimum of three pillows, covers, nightwear (different from day-wear), a comfortable mattress, and in all of that comfort, I find much sleeplessness. Their sleep seemed to be natural. It was deep. At the core of that rest was resignation and a kind of survival trust.

I've lost count of how many times I've been to Egypt, but I believe it is more than ten. I've been in Egypt for short lengths of time and longer lengths of time. I've led many tours to Egypt, and much of the time, Mt. Sinai was a place we visited.

I have come to love and respect the Egyptians. I have come to know many. Each time a new person became a part of my knowing, I marveled at what I could learn from them. Many were inspirational. They were hospitable in the spirit, even when you weren't in their house. They seemed to see in the spiritual realm, where many of us don't see very well.

In 1988, I met two Arab Christian leaders in Oregon. One man was Egyptian, the other man was Jordanian. We were at a home dinner, and we spent the evening listening to them talk about what was going on in the Middle East. I was deeply impressed with these two leaders, and decided that I needed to know more. In 1989, my husband, Jerry, and I decided to visit Cairo, not to see the sights, but to seek and find out what the social work conditions were in the country. We visited many social institutions. We were escorted by the Egyptian we had met in Oregon. I wanted to know if there was any Samaritan ministry there. I wanted to know, would it be such a call of God there? How could we provide and be different than what was already being provided? They were two hard intense days to ponder, and then ponder some more. We stopped at a Palestinian hospital and went upstairs to see where the Palestinian leaders often met. We studied children's work. What counseling was offered in the country? Were there addiction programs? Were they quality programs? Was there training available in this field?

When we went home, I determined that we would take a very special tour group to Egypt and to the Holy Land in 1990. We requested this tour through the Egyptian man I had met in Oregon. We asked for the very best Christian guides that would really connect with us, not only with what we would see, but connect with us as to who we were, and who they were. Amir and Mourad were the two guides chosen. Amir decided to invite a young Christian woman, Manal, for whom he had great respect, to join us. We began to connect personally with people living in Egypt. What I saw was enormous spiritual development. Here were young men and a young woman who saw what was important and what wasn't. Here we were, learning what is important and what isn't. It was a remarkable time for them and for us, and since 1990 we have continued to be close personal friends.

I continued to search for a Samaritan Ministry in Egypt. What would it be like? How would the counseling ministry go forward? Who would take it? In 1990, when we came to the border of Israel and Egypt, where we would be handed over to the Israeli side, a prayer was said at the fence that divided Israel from Egypt. I had crossed over to the Israeli side, and Amir and Mourad were on the Egyptian side of the fence. We touched our hands through the fence and prayed they would find a Samaritan person who is doing such a work in Egypt. We had talked much about the work that needed to be done, and what could be developed; but it was this prayer on each side of the fence that was the final piece in place for finding such ministry to develop in Egypt.

A few months later, they had identified a man named Moushir. Moushir was a commercial artist. He was born and raised in Cairo. He was an evangelical Christian, and he had a keen interest in counseling, practicing some caring ministry in his church.

How he came to have an interest in counseling is a very interesting story. When he was born, his father could not decide what to name his son. He went to the Bible, and in reading these words from Isaiah, "Wonderful-Counselor, Mighty-God, Eternal-Father, Prince-of-Peace," he decided to name his son Moushir. From his birth, he was named Moushir, the Arabic word for counselor. From scripture, his name was inspired.

Moushir went through a horrendous shock when, one day, his father was killed in the streets of Cairo, as he fell under a bus. This accident occurred the day he had received a letter from me inviting him to meet me in Kenya. We needed to know each other, study, pray, and plan together. He did not meet us in Africa in 1991.

Moushir was a man of passion, interested in classical music and the arts. He was a stubborn man. He held his own. When you hold your own against me, that's a good sign. It means you are a man who can balance and be strong in the Lord and in His work.

In 1991 we met. As I came into Egypt, there was a fertile quickening of the call of the Spirit to develop this work. Moushir was already reading, studying, paying attention to, and connected to this kind of ministry. How would it change? What would happen if he became encouraged with a wider picture with what we are called to do from Nineveh in Iraq?

Moushir founded a Board, and developed the ministry that is called "Counseling & Christian Maturity." The ministry was developed under the protestant church in Egypt; therefore, housed in a church. It was spiritually covered and encouraged by many Christians in Cairo, including the Egyptian man I met in Oregon in 1988.

In 1991, I met Fred Cooper in Egypt. Fred was an American advisor to the engineers of Egypt. They were building the sewers on the West Bank of the Nile. Fred was in Egypt for a number of months. We taught Level I Counselor Training. There were about 15 in the classes. After we started, I left Fred to continue to do the teaching. His training at Good Samaritan Ministries in Oregon suddenly was found essential by God's grace in Cairo, Egypt.

1992 was a busy year for me. I left for Africa, joining together Internationals from several countries, to study the ministry. Moushir was part of our team. We all travelled as a team to Kenya and Uganda.

On this trip in 1992, all of us personally met with President Museveni of Uganda at the Presidential Residence at Entebbe. The journey was an absolute turning point for our work in Africa. Moushir was given a chance to see the possibilities of the Samaritan call firsthand. Our call was to work among the people, not among the churches. It was a work that recognizes the needs of the people, and their great need for individual encouragement to grow beyond their circumstances. It was a fantastic journey and our great opportunity to travel together. We were forming lifetime relationships.

As Moushir joined us on the visit to Kenya, Uganda and Tanzania, his eyes were being opened to the bigger world that needs to be included in our own world. Moushir was challenged, and perhaps irritated at me because I was a woman. I don't say that with any negativity or malice. I say this with a spirit of humor. I'm a firm woman, and when I talk, I talk with considerable authority. I talk decisively. Usually, I am speaking from the deep inside, the Holy Spirit Himself speaking.

By the time we were returning on a train from Mobassa to Nairobi, Moushir was beginning to see the plans that must be laid in order for his counseling and caring ministry to reach out to many parts of the Middle East.

In 1993, it was agreed that I would come to Egypt for ten days to teach. The whole ten days would be a time of teaching, and a time of counseling in private for those who needed to see me. I flew alone to Cairo, but I will digress for a moment and say that on the way to Cairo, I spent a day and a night in Washington, D.C. I had a purpose in mind. Evarestus Anywanu was living in Washington, D.C. He was a student at Howard University. He was a foreign student that was sponsored by Good Samaritan Ministries. He is a Nigerian. In his parent's house, Good Samaritan Ministries Nigeria began.

I asked Evarestus to provide housing for me. He took me into his dorm, and said to the man at the door, "This is my mom." He invited friends over---college students and others. We spent an evening visiting. He asked me if I wanted a bubble bath. This was hospitality, love, and courtesy for his Mom.

The next day, we spent the day visiting special sights in Washington, D.C. We went to a site, sat and talked about it until our hearts were full of inspiration, and then we went to another. The place we both liked the best was the Lincoln Memorial. I can remember us reading aloud, together, the inscriptions inside the Lincoln Memorial. After we had been inside, we sat down on benches facing the Lincoln Memorial, and talked at length about the life of Abraham Lincoln, about slavery, and about how things came to pass that finally brought a healing to our nation. We talked about the vision of Abraham Lincoln, and his inspiration that hovered over our country, until we were out of this terrible 100 years after the Civil War, and civil rights were established for all Americans.

Evarestus was worried about the political situation in Nigeria. He felt an urgent call to make a difference. But how does one do that? There were so many problems in Nigeria that it would take an impossible leap of faith to make any difference at all. Nevertheless, the seeds were planted and the inspiration of that time encouraged each of us. After a dinner together at Howard University, we went to the airport, and I flew alone to Cairo.

In Cairo, I met many Egyptians and came to know them personally, because that is what a counselor does; they must know a person through and through in order to help that person find the next steps to wellness and wholeness. There was something unique about Egyptians and what they had to say, because usually, when they came in for a private session, they would say, "I have this problem." Then, they would describe this problem. It was interesting as there was so much clarity; they saw the problem they had. Here, people never say that. They just wander around from problem to problem. The Egyptian minds were clear, "they had this problem." There were other related issues, and maybe there were many, but they could pinpoint the problem.

So began the teaching in Cairo. It was a wonderful time. Most of the people attending the teaching were young; young women, young men, all looking for growth. There were over 100 in the classes. I taught about counseling, communication, and can you believe this, I gave them sexual education training! This was very important because there was nowhere to get a class on human realities of sexuality, and nothing much was written in Arabic to help. It was very important developmental training. I taught about marriage and children. I taught about the person inside, each of them. God trusted that person. He was training that person, through the Holy Spirit speaking to the heart, not just to the brain. Great breakthroughs occurred.

Our son, Mohammad Bader, went to Jerusalem at this time to visit his sister, Aida. He was then to get a visa and come to Cairo where he would meet me, be part of the teaching team, and then fly home with me.

He did not arrive. He was supposed to arrive around midnight at the Cairo airport. He did not come out of the gate! I was desperately worried, for I knew that his level of integrity was such that only the worst possible circumstances would detain him from meeting me.

After considerable search and desperation, I found out that he was being held by Egyptian Security, and that he would not be allowed to enter Egypt at all. He would be held until our tickets were good for us to leave Egypt together. This was two days, hence, and considerable strain on Mohammad. He had a valid visa from the Egyptian Embassy in Tel Aviv. I was deeply concerned. At one point, I went to the man who was making the decision to hold him and asked him to let me see Mohammad. The man finally relented. He let us see each other for a few minutes so we could make an agreement of how we would meet at the Egyptian plane. The fears of each of us subsided as we submitted to the present reality. Security escorted Mohammad onto the plane when we left. We each suffered some residual trauma when we left Egypt.

As my Egyptian friend drove me home from the airport through the streets of Cairo the night when Mohammad had not arrived I was mindful of the hardships of so many people; not only economic hardships, but serious, painful experiences of prejudice in rules that prevented people from being who they really could be.

For example, you could go to University, but you were often told by authorities what your major would be. It was hard to get a choice of university. Other people, who knew you little to not at all, were making your choices for you. The cost of education was cheap, the price was high!

In 1993, my biggest goal was to help developing the concepts of Family Therapy Camp I had developed here in the United States.

The concept of Family Therapy Camp was taught and experienced at grassroots. Over 100 people attended the Family Therapy Camp: families, children, and seniors. The camp was held at the Coptic Monastery at Beni-Suief in upper-Egypt.

God did great things at this Family Therapy Camp. Tremendous bonding occurred, lasting spiritual growth and breakthroughs. From the impossible, God was moving in His Spirit realm. Family Therapy Camps continued in Egypt for several years.

At this camp, I met William and Sonya from Cairo. We came to know each other quite well, and we liked each other a lot. I met their children and other family members. Many years later, Sonya and William would take responsibility for our work in London.

There are two events that happened at the Family Therapy Camp which stand out in my mind as permanent markers in the history of the ministry. First, while we were at the Coptic Monastery, Father Engels, a Coptic Priest, agreed to help me dedicate 30 children in the camp unto the Lord. Together, we anointed the children with Jordan River water and olive oil. I still, today, consider that a miracle along the road. Many of those children have gone on into Christian work, and they are having considerable influence on the development of Christian ministry in Egypt.

The second impacting memory was the special singing time; sometimes in Arabic, sometimes in English, but very powerful. The singer stopped, took his hands off of his guitar, looked out at all of us and said these words, "We are suffering for Jesus. Let these words stand in your mind and speak to you as they will." It was a profound statement spoken and must be remembered across the Christian world.

In 1995, Sonja Gurguis asked to come to Oregon, and spend a minimum of two months in training. She was extremely gifted in deliverance ministry, and had many ideas that were helpful to us too. It was a marvelous experience having her here living with us.

While she was here, she had a strange call from Cairo. It was the last time she spoke to her daughter for a number of years. Her daughter was crying, but not saying what was the matter, and then her daughter disappeared.

We always think God will protect us. We forget that He gave his own son to the cross. There is protection eternally, but there are trials and horrific circumstances in many lives here. Sonja went home and spent the next years looking for her daughter.

As I was getting ready to leave Cairo and fly home, these are the circumstances of my last night:

I was put in a car and transported across Cairo to a church. I was sitting in the car backwards to the direction we were going, and I got more and more nauseated as the ride went on for miles through heavy traffic. Finally, when I entered the church where I was supposed to speak, I was almost positive I was going to throw up. I was to stand on the platform and give my talk. It was quite a desperate situation. I did not know what to do. How would I manage?

What I did do that last night is quite another story. I decided to teach two scriptures. The first scripture, *"Jesus wept."* The other scripture was all of Psalms 119. Psalms 119, is the longest chapter of scripture in the Bible. It is also the half-way point in the Bible. I remembered Jesus wept at the tomb of Lazarus.

In spite of my increasing nausea and all that went with that, I knew that there were enormous spiritual problems in this church, and that their priorities were not clear. I sensed that Jesus wept over this church. As I began to read, I would say, *"Jesus wept,"* and then I would read a small portion of Psalm 119. Each time I finished that small portion of Psalm 119, I would say again, "Jesus wept." I am sure they thought I had gone mad, and perhaps I had, but I persisted until the end. They brought a couch for me to lie down as I could no longer stand up. I had somebody continue to read Psalm 119, and I would say, *"Jesus wept."* We went on to the finish. By this time, I had nearly passed out. A group of people came up and prayed for me. They wanted me to pray for them. I knelt down on the platform, practically lying on the platform, and put my arms around each one of them. Perhaps we poured out the tears of Jesus weeping, and our hope for the days to come.

If you read Psalm 119, you will notice that the whole chapter is about the law and the desire to keep the law. For example, in verse 164, *"Seven times daily, I praise you for your righteous rulings."*

I give no justification for what happened that night. I'm not sure if anybody knew what happened, but I believe the Lord knew what happened. I believe He was present.

I had been insisting for two or three days that I had to see Sonja before I left Egypt. I knew she was in hiding and that it was almost impossible to see her. I begged and begged, and so from that time at the church, they took me to a secret meeting with Sonja. In spite of my tremendous illness in the body, and the discomfort I felt, she and I deeply connected and our anguished souls touched one another by His Spirit. There was much she could not tell me. All I knew was her life was in extreme danger.

Around midnight, I was taken to the airport to fly home alone. I asked for a wheelchair, and I managed to make the flight home by myself.

Jesus came into the world to face the spiritual disasters of His time. In fact, he came into the world to face the spiritual disasters of all time. It was a spiritual disaster that had come upon me. As I journeyed home, I knew the ministry in Egypt, among the Egyptians, must never come to an end.

I want to clarify that this ministry is not a ministry of religion. It is not founded by a religious spirit; it is founded by a divine call from above. It is founded for our common ground to be found among the peoples. The ground we hold in common makes possible uncommon, unexpected events. The greatness of God continues to break through. It is God's greatness that has carried this work from the beginning.

Moushir developed a remarkable team. People wanted training. Counselor training began to really take hold in Cairo. Classes grew in size. Curriculum developed, changed, and improved. They could learn from the past, and learn from what the day brought. Maturity was coming in the spiritual realm. It was exciting, and in some ways terrifying.

Dr. Emil and his wife, Alice, were doctors in Cairo. Emil was a psychiatrist. He came to Oregon and spent several weeks in training with us. He was pondering, "Where would psychiatry go? How would inner healing affect the work of psychiatry?" Others came and trained.

In 1994, fifteen Internationals came to Beaverton for six weeks. We held an International Conference. We were putting together many nations. Moushir came. It was a time for each man and woman involved in the work to be able to not only relate to the needs they saw in their own countries, but to be able to understand the bigger picture of the needs in several countries. Could countries help each other grow and mature? Could they be an influence on each other? How would that be? Do we care as much about the needs in other lands as we care about the needs in our land? Our eyes opened wide, and our ears deeply heard what the Spirit was trying to tell us.

It was quite a remarkable event, this International Conference. We did very strange things. We had asked three to come from Kenya. One of them was a man named, John Oundo, who was developing an Addictions Recovery Program. I had a particular love for John because I baptized John in a river in Kenya, and he had received Christ because we met. John did not arrive. His passport, with his visa, was stolen in Nairobi. His ticket was stolen. He called me in tears. I spoke firmly to John and said, "Take care of it; you are to be here in ten days." John was ten days late, but the Lord met the need. This was an enormous miracle because often it takes months for a replacement passport. The government is not sure where the original went.

I took the men outdoors to play basketball. When we came back in, I said, "You probably need some deodorant now." (It was a very hot time of the year.) So, they tried to put the deodorant on over their shirts. These are humorous events. These are the things that make you laugh in a ministry where pathos can be so powerful, it steals our joy. I tell you, laughter was healing medicine.

One day I asked all of them to write down a list of the things they would like to have from America, things they felt were essential to their work. They were very interesting lists. They all had long lists that included things like musical instruments, computer, camera, copy machine, very long lists. The lists were materialistic. This was an opportunity for each of us to look at our lists and find out what is on God's list of priorities. They never made those lists again. They learned what we had in common with each other was not based on "things," but on a divine call and a profound relationship that would change all of our lives.

Another funny story about the International Conference was I decided to take them shopping to see the differences in prices in the United States. I took them to a grocery store, and as I looked myself at the grocery store, I almost got sick. For the food we have, our number of cereals, for example, is overwhelming. Then, I took them to the Goodwill and showed them the prices there. We went to a middle class store, like Fred Meyers, where you could buy new at reasonable prices, and then we visited Nordstrom's, where they saw a pair of men's shoes selling for $185. I showed them the differences in our culture. They learned a lot. It became a permanent part of the impressions they had of what is valuable and what will never be valuable.

Majed Alloush, from Palestine, was the only Muslim present. With 14 Christian leaders and a Muslim leader, it was quite challenging for everyone to be fully inclusive and to judge no one. After much inner struggle, and many questions, some voiced, some not, the union was achieved, and God had put together a team of leaders from many nations, a team that would continue to work for His Kingdom. They would always know each other, they would always pray for one another, and they each would always be included in the bigger picture of Good Samaritan Ministries.

In his own words, Moushir experienced, for the first time, the smell of freedom. As he lay on the grass outside of our offices, he said, "It was the only time I had ever smelled the real oxygen."

Moushir had many struggles. It was too hard, but he was always seeking God's will and the higher road. Eventually, he received a Master's Degree in counseling. He completed the Master's in Cairo, but one professor prevented him from getting his degree. He then had to do the degree over from a seminary in America through correspondence.

Moushir became more and more convinced that people need spiritual development; spiritual development is the food they need. He was convinced that a problem-centered ministry would not solve anything because it did not give them any depth of perception or spiritual development that would make a difference. He was right, and in that he has been a leader of the ministry as a whole.

He suffered much pain. His wife, Evette, and he have been childless. (Now they see that as a blessing!) She has a severe hearing loss. They have laid down their lives every single day, laying down loves they had that were important to them, like his art. The Lord continues to reveal His Spirit. He challenges our spirit as He must bring us into genuine, true maturity. God help us all. We must make a difference in this world!!

The ministry in Cairo had several beginning offices, but eventually they had a nine-room office in the top of a church. It is a very wonderful light and airy place.

There has been enormous fruit that has influenced the whole world from this seed planted in one of the largest cities of the world, Cairo, Egypt.

Samuel and Mona were very active in the Cairo development of their work. Samuel was the assistant director of the work in Egypt. They moved to San Diego and founded an International Arabic Christian Broadcasting Station that now operates 24/7. They came to Beaverton, Oregon, to meet with us and talk about their vision. We seeded the first funding for the vision to become reality. They are interested in the development of people, not just religious dogma, so the station gives parenting training, marital training, all kinds of training is offered. They bring in the very best training available. The door is kept open for many to come in and learn. They are a worldwide cable network, to all of the Middle East, North Africa, Indonesia, Europe, Australia, New Zealand, Canada, and the United States.

Sonja and William moved to London. Their daughter was found, and they founded the ministry in London. They have worked with us for many years.

Dr. Emil founded a work of his own, as did others. But, the core of the experience with the whole was each ministry came out of a handful of people that had the call upon their lives, a call they kept active and alive.

Amir and Mourad have ministries. We remain close friends. Manal became Amir's wife. She and her son came to Beaverton and spent two months staying with us.

Most of the tours I have led have visited the ministry in Egypt. Today, there are offices in three locations, one outside of Cairo. The work continues to expand because that's what is needed. They are not expanding a ministry, they are expanding the quality of human life. Expanding their horizons gives them eyes to see and ears to hear. As each profoundly becomes well, this sends strength and encouragement to others.

Recently, Moushir and his team have been doing trauma therapy and training to provide comfort and give a voice to those involved in Egypt's uprising.

With man nothing is possible. *"Jesus gazed at them. 'By human resources, he told them, 'this is impossible; for God everything is possible.'"* (Matthew 19:26)

One of the hardest and most painful parts of my heart is "Where are the leaders who will be servants to many, who will not seek position, who will not have their eyes on recognition, but who will be the genuine leaders in this world? They will not work underground, but they will never work in the eyes of man. They will work in the eyes of God alone. Where are the leaders? Where are you?"

CHAPTER 20

The House of Israel

My first awareness of the Jews was during World War II. As a child, my parents and I went to the movies almost every week and we were exposed to the newsreels. Gradually, during the war, the newsreels revealed what was happening to the Jews in concentration camps. Since I had limited friends and no siblings near my age, I took in much of the adult world. I developed in me a sense of history that remains today. History has become part of who I am, not only here, but also through the bigger picture that brought us all here.

It took many years, but along the road, God was doing something inside of me-- a hidden work, a work that reflects His character.

There are many tourists that go to the Middle East, sometimes multiple times, and they come back in support of Israel, or they become Messianic Christians, or they convert to Judaism, or they find themselves trying to enter into the spirit of prophesies of the Old and New Testaments. None of this was the path that God took with me.

Although I was historically conscious of the world around me, there was a very deep work of the Spirit going on in me. I did not jump to news, and I was not drawn to the prophecies fulfilled. This spiritual revolution came highly charged within a portion of the Christian community. I was slower to develop, and the song inside of me could only be finished by God Himself. I did not know the words. I did not hear the music. I lived the words. I lived the music.

In this chapter, I will highlight experiences that prepared me to know the song. It was as if God all along had given me, a growing knowing, and a way of understanding that we belong to the House of Israel. We are not advisors, or more important than they are. We are one in the Spirit, through Jesus, who chose to come through the House of Israel. We therefore are one with the House of Israel.

As I travelled a great deal and met many people, there were certain relationship milestones that stood out. Meeting Sam (Sternberg) Bar-El in 1968 led to a long friendship that has weathered our generation. Sam became a significant mentor to me. This did not happen through our wills. It just came to pass!

Sam and I lived our friendship and experiences in the spirit of reconciliation, the healing work of Christ, the understanding that without forgiveness, there will never be growth or wholeness. Without living a life free of negative judgments, a people cannot grow. This is our only hope to know God.

As the years passed, I became a member of the Bar-El household. I did not have a brother, and Sam Bar-El became my brother, his family, deep and personal friends to Jerry and myself.

It was Sam Bar-El, on my third journey to Israel, who told me I was ready to lead tours. I would never have done this. It would never have occurred to me. I wasn't even capable of doing it, but at that time, the capability was slowly being given to me.

Over the years, I was in Israel so many times that I was often there for special Jewish holidays. For example, I spent three Seders at the Passover table with the Bar-El family. Others I brought with me to the Passover table became part of the House of Israel.

There is one memorable holy day that stands out in my memory. I was in Israel for Rosh Hashanah and Yom Kippur. I was with the Bar-El family. I had come as a member of their household.

During the week before Yom Kippur, the Jewish people,

from Rosh Hashanah (The New Year) to Yom Kippur (the Day of Atonement), live a life of reconciliation, deepening relationships with one another, and really helping one another understand the greater importance of our birthing to God's will – One People.

Israel is a very political nation. At one time, I knew for sure they had 18 political parties, all of them fighting for importance and dominance. It is a country of argument and hostility in its relationships, but during these special days, this all is laid aside. A new time comes, and a new peace is received among them, one to another, a peace that is far more important than the politics of the seasons.

Israel has struggled and suffered much in their wars for survival. The holocaust lingers in their memories. Many Jewish people had incredible stories to tell. Almost all of the families had experienced the greatest possible suffering and loss. I found God's holiness, the Comforter, among them.

Leading up to Yom Kippur, when I was in Israel with the Bar-El family, I had this personal experience of reconciliation, and preparation. Families and friends went to the public squares to meet with each other and talk. It was not just conversation, but reassurance. When Yom Kippur arrived, we began a 25-hour fast, no food and no water. It was a quiet day. We visited living relatives, and remembered those who had died. We rested in the Spirit.

Sam Bar-El loves to play chess. In the afternoon, sitting at their kitchen table, he was alone having one of his chess games. I came in to talk to him. I knew the Jewish people read the Book of Jonah towards the end of the day of Yom Kippur each year, so I told him I would like for us to read the book together, which we did. I was somewhat feeling to challenge him spiritually, which is a natural response when you don't understand the deeper intent of the book. Sam challenged me spiritually. When we finished the reading, he said, "What happened to you? What does this mean to you? What is going on here?" This was the kind, firm, but gentle mentor watching over the House of God. We wrote faithfully to each other over all of the years. As couples, we travelled together. We knew each other's families well.

He faithfully visited us in Oregon. When my mother was dying of Alzheimer's, we had a great party in her honor. Sam flew from Israel for the party. As he visited my mother, who could no longer talk, he asked, "What do you want me to sing for you, Laura?" The last words she ever spoke were to her beloved Sam, "Pagliacci." We made sacrifices for each other, and we made sure each side was all right. To this day, we still cover each other's families in prayer and kindness, 43 years later.

When I say "The House of Israel," these are words that are not usually said among gentiles. I am not speaking of the country of Israel. I am not speaking of Judaism. I am not speaking of religious connection, either between the Christian and the Jew, or the Jew and the Christian. I am speaking of the House that Jesus knew personally, a House he bled and died for, a House he longed to see well and whole, a House to finally be called a Nation of priests to the world.

In Oregon, one night, I had a dream, and as the dream came to an end, I was told to go visit Rabbi Joshua Stampfer at Neveh Shalom Synagogue. I was told to tell him that I would help with Israel in any way that I could. I went to see Rabbi Stampfer. I had never met him before. I told him of the dream. He believed me, and I became part of the Israeli Task Force of the Portland Jewish community. I served on the Task Force for three years. I was the only gentile and the only Christian. It was a chance to see the difference between the House of Israel and the survival of Israel as a political nation.

Through Good Samaritan Ministries, we often served in special ways to encourage the Jewish community. If the community was having a special event, we offered to be servants at that event. I want you to understand, I was never posturing; we were living these events with the Jewish community. I was imitating no one and following no one, but only knowing what we were to do!

I served on other committees with Jewish and Christian people. I realized the enormous intent that each of us must have to bond and trust one another.

There was a special day, I will always remember, in Rabbi Stampfer's office several years later. I was attending a committee meeting of Christians and Jews. There was an argument going on. One of the men present said, "Well, let me be the devil's advocate for a few minutes." I will always remember that Rabbi Stampfer stood and said, "We will have no devils in this room." That profoundly impressed me. I could see that if we do not stand up, we will have devils in many rooms. Are we going to be a people of "issues," or are we going to be a people of God?

I watched Rabbi Stampfer struggle with the Palestinian question, and I was present for a service in the Synagogue when he announced to his people that he had decided to support a State for the Palestinians. He had decided that it was important that nationalism not overpower justice and relationship. It was an enormously important stand received with mixed responses. He not only said these things, he acted upon this stand. He began to lead tours to the Middle East with Arab counterparts as his co-leaders. He made friends of the Christian, Jewish and Muslim communities. The first day I had met Rabbi Stampfer in his office, I noticed on his desk was the book "The Last Great Planet Earth," by Hal Lindsey. The Rabbi was a man who thought deeply and lived bravely.

I found myself more and more experiencing the presence of Jesus inside of me. He had an access to me that was new, and He brought understanding to me that was not verbal, but permanent and eternal. I found what it was like for Him to come and join the community of the Jewish people, and His battle to save that community for their just purposes with God.

As I have said in another place in this book, I became more and more aware of the holocaust. We made a decision, with my husband, Jerry, and our daughter, Jennie, that we would go to Poland, and see Auschwitz. I had earlier visited Dachau in Munich, Germany. I wanted to know and understand what it would mean to kill half of the Jewish people in the world just because they were Jewish. I wanted to know and understand that "how" one truly kills is to bring about total annihilation of the Spirit, the Truth, and the Life.

I continued to grow in understanding. I continued to identify with the pain of God, watching over the Jewish people. I felt the terror of the German people, as well. I came to know His suffering in a way that would mean I would know His suffering for the rest of my life.

I spent years teaching the Old Testament, as well as the New Testament. I became more of an Old Testament scholar: studying, learning, growing, teaching, speaking it, living it. One day I discovered that Abraham really was my father. Those are strange words, but I completely understood then that I was a descendant of Abraham. Is Abraham our father? Was he defining a life of faith, and a life of exceptional courage that could break through all of our generations and our games?

More years passed. I read significantly. I did my Master's Thesis on the last 150 years of the history of Israel and Iraq, comparing the struggles of each of the nations.

One day, very unexpectedly, seeking nothing, I received my freedom.

I became a descendant of Adam before the sin and the fall. For the first time, I realized how total and complete forgiveness is. Forgiveness wipes out the sins of this world. We are taken back to the freedom of that garden before the fall, a powerful relationship with the God who is with His people. This was not a passing spiritual experience. I wrote no journals about it. I did not collect events and meditate on them. It was the continuation of me becoming a part of the House of Israel as God defines this. The term, "Israel," "or "Ishrael," means, "God rules me," or "God rules us." It is this definition that would define my life in the House of Israel.

When I became a part of the life of Adam and Eve before the fall, when I entered into that sinless state where the righteousness of Christ destroys the power of sin, it was a permanent event. Never had my conscience worked so clearly. I did not worry about the conscience of others; I used my own conscience, one of the great gifts of God to make us weigh every action we take against His breath, and the time He has given us. It is not that I became sinless and blasé. I became aware of the separation that sin had caused. I was free of the separation. No, this was not a religious experience, but an entire change of everything inside of me. It was an entire change in who I was, who I am, and who I will remain.

I continued reading and researching. I want to make it clear that I have always read broadly and on many subjects. Since I was in the eighth grade, I have chosen to read significant literature.

I will always remember the summer before the ninth grade, because I got the English reading list from high school, and read all the literature on that list. I experienced a hunger and a need to experience words. Films had a great influence on my life. I watched for great films, and I made sure that not only I saw them, but also our family saw them. I can remember significant films that touched me to the very core of my being.

It is hard to be educated. Most people are experiential, but when it comes to a deeper education of the spirit, where does one find that? From time to time, I delved into Jewish literature.

I want to talk about an Israeli Rabbi, Pinchas Peli, and in this way, introduce Rabbi Abraham Joshua Heschel. Heschel died in 1972. He was one of the world's great Rabbis. He walked with Martin Luther King in the Selma March, although at the time he had profound suffering with heart problems. Heschel read and wrote prodigiously, producing some of the greatest literature about the Bible and about the life of the Spirit.

Heschel met regularly with a Christian Professor, Dr. Reinhold Niebuhr. Reinhold Niebuhr was a noted professor at Yale Divinity School. Heschel was a professor at the Jewish Theological Seminary of America, in New York City, the main seminary of Conservative Judaism. He served as professor of Jewish Ethics and mysticism until his death in 1972. Heschel and Niebuhr often met on Friday night and had a Sabbath dinner together. During those dinners, they explored the road Christians and Jews could take to come back together. Through patience, love and prayer, we could become whole with God. These two men quietly led the Christians and Jews to an entirely new level of friendship.

Rabbi Peli, a famous Israeli Rabbi, was a disciple to Rabbi Abraham Joshua Heschel. He was coming to Oregon, and the Jewish people contacted me to ask me if I would spend a day with him and take him to significant Christian people to meet and talk. I knew little about Rabbi Peli, but I learned a great deal during the time we spent together.

What he shared with me was that when Israel went back to the land, in the early 1900's, they had little to no spiritual development. They barely knew anything about prayer. In the diasporo, they had lived harsh lives, retaining certain form, but no substance. He said the Lord had called him to develop the spiritual material for the training of the Jewish people. Heschel had shown him what had to be taught, and he was to fulfill the assignment.

On one of my many journeys to Israel, I decided to go see Rabbi Peli and his wife. I called him and asked if I could come. Sandy

Gunderson and I made the visit. His wife was contentious as we were talking about the Palestinian/Israel issue. Her feelings were negative and strong. We asked Rabbi Peli one question, a question he could not escape, "What would Heschel say and do about the Palestinians?" He said, "I cannot answer that question, but I'm going to send you to a place where you will find the answer." He sent us to an apartment in Jerusalem to visit the wife of the late Leyb Rochman.

When I called asking Mrs. Rochman if we could come, she gladly received us as guests. We found an astonishing woman, and a story of their daughter. Mrs. Rochman and her husband lived through the holocaust in Poland. For a long period of time, they spent up to 18 hours a day living between two walls, only coming out at somewhat safe times to eat and refresh themselves. Several shared this hiding place with them.

The last year, before the end of the war, they lived underneath a barn floor. In the winter, when it was raining, they often had to sit with their legs in cold water to escape being caught by the Germans. When Leyb Rochman and his wife survived the holocaust, they came to Israel to live, and Leyb wrote a book called, "The Pit and the Trap, A Chronicle of Survival." She gave us the book in English and I read it. I learned one thing from this book about their story of survival. There was one major statement repeated and then repeated again, "We live to give testimony." It was a life-changing sentence. Again, The House of Israel had brought a statement that would define my character and influence the ministry.

Do we live to give testimony? What is your testimony? What is mine?

While we were in the apartment, we were astonished by all of the walls and doors. They had huge drawings on them. The mother explained that when their daughter was about ten years old, she began to make these drawings. They were all life-size drawings. As we went from wall to wall and door to door, we saw them everywhere. They had never been covered up with paint or washed. Their daughter told them these are the prophets. The daughter had drawn them as her father was dying of tuberculosis of the bone, the result of those cold-water days in Poland. At the bottom of the drawings were moving fish in water.

Rivka Miriam, the daughter, came in. She explained to us the on-going theme of the water and fish, found at the bottom of each of these drawings. This was the silent part of us--the silent part, the spirit.

I learned that their daughter was a noted artist and poet. Finally, I asked the question we had asked Rabbi Peli. "What is the right thing to do in the issue of the Palestinians?"

Her answer was, again, a holy and life-changing moment. It came from far beyond her years and her understanding, beyond mine as well. She said, "If it comes to the point that one or the other of us must leave the land, then the Jews must leave." Here was Rabbi Peli's answer. This is what Heschel would say. It still shocks me today that she wasn't afraid to say it. Is it true? Was she telling something that is valuable, or just taking an opinion and broadening out with it? I don't believe it is true, I believe it is truth. *"Treat others as you would like people to treat you."* (Luke 6:31) It was the great Biblical truth, *"You must love your neighbor as yourself."* (Matthew 22:39)

Although Rabbi Heschel died in 1972, I chose to spend time reading some of his work. His one book called, "I asked for Wonder," again made a permanent change in my spirit. He explained in the book, in clear and true words of deep conviction, the greatest spiritual gift is the gift of wonder. I thought about this. We might say, "I wonder why God is doing this?" Or, "I wonder why that happened?" That is not the gift. The gift is that you marvel at the wonder of nature and at all you see. In the midst of discussions, negativity, or political bias, you would choose to come into this midst, and find the wonder of it all. An example of this could be "It's a wonder that man, of the whole creation, has the gift of speech."

I decided to train in this spiritual gift to see if Heschel was right. My husband and I often went to the Trailblazer basketball games together, and I decided to see if there was a gift of wonder in that coliseum before, during and after the game. I began to see the gifts of many. I saw the people coming in as individuals, not just as basketball fans. I saw the players working together, showing respect for one another, and helping each other. The greatness of God's wonder was even at the basketball game. As I continued to wonder and test this great spiritual gift, I saw that there is something here. The gift of wonder, completes the House of Israel. Just this week, I went to visit a very significant friend of mine. She is ten years older than I am and we share the same birthday. We both have the same name, Bettie (Bette). She pulled a saved slip of paper out of a drawer and asked me to read it. Here were words I had spoken a number of years ago, that she had written down. She wanted me to hear the words again.

"The gift of wonder can be described as the spiritual gift of being surprised at the greatness of God in all the things one sees and experiences. It is the element of being surprised into a healthy and acutely sensitive reality that God is good at every turn."

Live a life of wonder and you will come to know surprise!
See for yourself. "*Ask and it will be given to you; search, and you will find; knock, and the door will be opened to you.*" (Matthew 7:7) Refine your character with a new vision of God's Kingdom. A gifted life lived profoundly helps to create the love of God among us all.

Many years ago I was conducting a group therapy for Good Samaritan Ministries at our church. It was a large group, and my attention was on getting ready as I went into the room. There was suddenly an interruption from Heaven, and I heard the question,

"What is your new name?" The answer came clearly, "Keeper of Israel."

> *"Peace and mercy to all*
> *who follow the Israel of God."*
> (Galathians 6:16, Jerusalem Bible)

CHAPTER 21

Spiritual Chaos and Hard Lessons

Defining and living out the meaning of words is challenging. It is particularly challenging in the Christian world because we have our own vocabulary, and we presume that everybody knows the vocabulary and understands the meanings.

I was actively involved in church all of my life. I was not just attending church, but going to Sunday school classes, choir, and so on. It was not until I was in my late 30's that I learned of the word "grace." Grace was the prayer you said over meals. Grace is a very important Christian word defining the essence of Christ's work.

Where do people learn the vocabulary? How many are willing to admit they don't know what is going on, and ask what some commonly used words might mean? In the counseling office, I found confusion and spiritual chaos in everyone I saw. This included pastors, the highly educated, and people off the streets. When I asked a person if he/she was a Christian, some of their answers were disturbing. They often defined being a Christian as whether they went to church or they did not go to church.

Now let's look at the word "spiritual." We have all sorts of ideas thrown at us about this word. I just looked "spirit" and "spiritual" up in the dictionary and there was a huge, long list for the word "spirit." We have spiritual programs in AA. What does spiritual mean? Who defines it?

Spiritual has a lot to do with our character, and that part of us, undeveloped, leads to spiritual chaos.

Then we have "Holy Spirit, Holy Ghost, and The Spirit of Things. We have the spirit of a school, and team spirit. A spirit can be collective, but it must reflect individual development to be real in our actions.

With this introduction, we may now enter the world of spiritual chaos. I will reflect on my own spiritual confusion in my early life, and the consistent absolute confusion of the people that came in to get help.

Over my lifetime, I found I learned most things the hard way. I was often struggling to know or to understand – really struggling!

When I was in my early 40's, a very hard incident happened that broke my heart. I had a special brunch on Christmas Eve for valued and wonderful friends. We brought gifts to give. It should have been the most delightful day, but the event turned into a spiritual disaster.

One of the women present was living in the constant of spiritual chaos more than we knew. She became insanely jealous of her husband who gave a beautiful piece of jewelry he had made to one of the other women present. When they went home, she shut off his life from everyone and punished him until he died.

My concern, definitely, was for both of them, because I greatly loved this couple. They had been very special in my life. My other concern was who was to blame. What was going on here? Was there anything that could be done about it?

"Who is to blame?" is a very profound question isn't it? I don't know how your brain works, but my brain often worked overtime trying to figure out where the fault lay and what to do about it. I found situations could bring tremendous confusion. It seemed everyone was pretending that someone else was to blame but, usually, either over-blamed, or under-blamed, themselves. Therefore, repentance was impossible. How could you change what you do not understand in the first place?

After this incident, I agonized for six weeks. I asked God who was to blame. I did not presume to know. This is very key. Often we know less than we think we know.

At the end of six weeks, the Lord spoke to me. To give a little background on what He said, I want to say that the wife of the above-mentioned couple had taken classes with me at Portland State; she had travelled to the Middle East with my mother, one other person, and myself. We had been to Damascus in Syria. We had shared so much together.

When the Lord answered my question, He removed the shame and the blame totally. He said she was on the road to Damascus and not yet healed of her blindness, and I was on the cross with Jesus to accept the sorrow, the loss, and the redemptive chain that could bring peace to each of us.

I have said I learn by experience. Here was an experience. Here I was seeking the face of God, seeking to know, and seeking to do all I could to not only relieve my own suffering, but to relieve the suffering of others as well. This experience was hard, but I learned what the brain can do when it goes into chaos, over-trying to analyze events.

You often hear the words, "the blame game." Shaming is more subtle. It has many shades, grays, and blacks. You can shame yourself, shame others, or feel ashamed. We have to finally learn that shame is connected with our pride. The power of Shame disconnects us from the mercies of God. Shame makes us hide, as Adam and Eve did, in the Garden.

I would recommend to anyone reading this book, take one incident which happened in your experience with life, an incident that had a shattering effect on you. Ask God to redefine what really happened. What is the meaning of the event in the development of your character? It is my experience that most people run away from these events because they feel overwhelming sorrow. Many have a vague relationship with God, defined through Jesus, but the accessing and development of that relationship is very confusing.

We presume people know how to pray. Do they? Do they even know who they are talking to when they do pray? Are they talking openly and freely to a God who cares, and hears whatever they have to say? Do they hear Him?

In recent years, I have noticed many churches do less praying and more talking. It has troubled my spirit. Why are we talking so much about God, instead of talking to Him, and letting Him talk to us?

The Bible defines spiritual chaos with many dark and heavy words: jealousy, anger, lust. We could say spiritual chaos is the fruit of lack of spiritual training and development. Where are we going?

When I was a young teacher, in my first year of teaching, I had a new baby at home, and a husband, who had extremely serious trauma problems. He was teaching too. I was fragile on the inside, and in total spiritual chaos. I met with a class every day – 29 students who were also in spiritual chaos. In that whole process, I tried to develop a plan that would improve the situation, as we were supposed to keep discipline and order. I tried many plans. Eventually I learned, in the years ahead, stick to the plan you have, and refine it! Changing plans just adds to the chaos.

RECOVERY FOR ADDICTS

Sometimes, I hear almost snobbish Christian behavior. Many people use the words, "That isn't Christian." I particularly have heard this about the AA and 12-Step programs. It made me almost afraid to look at them because they weren't Christian enough.

Less than five years ago, I decided to read the AA book for myself.

I had always been told it was a spiritual program, but if it was a spiritual program without Jesus, it wasn't a correct program. As I studied the program, I began to see how God had put together the steps to heal the spiritual chaos in the minds of addicts. The steps for recovery had carefully been laid out through prayer and intercession. This material was authored by Christian writers who had experienced the agonies of addiction. It is a healing book, a healing plan, and a healing way that makes spiritual development possible. People who are addicts often start at ground zero. They may have thousands of miles to go before they will be free, accepted and whole. We as Christians must be careful in our words of condemnation. May we seal our lips to the Holy Spirit's right to speak. Use less, "This is not Christian."

I became convinced that the members of the counseling team at Good Samaritan Ministries needed to study the AA book. I also became convinced that I needed to invite people from all titled 12-step recovery programs to come in so we could talk together. We needed to find out what their problems were, and what we, as counselors, could do to improve the hard road of addicted clients. We had the Christian programs come in and meet with the traditional anonymous programs. As we talked together, the walls could be felt and seen. The walls came down as we worked together. In these meetings, we made a decision that a major problem addicts face is finding a sponsor who is well enough trained and able, through their own spiritual freedom, to sponsor another life bound in total darkness. I met with many who said the program works. The bigger question remained, "What would Jesus say about all of this?"

As we worked with addicts, we committed to help them find well-developed sponsors, and to stick with the program faithfully working the steps.

At least 25 years ago, I was attending a conference at the

Christian Renewal Center, a Christian camp. The speakers were the Sanfords, from Boise, Idaho. The Sanfords had a very important healing ministry to pastors and their wives. Something John Sanford said stuck with me:

"We have worked with pastors and their wives in therapy and inner-healing for 25 years. In the whole 25 years, we have only seen remorse. The exception was one couple who chose the road of repentance; all others kept on the remorse road."

Feeling bad does not change anything. Repentance is one of the most powerful words in the Christian faith. It means radical change—a radical change of direction, a radical change of who you are and whom you serve. We can know the word repentance. We can even know that it means change, but people are gasping for survival. We know that change only comes through the grace of God; therefore, are we shocked at His mercy? How well do we know God? What is repentance? Is it permanent, or just temporary?

We feel anger because we pass the blame between ourselves and others. We repent because of God. If God would choose only one thing to give us, He would give us the power to change. He does. Will we?

CODEPENDENCY

Codependency is a big word in the vocabulary of psychological problems. It has been popular to read a book called, Codependent No More, by Melody Beattie. People who read it can possibly identify themselves as codependent. They can be warned that it is serious and life-threatening, but what will break this emotional stronghold over their lives? Again, we see spiritual chaos, many theories, little action, and much reaction.

Codependency has become such a powerful force in spiritual chaos that 12-step groups have developed to deal with people who have codependency issues. Could we be codependent with God? I say, possibly.

Codependency is expecting your emotional needs to be met by someone else. It is a need for that perfect relationship where everything is just so perfect. It is a "dependent personality," not being able to function without the other person being there to help you function. It is strong reaction to the actions of others when they don't see our needs. There could be many definitions of codependency, and each person probably has their own definition, but it REVEALS A PERSON WHO IS BLIND WHEN THEY LOOK UP, AND TOO VISUAL WHEN THEY LOOK AROUND.

"Jesus gazed at them. 'By human resources', he told them, 'this is impossible; for God everything is possible.'" (Matthew 19:26) When we look for the perfect mother, the ideal sibling, a steadfast friend that always makes us feel better; we may not be looking up. You can easily become entrenched in looking around for your needs to be met.

The codependent is lonely if they can't find certain nourishment. They have abandonment issues from when their perceived needs were not met. The Scripture says, *"And my God will fulfill all your needs out of the riches of His glory in Christ Jesus."* (Philippians 4:19) There is a solution, but how does one get there?

We often strive after people to like us. We strive to please them. We strive to do good things for them so they will like us. We can't even strive after God, for He is fighting the battle to get to us. He is fighting to save us. He is the One fighting to change us.

When we go back to the Garden of Eden, at first, Adam had a very trusting relationship with God, and in the beginning, an ideal marriage with Eve. Soon, the blame game started. The codependency began. They both had to hide from God. Neither one would take full ownership of what they had done without being prodded by God. Even then, their ownership was weak. The thing we must see was that God did not stop fighting for them. He stayed with them. He provided for them. He knew they would have a hard life, but He would fight for their generations.

Codependency with God has to do with expectations. Perhaps we expect too much from Him, and feel that He expects too much from us. "He didn't heal me. It has weakened my trust, and it has weakened my faith." "He didn't save my daughter's life. He has disappointed me. He does not see the vital treasure I had in that girl's life." Our expectation can create impasse instead of growth.

Expectations are dangerous because God moves in unexpected ways. Expectations mean we set a path for God, and we tell Him what direction to go. Then, when He doesn't take that path, when He doesn't appear at that moment, and when things do not go right according to our plan, there is a gasp of loss from us.

We must meet the God of surprise. We must wait for Him to surprise us. He will. He does. It is going on, but so often we miss it, for we expected God to have a certain manner towards us.

A codependent with God sets a course for God to follow. Then, when He doesn't take it, they are disappointed. It is about emotional upheaval. It is about a war between yourself and God that does not seem to resolve because you just plain don't agree with Him. If you are God, you would see me and you would give me my way. Can we be that direct with ourselves? Otherwise, we miss the mark!

SPIRITUAL CHAOS TO ORDER

We tell people to "Read the Word." "I love the Word." But, oh my, spiritual chaos can break out at an incredible level when we take words and we use them the way we think they should be used. Can you imagine? There are over 800,000 words in the Bible, 66 books, and a general population who are not always good readers. Can you imagine the chaos? Little system, little organization, little understanding of what is happening, they grab at words as if their lives depend on them; which, indeed, it does!

Recently, a group of teachers at Good Samaritan Ministries, teachers whom I have been training to teach the Bible for three years, taught two different weeks on the Sermon on the Mount in Matthew 5-7. The teachers struggled to know and bring the words to life. It is hard for us to remember that each person in the room is different, and each person in the room must individually hear something that changes their life. I stopped the last class. The room became silent. I said, "This is Jesus, the Christ, speaking to you. Do you want to hear what He has to say to you?" Suddenly, the five thousand people faded, and Jesus was speaking directly to each of us.

Almost all clients I saw in thirty years had little or no comprehension of the "Power of Forgiveness." The common problem I saw; they want to control the power to forgive!

People can talk and talk and talk. They can give us the most wonderful sermons. They can give us the most life-changing instruction, but what will happen inside of us, is the cause for which Christ came. He is speaking through words and actions. When you hear Jesus speaking, He is not speaking from 2,000 years ago. He is speaking at that very moment when you hear. He is touching inside you, creating something you did not know. He is bringing you to the point, where you cannot give up what He has said. His words and actions unite us to Him, and profound change occurs.

What kind of learners are we? Do we learn and then forget? Do we try to teach using too many words? Do we cause confusion, or are the words speaking into the lives of individuals in the most astonishing way, bringing the fire of change? Can we hold the Bible in our hands and be shocked that it is in our hands? It has been given to us through ancient man from the Living God. We have it in our hands. We have it before our eyes. Do we have it in our actions? The Word will become life and dwell among us if we let it fully come into us.

In the Bible, a person's name created substance for who they were. When Jesus said, *"If you ask me anything in my name, I will do it,"* He is releasing the power of His Name to shatter the weakness of our powerlessness. (Matthew 14:14) We teach children the song: "Jesus loves me, this I know, for the Bible tells me so," and they store it somewhere in their memory. Perhaps, the last song they will sing in their lifetime is that song; but, in the raging storm of spiritual chaos, how imminent is that love upon your life or mine?

I spent five years trying to wake up in the morning and remember God first. At the end of five years, I could only do it less than half the time. At that moment, The Lord spoke to me. He said, "I always remember you and you will never have to try to remember me again." I will never forget what He said. Can you imagine a relationship so personal and so deep with the Living God? He did not and will not leave you behind! He will cherish you when you do not cherish yourself. He will forgive you when no one else will. He will weep over you or with you because He is a personal friend, and someone who is willing to keep that friendship with you forever.

People get married and say vows. The vows are taken before God and man. Then, spiritual chaos comes because expectations have weakened the relationship. God has become less, and what they expect from one another has become too hard, unmanageable. What happened to the vows? What was said at the wedding? What did the vows ask you to remember, as an individual, all the days of your life? Point not ever at the other person who did not live the vows. Did you?

1 Corinthians 13 is a favorite scripture for many. It is called the love chapter of the Bible. It is familiar. We pronounce the words like poetry when we use them in a marital ceremony. We may use them in marital counseling, we may have heard them read, and we may go to them often. Are we shaken by the redefinition of love

itself? When people came to me for counseling, they pointed out what their neighbors, friends, and family did. They never saw what they did clearly. I mean it—almost never did they see what they had done. Did they choose blindness? Did they know they made that choice? They didn't hear, *"Take the log out of your own eye first, and then you will see clearly enough to take the splinter out of your brother's eye."* (Matthew 7:5) Where did this word go? Why did the words not penetrate the hard shell in which we too often encase our problems?

THE HOLY SPIRIT

The Holy Spirit is part of the Trinity, part of the One God. He is the person who is willing to share with us. This gift of the Holy Spirit leads us to know God better. It opens the door to a relationship where all things are possible. In the 1960's, the Holy Spirit movement was strong. Many were being prayed over that they might receive the gift of tongues, and be filled with the Holy Spirit. Now, 50 years later, the Holy Spirit has lost its essential purpose inside of many. The desire to receive the Holy Spirit has been watered down. There are new ideas. New parts of the scripture are important, popular, and taught; and yet, we cannot bear witness unto the ends of the earth, without the Holy Spirit. Did the movement of the Holy Spirit among us fade, or did we lose interest and go seeking elsewhere for power?

Examine your life. Are you able to bear witness? Do you bear witness? What is it you say? What is it you do not say?

I will always remember when our daughter, Laura, received the Holy Spirit and the gift of tongues. We were going to a praise service at the coliseum. She, being Laura, had a date with two boys that day. She got home late from the first date; her second date was sitting in our living room. He was going with us to the coliseum to the praise service. 8,000 people were present and all were praising the Lord together, all denominations, all seeking unity, and at that time worshipping in a new way.

We sat in the first balcony. Laura suddenly jumped up and said, "I must go downstairs." She went downstairs and came back shortly thereafter. Then, she jumped up again and said, "I must go down again." Among the 8,000 people, was a man who had been a pastor. He had been one of the students in the first Bible class I taught through Portland Community College. At the time, he was in this class, he had terrific financial problems and worries. By God's grace, I had been able to help the family in quite significant ways. I had not seen this man for a great length of time. When Laura came back the second time, she said, "A man prayed for me, Ron Aikens. I received the baptism of the Holy Spirit. He told me He knew you." A living God makes living things happen. Don't give up. Keep your search simple. The scripture says, "*Seek my face and you will find me.*" (Matthew 7:7) and (1 Chronicles 16:11)

Your problems will change, but God's face never changes. Problem centered, or Christ centered, an absolute of decision making!

CHAPTER 22

Interlude

I had known this man for several years. I knew him as a schoolteacher and a counselor, but I did not know this man! One day, this man called me at home and asked me if I would see him for counseling. He said he needed help badly. I was deeply surprised at the phone call, but agreed to meet him.

He was approaching the final stages of alcoholism, moving rapidly in that direction. He was as a drowning man, desperate for answers, but he did not know the right questions.

I knew we were in a life and death battle, and the battle could easily be lost. I knew that I had to persist hard and determine by faith to the breakthrough of this man.

He had been fired from his job. He attempted many treatment programs, and in the process of all of his experience, he had lost the value of himself. In fact, he stated, "I tried them all and beat them all!"

We sat down at our dining room table and spent several months searching for the agonizing child on the inside, and the man who wanted to be, but could not.

His father died of alcoholism when he was a young boy. His last memory with his father was going to the tavern and being asked by his dad to drive him home. He could barely reach the pedals. Then, one day soon, his dad was dead.

This was a man who had developed many complicated games

to keep himself fooled into rationality, always hiding the boy, never allowing the hurt boy to be seen or to grieve. The battle continued to rage for his life. Sometimes alcohol had a seemingly weaker hold on him for a moment, but it had a determination to finish him.

He and his wife had a very handicapped daughter. She was in such a severe condition, she had been placed permanently in a children's hospital. She was blind and could barely sit up.

One day, he drove to that facility, picked up his daughter, and took her on what one might call a "joy ride." He got very drunk. It was a very serious situation, and no one knew where they were. He eventually got her back to the care facility, and came home.

His wife called me when he got home, and I said I would be right over. Now, you will not believe this! He was prostrate on the couch. I crawled up on top of him, went nose to nose with him, a man coming out of a drunken state, and told him he could not feel guilty. He would be forgiven!

One day, he brought his daughter to our house. I met her. I could see how much he loved her, and how heartbreaking her condition was to his soul.

Sometimes I went to his house, and I can vividly remember a time when he was in such a destitute condition, that he was sniffing lacquer thinner, as well as drinking more than a fifth a day. Time was running out. I met with him anyway.

In his lifetime, I was the only person who ever prayed with him. He had some exposure to church, but found it of little interest. His life was too broken to understand the words.

On one occasion we went into an intense battle during a telephone conversation. In my spirit, the Lord had revealed to me that he was hiding a secret, and that he had to tell me that secret. This battle raged for over an hour, and then the secret came out. He perceived that he had hurt his child when she was five and this had caused her to be in an in-patient care facility for the next five years. Was the perception true? No. She was born with a condition that was going to take her life. Was his perception real to him? Absolutely! He lived in a haunted house of guilt and shame.

When the secret came out, he began to change. He began to have a will to live. He began to have some hope. He could breathe, and he could understand he was breathing.

After several more months, we decided that we probably would not have to meet again. He said to me, "Do you want to know a secret?" and I said, "Yes." He said, "You are the worst counselor I have ever seen, but I could not beat your sincerity. I have chosen to live."

One day he and his wife called. Their daughter was in intensive care at the hospital and they wanted me to come right away. We were together all night, seeing the child from time-to-time, and then leaving to go to another room in the hospital. About five in the morning, I said, "Your child just died." I knew the exact moment of her death. Her purpose on earth was finished.

They asked me to do the funeral. It was a very special honor. Her life meant so much to each of us, as we prayed together in those final hours.

Almost no one in the family had any foundation of faith. They had almost no recognition of Jesus, or comprehension of Christianity. Their higher power had been, "Can I play the next game and win?"

Now, here I was, with the whole family, to honor and to bring to them the memory of this child and her purpose of life lived among them.

She was buried on a hill in a place where we could all join hands. It was quite a large group of people. I began the song, "Jesus loves the little children, all the children of the world. Red and yellow, black and white, all are precious in his sight. Jesus loves the little children of the world." After I sang it, we all sang it together. The day ended with Jesus among us.

Several years later, the man came to my office to visit. He said, "I've had the most wonderful experience with my dad today. I went out fishing and I found him with me."

The Lord restored what he had lost. He went on to be a teacher again, and became a principal of a school. He found he could keep his sobriety because he knew why he had lost all those years. Shame and guilt did not defeat his recovery.

I will always remember that a broken little boy came to see me and together, with God's help, we found the man. The months and months of prayer had given the little boy his manhood, his conviction for life, and his strength.

I never sought to be a good counselor, never. I sought to be sincere, and to share in the pain of the one who was broken. The first three steps of recovery are these: "I can't. He can. He will."

CHAPTER 23

Money Matters

When I was five years old, my parents started training me about money.

They gave me four small jars, each with a label on it: God, Gifts, Spending, and Savings. Each week, I was given a nickel for each jar.

As I grew older, the amount for each jar slowly increased. I learned that I could borrow from a jar, if needed, but I had to pay it back into that jar. The allowance I was given was never for work I did, and it was never withdrawn as a punishment.

When I wanted skates or a bicycle, I had to save my half of the money, and my parents paid half. I was eleven before I had my first bicycle.

In this way, I learned the great balance of money matters: God, others, and myself. To this day, these are the money matters principles of our home.

"You received without charge, give without charge."
(Matthew 10:8)

This is what matters to God Himself.

It may shock you, as it did me, that 25% of the New Testament is about money and money-related matters. Do we read the New Testament and understand that money matters?

From the beggars on the streets in Jerusalem or India, to the shopkeepers, the innkeepers, and to God, who collects our tithes, money matters. What is the matter with money?

Are we grateful for what we receive? Do we watch for balance in what we do with our money? Is it our attitude? Does money matter more than gratitude?

My lifetime experience with money, and I'm sure yours too, has been learning about the purpose and use of money.

The average family, today, is spending their money. Some are saving money too. Some give a certain portion and measure to God, and more might consider the gifts they give to be part of their money story.

Jerry and I listen to NBC Local and National News for an hour every day. Our local news broadcasting station has been having a one-month food drive to raise money for needy families. We are already over halfway through the month and only 10% of the funds that are needed have been given.

Some are suffering from compassion burn out. Others suffer from disgust, as "Why should the church take it all?" Others are very spoiled, very selfish, and only willing to budget for their own use of their own money.

Currently, we have a war starting between unions and business. The war is in the beginning stages. When is the stage when giving becomes more important than receiving?

One of my favorite stories in the New Testament took place when Jesus noticed the widow putting her two mites into the temple treasury. As He knew her heart intent, and the spirit of this widow, He turned to his disciples and said, *"I tell you truly, this poor widow has put in more than any of them; for these have all put in money they could spare, but she in her poverty has put in all she had to live on."* (Luke 21:3-4)

Another day, Jesus went into the temple and knocked over the moneychangers' tables, whipping them as He did it. Here are two extremes: the collectors of money, and the small givers who sometimes make the greatest sacrifices.

When I was teaching Bible to children, I used to call the Temple Authorities, "The Money Boys." They were always weighing and measuring the amount in the Temple Treasury. Everything was exact. Everything had to be paid exactly. The tithe was an exact amount.

Jesus came to redefine money. He came to bring new light to it. No greater definition of this new light is there than the contrast of the two stories: the Money Boys and the Poor Widow. Somewhere, we can be found on the road, perhaps between those two places.

I am sure each of us could think of dozens of scriptures about money or valuables. Which scriptures are important to you? What scriptures move you? What scriptures set you free, that you might receive freely and give freely? Should I give you the answer, or are you challenged and willing to find your own answers? Don't just move on! Take this challenge seriously!

I think I will not give you the answers, for if I do, you will learn little!

When Jerry and I were married, I asked him what he wanted us to do about money. Since I had been a bookkeeper before our marriage, it was decided that I would do the bookkeeping, but I wanted to know his decision. He repeated over and over to me, "All I want is for you to pay our bills each month in full."

Sometimes this statement made me angry. I wanted more specifics. I wanted him to see money in a broader way. Jerry came from a family where lack of money was a constant anxiety; poverty was a constant member of his childhood household. As an adult, Jerry experienced a constant and profound anxiety believing we had no money. Even to this day, after 59 years of marriage, he has days when he still believes we have no money. It is not based on truth; it is based on the illness that poverty can cause in a child's spirit.

In my life, as a teenager and young adult, money was used to punish. It was silent punishment—a silent, powerful disapproval, which led me to work two to three jobs as I worked my way through college, paying my own way in circumstances of great difficulty and hardship.

I am sure that in each of our lives, there are money stories. I really challenge the reader to think of their own money stories, for what good would it do for you only to hear mine? You would find mine interesting, and you would find my stories would get your attention, but your own stories can keep your attention and help to retrain you.

One day, an older woman who was a teacher and friend to my mother, called me on the phone and asked me to come by her house, as she had something to give me. I went to her door and she handed me five dollars. That day, I began to learn what it would mean to freely give, instead of squeezing, fighting, demanding or whining. I began to learn what it would mean to simply give.

We like to hear God's voice telling us the things we like to hear, and, although it is hard to hear God's voice, we strain to hear our will fulfilled. When it comes to giving, I'm not so sure we want to hear God's voice. He does not stop with Biblical regimentation. He does not stop with the law, but He is building, within each of us, a life of grace, a life that gives full measure and running over.

In the early years of counseling at home, I had a family come to the house. They didn't have enough money. The man did not have skill for a job to make a sufficient living, and they had four little children playing on our living room floor while I talked to their parents at our dining room table. The conversation was not just about money, it was about many problems, but money seemed to be a little part of the conversation, so I asked the man a question, "How much are your bills? How much is your debt that you cannot pay?" The man said, "five hundred dollars." I went into the other room, wrote a check for $500, and gave it to the man for those debts. Did the Lord tell me to do this? I want to say to you adamantly, the Lord trusted me to do this. It was a trust issue between God and myself.

After several years, the money hardships fell away from this man and his family. One day, we began to receive checks for $600 a month for Good Samaritan Ministries from this family. The monthly checks came 100% of the time. We were having trouble paying ministry bills. It was his turn to lift our burden!

Money can cause us great anger. When our daughter was five years old, and I was pregnant with our next child, my dad was going to Denton, Kansas, to visit his parents and family. I asked him to loan me the money so I could go with him, as I longed to be back in Kansas with the family. He did. It was $150 dollars. While he was in Kansas, his dad took out a shoebox and handed him $5,000 in cash. In fact, he handed each of his sons $5,000. Now, when I came home, I had a moral dilemma, which produced a large heart hurt. Why, oh why, could my father not see how much struggle we were having? Why would he not say, "The first thing I'm going to do with the $5,000 is tell my daughter the loan is paid." He did not. I wept, and I did not pay the loan. We never spoke of it. I never sensed that he was unhappy, but I wondered for a long time, "Did I do the right thing?"

In the early years of our marriage, how much money was spent on things that would be important to me, personally, brought lots of anguish. It was hard for me not to measure my husband's love for me by money he spent on a gift, or the money we spent going out to dinner. For five years, we went to McDonald's on Friday nights for dinner. Each Friday, my spirit agonized over my value. Now, today, I've outgrown that spirit, that agony, and that attitude towards money and my husband. I don't need to receive to have, and I can give from my heart, gratitude for the smallest gift. I can give gratitude if there is no gift. I can give gratitude for the giver, and not be tied down with the gift. That took a long time. If we want to achieve maturity, we will have to measure our money story very carefully, and learn from it.

Tell one of your money stories. See what you can learn now from your story.

Recently, I learned, from an article I read, that many Jewish families have a charity box visible to each family member in their house. I like the idea very much. Then I remembered there were two things that occurred during those first five years of the ministry in our house. There was a charity box by our front door. The box was made by a man we had helped. If money was in the charity box, and someone came who had a need, the money was given from the charity box. There was not once during the whole history of the ministry, that any of the money was kept for us, for charity begins at home. Another lesson, which also is a money story from that first five years, we never locked our doors. When we put the angels in charge of our house, we were willing to have everything we had stolen. Nothing we had was as important as an open door. Nothing was more important than believing that whatever was taken, our need would be met by what was given. It was amazing. We had no fear of robbers. We had no sense of needing to secure any part of what we had. Here is the power of spiritual freedom.

I've always had a rather insane belief that no church should ever be locked. They need to be open 24 hours a day, for many would slip in and pray, and many would find solace in a holy place that really was holy. To my knowledge, the churches are all still locked. Are we wrong?

This reminds me of a story. The Church of the Holy Sepulchre in Jerusalem was built by the Crusaders. It is a very holy place, a place five Christian faiths share. Over the centuries, there was division and argument about the space inside the church: who shared what, and where each altar would be placed. Finally, four Muslim families were given the only keys to that Christian church. Each day, the family chosen came faithfully to lock and unlock the doors. Is this a parable we don't like to hear? It is the Lord who speaks.

In the history of our marriage, we have only borrowed money once. We borrowed $300 from the bank because my husband's mother died. We had to fly to Oregon from Kansas City. My husband was working on a Master's Degree at the University of Missouri, Kansas City. He had to fly back. We were able to pay off the $300 in three months.

I do not include the buying of our house in the story of loans. I'm talking about the loan you would get from the bank for something you thought you needed. We learned to value and appreciate what we had. We were not unhappy with an older car, odd furniture, and other comfort delays. All of our needs have been met.

Even today, if you went through our house, I would tell you the story of most of the furniture, and how we received it. There is a chair in my home office that I bought at a garage sale for five dollars. There is a desk in this office that I bought from someone in the ministry for $50. There is an old kitchen chair that I sat on for the first five years of the ministry, a cheap, plastic-covered kitchen chair. There is a second-hand bookcase. A man and I traded bookcases. His was bigger and he needed the smaller one. It worked out well for both of us. But then, in my office, there is one thing that is very special.

One day, I was having a meeting at Good Samaritan Ministries with the Assistant Director of the Ministry, and a man named Bill, who came in to meet with us about various issues. As the meeting went on for awhile, and I had already made a plan to leave the office early and go buy myself a new office chair (as I was having considerable problems with my back), I told the men I was leaving. Bill said, "What kind of chair are you going to buy?" Of course I knew because I had a picture of it. He said, "That chair is a piece of crap. You are to go buy the best chair you can find and I will pay for it."

Even in my retirement at home, there is the chair that was given through a miracle of grace.

My office began at home. My retirement office I have just described is the same office space at home, the entire bedroom. We took more stock in giving than in receiving. There are two chairs in the office, the old plastic one, and the grace chair. They are symbols: *"My grace is enough for you: for power is at full stretch in weakness."* (2 Corinthians 12:9)

I will be really disappointed if you don't search out your own money stories. The New Testament can teach you more about your money stories than you possibly can imagine. I will be disappointed if you miss this great opportunity to seek and find that which is so easily lost.

Jerry and I have always been glad to pay our taxes. We are extraordinarily grateful for what is done with them, how many people are helped, how many people's needs are met.

When there is a bond issue, at least 90% of the time, we vote "yes." We do not resent or speak poorly of our government, our schools, or our people.

This reminds me of a funny story that I think you will enjoy. The story took place during the Cuban Missile Crisis. At the time, I was Assistant Civil Defense Director of Washington County. Since a dangerous war or nuclear explosion was possible, there was a great deal of preparation for the day the Cuban Missile Crisis was resolved. I called a meeting of educators from the school district, including the Superintendent of Schools. Forty people came to the meeting. Now, our living room can handle twelve, but forty is quite difficult. I will always remember that the Superintendent of Schools sat on the floor behind the front door. It was an important meeting.

Shall we have it somewhere else, or shall we examine the value of life in the living place of the people? Out of that meeting, came identity bracelets for the children, and any health information needed. Out of that meeting came decisions that, at the time, were very wise.

Most of us know the scripture, *"The love of money is the root of all evil"* (1 Timothy 6:10), but do we then know the act of giving of our provision is the root of all good?

Going back to taxes, and all the money we pay for the things we need. I always see the people working at their various jobs. Through this tax, or through our basic purchase, their basic needs are being met.

Jerry and I have a very special relationship. When we give, or we do something, we do it out of agreement. I may manage the fiscal matters as a bookkeeper, but never as anything but a full partner to my husband. The management of the physical and spiritual aspects of finance and goods are a shared concern.

I know a lot of investors talk about how much money is needed for our future. Invest in order to make it through your retirement. The church might talk about the tithe. The mother might talk about the cost of groceries, and the father might worry about the cost of gasoline, but in all of this, there is a deeper issue all the way around those subjects. Do we daily, hour by hour, receive with gratitude what has been provided? Do we never forget the greater privilege of our life is to truly and freely give?

One day, I was in Nairobi, Kenya, in a very large populated slum area called Baba Dogo. We were visiting a widow who was interested in, and part of, Good Samaritan Ministries. Before we entered the house, a Kenyan woman rushed up to us, out of breath, as she had raced to get to us in time. She brought us two loaves of bread. When we went in to visit the widow, I laid the two loaves of bread on the table between us, and I explained to her, "one of these loaves is for you and your children, the other loaf is for the needs you will meet in Baba Dogo, for you are called to be in charge of the distribution of food for the needy." We prayed, and we left. She remained a Samaritan.

One day, a man brought me a gift. It was near the time of my retirement, and he wanted to give me something special, so he handed me a gold $50 piece that his mother had given him as a special gift. He warned me it was worth a great deal more than $50.

My husband and I decided to put it in a safety deposit box. This gold coin is available if one of our children has a major health breakdown. This is a different kind of savings. It is a savings for mercy, a savings account for love.

Money matters. Don't ever be fooled that it does not. Money matters are worth looking at each day. Do not just budget where your money goes, but know the budget of your heart, your gratitude, and your life purposes. You are part of the community of humanity, the Kingdom of God.

CHAPTER 24

Lessons From Hiroshima

In 1945, The Enola Gay was on a dangerous mission to drop the first atomic bomb on Hiroshima.

When Jerry and I visited Hiroshima in 1982, we learned the name of that bomb, "Little Boy." The bomb that was dropped three days later at Nagasaki was called "Fat Boy." This is the beginning of lessons from Hiroshima.

Jerry and I spent two nights and one day at Hiroshima. First, we went to the Peace Center. It is a large park area with a museum. Walking through the museum, you see, close at hand, not only the disintegration of bodies, but also the level of suffering that went on and on. It is not about the war. It's not about who was right or who was wrong. It is about human suffering. It is about agony, Deeply and powerfully it's about who is God? As I looked at the real picture, I felt the deepest pity, the deepest sorrow I had ever known.

We went to the large cathedral built over the epicenter of the bomb. The cathedral was empty. We went down towards the front to sit, meditate and pray. As we were getting up to leave, three teenage Japanese girls stood looking at us on the side of the aisle where we were sitting. I cried out, "I'm so sorry." I cried out a sorrow that would not be comforted. The first Japanese girl, on the right, gave me her handkerchief to wipe my tears. I still have the handkerchief. I am still so sorry to see the grief of innocent people who had nothing to do with the decisions that were made by others.

As we moved to the back of the church, there was an American woman sitting in a pew. She called us over. She said, "I have been waiting for someone to come. I have asked the Lord to send someone to me, as I wish to go to the hospital to pray for my husband's boss, who is dying of cancer. Would you go to the hospital to pray with me?"

The woman was from Tacoma, Washington. She was married to a Japanese national. She was a Christian of faith. She needed the Holy Spirit over this man's suffering and his need for salvation.

We agreed to meet at the hospital. In the afternoon, I made my way alone to the hospital and went upstairs. I found the room. She was there. A shrunken Japanese man was in the hospital bed. His wife was sitting by his bedside. The Supernatural Spirit of God came upon me as I walked into that room. These words came out of my mouth, "I have come to welcome you in Jesus' name into God's Kingdom." A look of shock went across the man's face. I took his hand. We all prayed together.

As we were leaving the room, his wife followed us. She fell, sobbing into my arms.

When I returned to Oregon, I learned that the man died four days later. I learned that before his death, he spoke to his whole family about what had happened. He said, "I do not know why God has accepted me into His Kingdom. All I know is I always said 'Amen' at the end of my prayers." In a letter, the woman from Tacoma, who had brought me to the hospital, shared that she took some water from Lourdes with her to the hospital, and he asked to drink it. His baptism was complete.

Everything I had learned up to this point in my life was shaken to the foundations by what I learned in Hiroshima. The hospitality of God is greater than I had ever known. This hospitality is profound.

He sends. He welcomes. He is.

The Lord did not require the man to accept Jesus as his personal savior. He did not weary the man with religion. As the man was suffering, the Lord threw his arms around Him and welcomed Him into His Kingdom.

As I look back, I was led to accept Jesus. The pastor gave me the right hand of fellowship. No one ever threw their arms around me and welcomed me into the Kingdom of God.

This seemed to be the missing piece, the missing peace! We tell people what they must do. We tell them that their sins will be forgiven. We tell them to accept the faith. The Lord Himself exploded His gift of hospitality to the poor, the lame, and the weak. In Hiroshima, my faith exploded, my vision cleared. Is this not the Lord speaking to us? Who are we? Do we know the explosive power of His hospitality? Do we know Him?

Our assignment is clear. Make Him known to the world. Witness, and make Him known. As I look around the world in which I live today, I have seen little witness; even little desire to do so. I've seen pathetic poverty in the Spirit, and hesitation too deep for words. I have seen the Gospel forced upon people, but not the understanding of the Gospel. I have never seen the shocking hospitality of the Kingdom of God!

The days now were here when I saw the intent and purpose of the Living God. Only as He welcomes us with the explosive power of His Spirit, can we ever truly know Him as Lord and Savior.

In 1945, Hiroshima was the largest Protestant Christian city in Japan. Nagasaki was the largest Catholic city in Japan.
These are the lessons from Hiroshima. They are as alive this moment as they were that day in 1982. At that moment our weaknesses were exposed. His strength was revealed!

CHAPTER 25

Woman

I believe this chapter will be confusing to some, and that it will be okay for you to be confused. From earliest childhood we play, "Let's pretend you are the mom and I'll be the dad." It's as natural as breath to a child. Then, we turn to one other person and say, "you can be the baby." Papa Bear, Mama Bear, Baby Bear, the whole earth is speaking "FAMILY." [Who is woman?]

WOMAN

In 1990, I found myself unexpectedly at the home of B.K. Kirya, Minister of State for Uganda, Africa. As a team of ten, from several countries, we learned from B.K. that evening. He became a very great covering over this ministry and my life. He taught me one particular sentence, during this unexpected visit, on the first day I had ever been in Uganda. He said, "Thou art woman."

It reminded me that my grandfather Roberts, who was disconnected from almost everything all of his life, had always called my grandmother, "The Woman." Here was a word that connected in my spirit.

When B.K. Kirya said "woman," he was speaking of her from beginning to end, a woman. Thus, when a girl child is born, a woman has come into the world. This enlarged my understanding of the greatness of a birth child. The baby girl is not just an infant. She is already fully woman.

Then I thought about Jesus. He came in the form of an infant, but He was fully man.

The word "woman" became a trembling power of truth. It pierced all other parts of my being. Sinless Adam, before the fall, spoke the word in the Garden of Eden. When woman comes into her fullness of woman, indeed the blessing of God is present.

We have a given name and roles that we have in life, such as child, mother, or wife. There is only one thing greater: "thou art woman." Genesis Chapter 2, verse 22, "Yahweh God fashioned the rib He had taken from the man into a woman, and brought her to the man. And the man said: This one at last is bone of my bones and flesh of my flesh! She is to be called Woman, because she was taken from Man."

I heard, when B.K. Kirya spoke "woman," he spoke with authority. With the authority of the Holy Spirit over my life, I received the word "WOMAN."

That evening, we learned B.K. went to bed early, with no difficulty leaving guests. He arose every morning at 3:00 to pray the first hour, to read the Word the second hour, and the third hour, to come into contact with the important news of the day. He had made no exception to this schedule for twenty years.

MOTHER

B.K. spoke about how Jesus spoke to His mother and called her woman at the wedding of Cana in the Gospel of John, Chapter 2. In the Gospel of John, Chapter 19, verse 26, "Seeing his mother and the disciple he loved standing near her, Jesus said to his mother, 'Woman, this is your son'. Then to the disciple he said, 'This is your mother.'"

Three common words in addressing woman are these: "mother, mama, or mom." One of these words can stir the soul of woman; making her listen with respect when the authority of the word is spoken. Each time one of these words is used and spoken towards woman, the relationship between mother and child becomes an empowering relationship for the mother and the child. The child is speaking with authority; the mother must listen with authority.

My husband longed for a son. My mother had longed for a son. A longing for a son is part of my story.

The first day I met Mohammed Bader, it was in a classroom at Bethlehem University. A few hours later, he came with us on a bus to the Galilee. On the way, we stopped at Shiloh.

He said, "I want to tell you something, I want to speak to you." We stepped outside the ruins of the Shilo Church and went behind the building. We sat down on a broken pillar. He told me he had suffered a sleep disorder all his life; but that was not the real conversation. The real conversation was this: he called me "mom." It was at that moment that I was his mom. He was the first of many sons. He confided in me. I gave him my word, as a mom, that I would be with him, to sustain his life, until he was healed.

You can't be a mom if you aren't one on the inside of your heart. You really can't be a mom unless first, you're a woman.

I met Mohammed Bader in 1983. In 1989, I became his second mom forever.

MAMA

"Mama" is often the first word a baby speaks, "Mama, Dada." This is a natural word coming from the child. Every language has a special word for Mama. For example, in Hebrew, mother is called "Ema."

Now, this reminds me of a story that is worthy of being told here. I had an Orthodox Jewish friend named Daniel, who lived in Jerusalem. He lived with his wife and his son, Nissim. His wife suddenly died when Nissim was about three years old. Daniel shared with me that for the next six months, Nissim looked everywhere for his mother. He would open the cupboards and say, "Ema?" He would look and look and look for her. One day, he took his father's hand, looked up at his father, and said, "Ema!"

MAMA BETTIE

I gradually became known, after 1987, as "Mama Bettie." "Mama" plus a given name is the custom of respect when speaking to an older woman in Africa. They speak of a woman as Mama and use her given name. If the woman is younger and not married, they call her "sister." But, "Mama" is heard everywhere you go. It is a word that requires no other explanation. This is the primitive word of the bond between Mama and the children. It is to bring absolute honor and respect to the woman.

I was called Mama Bettie so many times that I gradually became Mama Bettie. At first, it was strange and not what I would have liked to hear. We're used to calling each other by our given names. We're not used to titles, and certainly, a grown person looking at me and saying, "Mama Bettie" was strange. I was not the person's Mama, but, it was their way of saying woman.

Mama Bettie did not denote to me that I would mother people. It did not denote to me that I would have certain rights over the person who called me Mama Bettie. It was only a word of respect.

I have found many people in this world looking for a mother, others looking for a father, and some looking for both, as they had none who truly ever knew them. It is a grave responsibility not to baby, spoil, or play too significant a role in another person's life. It was my responsibility to respect myself, and an honor to be respected by others. I gradually accepted "Mama Bettie" as a given part of my name.

THE TRUE MOTHER

A woman can be a mother who has no birth children. One of the greatest needs the world has is for mothers at large, a multitude of them, who stop for the lost and broken children along the road. They are needed not just by young children, but by children of all ages. The true mother has authority. She has a way with children. Mother Theresa lived as a true mother. She was a nun, someone in complete submission to the Church and to the Lord. She became spoken of worldwide as a true mother. She was known as a true mother in most nations.

A true mother chooses her children. Mother Theresa chose unwanted babies, and the most extreme, poverty-stricken bodies that lay dying in the streets of India. She, herself, made sure they were carried to a place where she could minister to them, and where she could train sisters to do this work. She washed broken bodies, prayed over them, and did not ask them if they had accepted Jesus first. She was a mother to the motherless.

I read a story about Mother Theresa and President Bill Clinton. Mother Theresa was the speaker at the Presidential Prayer Breakfast in Washington, D.C. President Clinton took her to the Prayer Breakfast in his limousine. While they were in the car together, she talked to him about the U.S. abortion problem. She said, "Don't kill your babies. I, myself, will take any of them that this world does not want. I will take them."

Mother Theresa was less than five feet tall. President Clinton was very tall. When they arrived at the Prayer Breakfast, Mother Theresa was to stand up and give a speech to 4,000 people from all over the world. The podium was almost taller than she was. She could barely be seen over the top of it. But, when this mother spoke, this mother meant every word she said.

Without firm authority, the word mother means little. With a mother's godly authority, Mama is given to those who need it most. Each Mama is called to a life that expresses the fullness of woman and the greatness of true motherhood.

Even if you are only 11 years old, you can be a great woman. You can be a mother to many, and you can be a friend to all.

WIFE

Wife, you too are woman! You are to be the fullness of woman and live out your great faith and His empowerment as a wife. Always fight for your husband, and never tempt him to ignore God or do evil. You may be a conscience speaking into your marriage. A conscience is not an argument. It is the truth being spoken because of love.

Woman, Mother, Mama, Wife, and the Holy Spirit. "Here are the children, where are the teachers?" God asked the question at Nineveh. Have we answered it?

CHAPTER 26

Mommy-Ism
and Soul Ties

Mommy-Ism is a panic disorder. Mommy-Ism is a relationship disaster. I was a Mommy-Ism child.

When I was seven years old, I had experienced several years of severe earaches. When oil was put in my ear, I was always panicky whether it would be too hot. One evening, I was struggling with an earache. My father was gone and my mother had to go to night school. (At 35, she was trying to graduate from high school.) She walked out the door and left me alone. I began such a wail and scream that finally the Craigs came down from the apartment upstairs to find out what was wrong.

One could affirm no seven year-old child should be left alone. One could also say that a child who was sick should never be left alone. But, deep inside, beyond my tension and the fear I felt, I believe the root of my problem was not the earache or mommy being gone; the root of my problem was Mommy-Ism.

When mommy came home, she was very angry with me for making such a fuss and getting the neighbors involved. Probably, she was experiencing her own guilt.

Mommy-Ism is a separation anxiety disorder. The child clings to mommy, as one clinging to a life raft. The sinking boat filled with the sea. Mommy likes the clinging if it gives her a sense of her own worth. It irritates her if she feels the child is clinging to her instead of the life raft. Mommy-Ism is rooted in an incomplete relationship with God, lack of other support systems, and a deep and profound lack of balance between mommy and child.

Over the years I saw many who had mommy-Ism problems. Some of them transferred those Mommy-Ism problems to me, expecting me to somehow provide for their Mommy-Ism insecurity needs.

In the counseling office, we saw Daddy-Ism, Husband-Ism, Friend-Ism, all rooted to an insecure relationship with God. The Lord Himself was not the Lord of their life. They wanted people to rescue them. We want people to make us feel good. We want people to support our house.

This brings me to the topic of soul ties. "Soul ties" is a very powerful concept in Christian healing. It must be addressed if a person is to become whole. A soul tie can be found in deep rooted "isms."

I was in my 40's when I received a phone call. The call was from a man who worked at the Christian Renewal Center the summer before. He had been attending Oral Roberts University, in Tulsa, Oklahoma, for a year, and he had just recently come back to this area. I barely knew the man. We might have had one conversation during the time I was at the Christian Renewal Center. I was very surprised at his phone call. He said, "I have a word for you from the Lord. May I come and give it to you?" I said, "Yes."

When the man came, he did not sit down and talk in generalities. He came right to the point of his visit. Since the man knew little about me, having had nothing but a distant relationship with me at camp, I knew his visit was a divine appointment.

He said, "You have a soul tie with your mother." I knew this, but I didn't know the term, "soul tie." I didn't understand the danger. A soul tie has the power to limit spiritual growth and control over freedom.

We went into my home office. He said, "May I lay hands on you and pray?" I said, "Yes." The Lord showed me my soul tie with my mother. Between her navel and my navel there was a thick tree trunk; not a cord, but a thick tree trunk; inflexible, solid, and rooted in each of us. We had no power to sever the soul tie to allow our individuality and wholeness to occur. During this prayer, I knew no one but the Lord Himself could sever the tie I saw. It was severed. My life was no longer bound to Mommy-Ism.

When the man left, the Lord told me, "You always felt responsible for your mother's happiness." This word immediately resonated inside of me as the truth. The Lord spoke further, "You are not responsible for her happiness. She is responsible for her own happiness." It was as if a million pound weight had been lifted from me, a weight I had carried since infancy. The soul tie was completely broken. I was an individual. I had been given freedom in Christ Jesus, my Lord. When the man finished his prayer, he immediately got up and left. I have never seen nor heard from him since. He was on a mission. My individuation rapidly developed. I was free to fully give my life to Christ. My life no longer belonged to the "Isms." My life belonged to God alone.

Whole family systems can be tied together or enmeshed with soul ties. Soul ties can be generational. An example of a generational soul tie was my mother's relationship with her mother. Since her mother was orphaned as a very small child, my mother felt responsible for her mother's happiness. I watched her struggle with this until my grandmother died at 92. She never ceased to feel responsible for her mother's happiness. My mother, too, was an only child, as my grandmother was. I can remember, at Christmastime, she bought my grandmother very lovely gifts, and I received something from the basement bargain counter. Was my mother rejecting me? No. She was trying to make her mother happy.

Generational soul ties can go on into the next generations. To be completely whole, each of us must be willing to address this issue. I had parts of me scattered in many places. I must have all of me together. He sets us free by His spirit, and out of that freedom we can truly love one another.

In the counseling office, breaking soul ties was a difficult task with clients. It had to be recognized that many clients had soul ties; some had several, some had only one. It was hard to remember this as clients came in with their problems and viewpoints. I could hear their struggle to be themselves. Yes, I often did not remember the urgency of helping them deal with their soul ties. It is for this reason that I am writing this chapter in order for you to find the soul ties rooted to your personhood, and to encourage you that the Lord Himself will break the ties and set you free.

I come to you as the man came to me. Soul ties are there.

Soul ties can be to objects, such as when you must have the right house, the best furniture, a collection that you absolutely obsess about. Soul ties can be to your own ideas that may be as inflexible as the tree trunk between my mother and myself. Soul ties are destructive forces that do not lead you to the goal of freedom. A soul tie leads you to more complex forms of dependency.

If a man and woman marry who both have soul tie issues, there will be an outbreak of war; devastation may quickly occur, and conflicted and complicated dealings will reflect the insecurity of each soul-tied person. Many marital problems are rooted in the soul tie issues of the individual. We seek marriage as the solution. We think somehow we can get away from our complications and get married. You think, "We'll have our own house. We'll make our own decisions..." But, the soul ties go with you until they are broken. If not dealt with, soul ties stay with you for a lifetime. Trauma seeps into generational issues, and it will manifest clearly in abuse to you and from you.

Once I had a client who had generational soul ties with mother and father. Family members of her father had belonged to the Klu Klux Klan. The mother's soul tie to the daughter was rooted in Masonism. The client was suffering really serious physical problems. When I could see the soul ties and her bondage, I could see why she was having physiological problems with her body. When I could see, I could pray. When I prayed, she could see. Deliverance occurred!

Cults demand radical soul ties to the cult. They do not offer personal freedom of the individual to develop and grow. The cult will offer to develop you, but then you must conform to their ideas of development. This could profoundly interfere with the responsible development of the freedom of your will.

Soul ties are rooted in imbalance. I've seen people attacked by consuming powers. These powers can unbalance them throughout all their days. They will haunt them at night, and prevent them from their progress towards responsible freedom.

For example, if a child is born and prefers mommy to daddy, a soul tie with the mother is being fed. This creates triangulation with the parents and child, a tug-of-war. Rather than developing the child's security, it prevents the child from being secure.

It might seem that I'm talking in absolutes in this chapter. I can only say that I've seen the absolute devastation of soul ties in many.

Sometimes soul ties are developed through long pressures from manipulation, guilt, and shame. This is torture that can be obvious or subtle; but it is, indeed, torture. The soul is being demanded to fully commit to another person. This vice of control is preventing the soul from being fully committed to the freedom Christ offers. Soul ties are powerful. If guilt and shame are used as a control weapon on a child, the child will later demand soul ties from mother or father. The soul ties become the feeding system of the child.

I believe every person has the option, the right, and the

responsibility to examine themselves. We examine ourselves to see if we have a lump in our breast. We can examine ourselves to see if soul ties are preventing us from being in balance. If we are to love our neighbor as ourself, if we are to love our enemy, then preferential love must be defeated. God must be free to keep you and train you to do unto others as you would have them do unto you.

If your personality is free to do unto others as you would have them do unto you, and if your personality is free from soul ties that have bound your soul to massive games and difficult responses, then your whole personhood can follow Jesus.

Again and again, Jesus set himself apart. His soul ties were to no one, but to God alone. He said, "Follow me." Will we follow Him?

Often, I have heard it said of marriage, "I was looking for my soul mate," or "My husband and I are soul mates." There is a vast difference between soul mates and marital union. Soul mates can become soul ties. If there is a lack of freedom, there is a lack of being able to give and receive freely. If you are married to your soul mate, be careful to not be so exclusive from others around you that you shut out an entire world for the sake of the love you have for your soul mate.

Some, who are restless in marriage, not married to their soul mates, look for a soul mate. If one is found, the break-up of family will be an avalanche of devastation.

How powerful are the words in the Old Testament and the New Testament, in the demand that God places on each of us, "*You must love the Lord your God with all your heart, with all your soul, with all your strength, and with all your mind, and your neighbor as yourself.*" (Luke 10:27)

WHAT IS YOUR ASSIGNMENT?

Are you just going to go on to the next chapter, or are you going to stop and take this seriously? Are you going to sit down and find the areas where your own choices of weakness have taken control of your life? You can easily say, "Well, I have an addictive personality." I want to say to you, "You have an addiction to a soul mate. Not only could your soul mate be a person, but your soul mate might be cigarettes, always being right and making others wrong, or claiming you are just like your father and can't help it! Never let the problem be more powerful than the solution!!

What will you do with this information? What will you do with this story? Is it too hard for you, so you want to talk about something else? Will you hide from this and say, "Well, my problems are not so serious." Will you stop, rest awhile, and let the Lord tell you the truth? Only the truth can set you free.

Set aside significant time.
God knows the soul ties that are
separating and isolating you.
He offers you your spiritual freedom.

It is my prayer that this chapter disturbs your waters and challenges you. It is my prayer that you find the sources of manipulations that plague your soul.

"Do you perceive not that you are Mine, and you are Mine alone?"

CHAPTER 27

Union

United Way is a union. It is a union between the needs of the community, and the united effort the majority of a community makes to meet those needs.

Marital union is not easily achieved. For this to come to pass, many forces must be overcome and obstacles defeated.

Over the years, I have taught with passion about sexuality. I learned the hard way. I experienced. I sought. I could see that there was something in sex that was missing. Was it better climaxes? Was it better environment? Was it more seduction and stimulation? In the development of human sexuality there are many dangerous roads. In my experience with most clients they did not recognize the dangers of ignorance, naivety, or lack of moral foundational boundaries.

The institution of marriage started in the Garden of Eden. Sin broke the institution of marriage, as it prevented union. Union is the goal of God for marriage.

A number of years ago, I wrote a small book called The Power of Conflict and Sacrifice, A Therapy Manual for Christian Marriage. The book sells for five dollars. The book speaks many parables and strong truth. If you are going to finish this book, you need to commit to finish that book.

At one time, I read thirty books about marriage and sex, seeking to learn, in a healthy way, what I did not know or understand. I can reduce, to a few pages, what I came to understand. The continuity of the family depends on knowing and understanding what is good and perfect and true!

Marital union is not about thrills and excitement. It is about the explosion of God's creative power, the creative power that created life itself. God put this creative power inside of us for life to come forth. Sexuality has produced all the generations. God is the author of sexuality.

The obstacles of union have an avalanche effect on the creative power that God placed in us. We are conflicted by our mood disorders, lack of willingness to talk about a problem, and various methods of manipulation that hold us to instability. Imperfect concepts of our body limit how we see this creative power within us. The human perfectionistic spirit may lord it over our imperfect, painful realities. The greatest damage can come in the unwillingness to be a willing partner, and the denial of the divine purpose of healthy sexuality.

Marital union starts with the recognition that it was God Himself who made each of us, and gave us this possibility of the creative power of union. A marriage starts with a family. Sexual union requires a powerful God, who grants mercy when we beg for help.

Since our lives have been rooted in sin, we must remember sin produces sicknesses that have the power to prevent sexual union. Never allow your efforts to die as you seek healthy solutions. This is not a lukewarm issue!

To put it in the simplest language possible: woman was created out of man; man was born out of woman. In sexuality, man comes back into woman. Woman must choose to give back to man the rib by her heart and her compassion. Woman can choose powerful acceptance of a man's life. Full acceptance one to another brings forth the fruit of continuity and union in marriage.

Now, I'm going to give you two assignments that will lead you to the completion of union. You are to read The Power of Conflict and Sacrifice. You are to do this as if your life depended on it! You are to read it as a couple.

As you share in this experience together, you become able to learn from it. This makes possible new pathways, new patterns that will bring shocking breakthrough to your marriage. When you read, particularly, the last chapter of the book, you must first read Genesis 1 and 2. When you have finished reading Genesis 1 and 2, and after reading the last chapter in the book, The Power of Conflict and Sacrifice, you are again to go back and read Chapter 1 and 2 of Genesis. You are not to do this because you are required; you are to do this to receive a great gift. God created the greatest gift He could give man and woman; He created the road to union. Talk, talk, talk together on what you learn and act upon the lessons. Without actions to follow, the words become as nothing at all!

WARNING: Do not think of a single excuse not to do this, whether you have abnormalities or differences in your styling, or your understanding. Even if you hate the scriptures, or you are too far gone to care, do not think of a single excuse that will prevent you from completing the assignments and making actions from the heart. All excuses are cancelled for this assignment!!

Papa Jerry and I almost gave up seeking to grow, to learn about or to understand each other. It took me more than ten years to see some of the problems I caused in his life. It took me 20 years to help connect a sentence to his sentence, and find a way to communicate that did not end in the entanglement of conflict.

We have both been sexual people, increasingly committed to a better road. We found union is not possible in a self-centered mind. It is not possible in rigid game playing. It is not possible if we do not give the sex act to the Lord before it occurs and after it has occurred. We found union. It has kept us alive, given us more wellness, and increased the God-given creative power within our family life.

We came from massive soul ties, dirty minds, considerable sexual addiction, and powerful confusion. If you seek the Lord with all your heart, He will give you the seeds of union. He will give you life. He will bless your home, and He will keep your hearts. Sex was an important area of concern in all of the counseling work I did. I taught my clients to love sex in a right and healthy way.

When two or more agree, then it will be so. For most of our marriage, my husband struggled with depression. He used a pretty consistent small amount of alcohol to manage his pain and diffuse his heartache. He was not an alcoholic, but he was using alcohol for the wrong reasons. I sensed that it was doing him harm and contributing to his depression.

I talked about this with him only once. I said, "I know you have a hard time with depression, and alcohol is a depressant. When you use alcohol, it depresses you immediately. What if you tried not using alcohol to see if it makes a difference?"

This brought about union in our thinking. It brought about cooperation, for I only made a suggestion, and I only made it once. I never suggested it again. My husband stopped using alcohol. His battle with depression was greatly lessened, and he never started drinking alcohol again. When the two of us agreed, then it was so.

CHAPTER 28

Counseling
And Generations

From the beginning of the church, the call was to train the young, and to provide for worship and community in a safe environment for the Christians and those interested in Christianity. I was at Ephesus in Turkey, in 1974. Four of us were travelling together, including my mother.

Ephesus was a large archaeological site. It involved digging up a Roman city. It is one of the most significant sites from early Christianity, for when Jerusalem was destroyed, the Christians gathered to safety at Ephesus. Mary, the mother of Jesus lived there. St. John, the Apostle, and Paul were there. The city was a great first century center of Christianity.

While visiting Ephesus, we went to the sixth largest church ever built, the Church of St. John. The ruins of the Church of St. John are largely excavated. The original floor of the church is there, and in that floor, is the original site of the baptismal pool.

It was at Ephesus that I learned something powerfully important. I'm just beginning to learn it again, and think about it. I can see that baptismal site, and hear the words that were individually shouted by those who were to be baptized. The fount was in the form of a cross on the floor. It was the original immersion site.

The person to be immersed took off their clothes, except for a small covering. Each person baptized faced away from the baptismal site and shouted three times, "Oh Devil, I leave you! Oh Devil, I leave You, Oh Devil, I leave you!" Yes, I said, they shouted. The strength of the early church was the new believer shouting out, "Oh Devil, I leave you!" If one is born again, they fully believe in these words. After this strong declaration, the person turned around and walked down into the fount of immersion. When they came up the steps on the other side, they were dressed in a new white robe. Something profound had happened. They had entirely faced the devil, and they had made an entire turnaround to go in another direction to follow the Christ. When the baptism finished, they were born again! Their lives were free. They had no past encumbrances. They had no past shames or guilt. Their lives belonged to God, and no longer belonged to this world. The saints of the early church fully confronted the devil himself, and they fully turned around and faced the other direction towards a new life.

Today, we encourage people to accept Christ, to give a confession of faith, and to be baptized in the name of the Father, the Son, and the Holy Spirit. But, as I worked for years in the counseling office, I can tell you, almost none of the people had fully turned around. They were confronted continually by their weaknesses, and the devil's strength to tempt them in every way. The more I think of this, the more I am sure that this one part, "Oh Devil, I leave you," was as important as it was to be baptized. Without this one part, "Oh devil, I leave you," this one powerful decision, this shout of freedom, there is no lasting rejoicing. The Devil must not defeat the new Christian!

I have studied and visited most of the denominations. I have personally fully participated in my own church. I have honored and respected, not only the individual church, but the church as a whole. However, in my whole experience of the church, one thing was missing: the connection through Christ Jesus in lifetime relationships.

What do I mean by this? The pastor was there for a time, and then he left. The people lacked a leader who could hold them into the full relationship of Christ Jesus among them. There was something powerfully absent. As I set out in ministry, I set out to find what was missing in all of these broken lives that poured into our offices.

I set out to seek, find, and develop what is missing in my fellow man. The powerful call of true relationship became the cornerstone of Good Samaritan Ministries.

As I interviewed several thousand Christians, I found a core issue of abandonment in most. There was no place for them to go and be entirely honest, able to fully disclose, and then be able to walk in dignity in the strength of Christian community. They went to church, joined committees, worshiped, and did the right thing, but there was still one missing piece. It was this missing piece that has truly been my life's work.

For 32 years, I worked in the counseling office. When I retired, I did not leave it. The relationships continue. Intercession, and our joy, love, and availability to the people remain a high priority of Good Samaritan Ministries as a whole.

Before Good Samaritan Ministries was even founded, I was on the staff of a Junior High School. I was on staff for seven years in one school as a permanent substitute. I was on staff to be fully available to the children and all of the teachers. There were 900 children in the school where I served, and 55 teachers. I made myself available to all, not just in work, not just by paycheck, but by giving lifetime respect and relationship.

Recently, in our church, there were two women who came that I did not recognize. I went up to greet them during the service and said, "My name is Bettie Mitchell." One of the women looked at me in disbelief. She said, "You were my substitute teacher at Mountain View School. The children loved you in that school and you changed my whole life. I have now been a substitute teacher for 5 ½ years. Every day, I remember your spirit in that school and your relationship with all of us." Her name is Leslie. What a powerful gift I received. I had not seen Leslie for 34 years. She was from out of town and only came once to our church.

As the years have gone by, hospitality, intentional and deeply profound listening, significant assignments, and the will to truly embrace the lives of others through Christ Jesus have been the testimony of this ministry and my life's work. It will remain so in the generations to come.

The ministry is open, available. It is a place across the world that gives much. The ministry is an opportunity for victims to be trained as Samaritans. As the years passed, I met with the generations of many families.

When children come into the ministry, this is our greatest of joys. Among us is a welcoming spirit for each of them. Good Samaritan Ministries stands for the reality of a sense of home, homeland, and peace for all who come. Over the years, I often said, "Welcome Home."

I remember the words of Jesus, "*So he called a little child to him whom he set among them. Then he said, 'In truth I tell you, unless you change and become like little children you will never enter the kingdom of Heaven.*" And so, the one who makes himself as little as this little child is the greatest in the kingdom of Heaven.'" (Matthew 18: 2-4) I remember the small lives around the world, children looking for home, looking to see if we are with them.

In the early days of substituting, I knew one thing. I knew that when I walked in a classroom, I had five minutes to affect the lives of the students. If trust was born in those five minutes, a lifetime relationship would take place.

Good Samaritan Ministries does a lot of family counseling. It is good to see the whole family, to learn about each of them, and help them to learn about each other.

I will always remember a visit I made to one family. I went to meet with the mother and her two children at their house. We were going to study the toy situation, and make some decisions on what toys were needed. We weighed how toys can affect the children's lives and the development of their healthy decision-making. We were researching their toys, and we were doing it together with the children. We were seeking ways to get the children more involved in appreciating what they had, and limiting what they had to what was truly needed at their age. We called the day, "Toy Therapy." We all liked it. We devised a plan to rotate the toys, as I recall, every three months. The children decided which toys would be removed and which would be staying. We talked about the purpose and use of each toy possession. The new system was set in motion, and it worked. Today, one of those children is studying to be a medical doctor. The other one is musically talented and successful in the university.

Another day, a family came in to see me. There were seven children and the mother. The father had recently died. They came in to talk, and I came in the room to talk to them. I was so glad to see them because I knew the father and mother. I knew the children. I knew them in my spirit, I knew them in my heart. I really knew them! Therefore, this knowing made each of them glad to see me. It made them glad to know someone understood.

We talked together for about an hour and a half. At first, the children were reticent to express their grief and feelings about dad's death and the current family situation. One boy hid in the hood of his jacket. Each one of them had their own way of avoiding. During our time together, every one of their needs was met because I was part of the family, their family, and they were part of my family. I was not "the counselor." I was sharing in their grief, and sharing in their hopes for their future.

One of the teen family members had stayed in the vehicle. He didn't want to come in. He was having a difficult time with his mom. I went over and spoke to him in the vehicle. It was a distant speaking, but it was a real speaking. The mother wanted to know what we talked about, but I said, "I talked to him privately and he talked to me privately. It is important that each person has their privacy." As we meet together along the road, we can be significantly life-giving to one another.

Sometimes, in family therapy, I saw grandparents, parents, children, and even great-grandchildren.

In this world, many just see people. They see people on Tuesday at 3:00. They see people at dinner. They see people occasionally. I saw each person forever. Perhaps I could say that our insides met with one another, not in outer form, but in the inner substance of real relationship. Even 20 or 30 years later, it is as if we are still meeting. It has nothing to do with occasionally seeing one another; it has to do with lifetime relationship.

Over the years I wrote letters. For some years, I wrote 400 letters a month. I dictated them into a dictaphone. A typist typed 40 hours a week, just on my letters. I wrote across the world. I wrote significant, individual letters through the Holy Spirit, letters of encouragement, and letters of empowerment.

I carried a box where I kept the letters that had to be answered. There were usually a lot of letters to be answered, but every time I took that box into my hands, I said, "Lord, show me the letter that needs to be written to someone who is not in this box." I wrote letters to children. I wrote letters to widows. I wrote letters to a former witch doctor in Africa. Although I'm retired, I'm still writing letters. This time, I use the computer myself. This is a great miracle! It took me ten months to learn how to use it. There isn't an ounce of mechanical genius in me. But, the will to write has remained steady.

Letters have come from all over the world. Just this week, I received a letter from Bisi, a Nigerian woman that came to Good Samaritan Ministries 13 years ago. Bisi is now 76. Although we have not seen each other for years, our lives crossed again in our letters. She is living six months out of the year in Nigeria, and six months out of the year in Michigan. In her letter dated April 14, 2011, she says:

"Whenever I can help GSM, I'll not hesitate to do so. I have benefited from your generosity and love by accommodating me while in Oregon. I had booked a flight to Oregon to spend time with Reverend and Mrs. Ajayi of the Apostolic Faith, who are age-long friends. The man taught my son in high school next door to mine. A few days before the trip, he got back to me to inform of his wife's illness. My son contacted the hotel I lodged in before GSM sent someone to pick me up after two nights. The Baptist church I contacted for accommodation help could not do it, but as your name implied, you picked me up and gave me shelter, food, spiritual, and physical love without a charge.

I recommended GSM program to a friend of mine who is into spiritual calling. She has a lot to learn from GSM, which can offer her the training she needs to make impact in her mission. Her name is Mrs. Julie, a nurse by profession.

P.S., As a mark of appreciation for the service I gave to teeming children in my town Ibadan, Nigeria, the king recently honored me with the Chieftaincy Title, "Chief." I don't like it attached to my name. I'm satisfied without being addressed by it. I prefer a title that will portray me as a relentless worker for the master. Love and Honor, Bisi."

People respond to warm hearts, to our love, and trust. It isn't always easy to give it, and it's not always easy for some to receive it. We are in a school with the Master who welcomed all, and who sacrificed rest to be a servant to the people. He did not keep a schedule, He kept a life, and He taught us to live the life He kept.

The goal of the ministry was not "My Ministry." It is not named Bettie Mitchell Ministries. The goal of the ministry was the empowerment of the ministries of all of the people, the empowerment of Samaritans who would work in one accord across the world, nameless people doing the work of the Father. Each worker is valuable, and each must receive the great call upon their own individual life. As you read this book, you might examine yourself. Have you learned of the great call upon your life?

Perhaps many have read this book out of curiosity about Bettie Mitchell. Now it is time for you to learn about the call upon your own life. Go ahead with your call. Respond to it well. Give because of your own faith in the Name of Jesus. Never hold anything back from His work! I pray you will be a lifetime Samaritan.

Last Sunday, Jerry and I were at Family Therapy Camp. Julia, from Maryland, was visiting with her adopted daughter, Veeka. I had not seen Julia for three years. Veeka was having her sixth birthday.

We drove up to spend two-thirds of a day with Julia, Veeka, and with the people in camp. The camp went well. The theme was "Never Give Up." It was a theme I really appreciated. There are many things we need to give up, but we must never give up seeking and doing what is right.

While we were sitting at the table, a young woman named Sarah was sitting with us. She was in her very early 20's. She obviously had a very hard and broken life. She had just sung a song at the worship service, a song in which her sobs mingled with the words.

As we were sitting there, I talked to Sarah. I talked to Sarah's deep down inside. She asked me what Good Samaritan Ministries was about, how did it come to pass? I briefly told her. I said, "If I hadn't obeyed, we wouldn't be here today." Julia spoke up then.

She said, "In 1981, Bettie was my counselor. We met in her house. All sorts of people were coming, the people that nobody would want, and the people who would never be received in a warm way by the Christian community."

Julia talked about the meeting with me, and then all the years we stayed in contact. I even flew to Houston to visit Julia when she worked as Religion Editor for the Houston Chronicle. I went to her office at the newspaper in Washington, D.C. We wrote to each other from time to time. We shared very personally. I have a great joy and interest in Julia's life, and of course, Veeka's life. Julia went to Kazakhstan to adopt Veeka. She is a child who is obviously gifted in her heart and spirit. Veeka is expressive. What joy to see this next generation celebrating life with us.

Julia had been out of work for ten months. It was not easy for her to fly out for family camp, but it was Veeka's sixth birthday. Veeka is one of her generation, precious and vital to the quality of survival in this world.

I just had a phone call. It was from Bill. Bill is an attorney, and a member of the Board of Good Samaritan Ministries. I've known Bill for a number of years. He was a District Attorney, and now he is a criminal attorney. He also teaches in the university. Bill is the one who bought me the chair that saved my back. Over the years, Bill came to Good Samaritan once in awhile. I knew Bill loved his dog. We talked about his dog a lot when Bill's dog died.

Jerry and I decided to have Bill and his wife, Vickie, over for dinner. I knew he had a new dog, and I said, "Bill, you must bring your dog to dinner." His dog's name is Chance. He is a very large white poodle with lots of energy.

Now, this afternoon, Bill called me and said, "I'd like to bring Chance over to spend time with Jerry." Bill and Jerry walked down the street with Chance. Jerry got to hold the leash. Bill knew that Jerry lost his dog, so he and Jerry shared Chance.

The stories in this ministry are simple stories. They are stories of an ever-widening circle of influence. Samaritans are servants of the church. We are not instead of the church, we are servants.

When I went to Africa, I saw that everyday the women went out to dig and hoe in the fields, and if they didn't, the family would not eat. When I came home, I brought a digging tool and hung it on my office wall. I said, "We are diggers. We're not evangelists. We're not a church. We're cultivators of the soil. We cultivate the soil in human lives every day."

"We want people to know Jesus. When the seeds are planted, they can bear everlasting fruit in the generations that lie ahead."

Saints Peter, Paul, and John are still part of our lives. Although they lived over 2,000 years ago, they are part of our stories too, part of our generation.

And so, we too must go out into the fields and do the hard work, digging in soil. Digging is sweat on the brow. It's a desperate work for the family to eat. Without digging, Christianity is choked out and we become less than conquerors, rather than more than conquerors in Christ Jesus our Lord.

CHAPTER 29

The Generations Of Our Family

Grandma Costin died at 92 of a stroke. She had some dementia, but a lot of presence through her final illness. When she slipped into a coma, my mother and I visited her at the nursing home. I put a small New Testament in her hand. She turned the pages, and stopped. I took the small Bible and read it to her on that page. I then put it back in her hand. Again, she would thumb through the pages and stop. Again, I read to her what was on that page. This went on until we could truly see what the Bible had meant to her. In my experience with her as a child, she read her Bible every day. The last thing she did before she slipped away to heaven was read her Bible.

The death of my mother in 1986 came very hard for her. She spent a long period of time with Alzheimer's, but there was something inside of her that was always alert; a knowing beyond the disease. I was worried because she was having death rattles and it had gone on for a week.

You will be shocked, but Jerry and I went to the beach. When we got there, I got out of the car, and cried out to God for his mercy in helping her go home. Soon, I had a phone call that she was approaching death and we hurried home two hours after we arrived at the coast.

For the next hours, I stayed in my mother's presence, snoozing now and then, but fully awake and alert to her struggling to go home to be with the Lord. It seemed that the struggle would not end, so I took out my Bible, opened it to the book of Revelation, and read her the last two chapters. After I finished the final words of Revelation, "May the grace of the Lord Jesus be with you all. Amen," at that very moment, my mother died.

The generations of our family have been profoundly influenced by the living word of God. It was never about Bible study or Bible reading. It was about Bible knowing, a knowing too deep for words that my grandmother and my mother each revealed at the hour of their death.

Jerry and I raised three daughters. The oldest one, Michelle, was six when Laura was born. Laura was three when Jennie was born.

We were an inclusive family, together, seeking the times and adventures of real life living. We worked together with a lot of accord. It was my personal goal that each of the children would be raised as individuals, they would be seen as individuals, their needs would be met as individuals, and God would be the primary source for each of their lives.

Laura was a spontaneous child. She never learned to walk, she only learned to run. She had an extraordinary giftedness and a passion for embracing life.

When Laura was seven years old, we were at our church in Beaverton. She was not sitting with us; she was sitting with our Chinese director of Christian education. Later that day, I was washing windows when Laura said she wanted to tell me something.

I sat down immediately and listened to her story.

There was a large wooden cross, at the back of the altar, on the front wall in our church. Laura said that as she was looking at that cross, she saw the feet of Jesus first, and then she looked up and she saw His whole body. Then Jesus said to her, "Now that you've seen me, you will always know me." I asked her to tell me this story twice. I wrote down everything she said and put it away. It has given me the greatest comfort to know that no matter what Laura has gone through, she will always know Jesus, and He will always know her.

Years later, as Laura was riding the donkey in the Palm Sunday Procession in Jerusalem, she picked up a four year-old girl. As they were riding into Jerusalem, and about to enter St. Stephen's Gate, the little girl began to cry. Laura asked, "What's the matter?" The little girl said, "They don't know Jesus."

Satan had a perfect plan to cause our family grief. His goal was to distract me by what our children and family would go through and, thus break me away from the "Call." Satan's plan was to cause each of us to destabilize. His plan was to cause two of our children massive difficulty in their marriages, difficulties that were so serious that we shook our heads and did not know what to do. I could have stayed awake every night all night and had no peace if I had let these problems control me. In my grief, I found my peace. The family and the work of Christ continued. I put the children and their problems in the Lord's hands. I was not avoiding what I was to do. I was to firmly keep their lives in my absolute trust that the Lord would see them through.

Michelle, our oldest daughter, was sensitive and as a child she had a whining problem. She was the most difficult birth the doctor ever performed. She struggled to fit in, but she always managed to do it. She significantly helped with the other children, and she really tried hard to do well in her life. Michelle went to secretarial school for one year when she finished high school. She found her first permanent job. She decided to join the Nazarene Church and make her own way in her Christian walk. She attended church regularly, and she joined the volleyball team.

At 19, while she was playing volleyball at the church, a man came onto the church property and connected with her. He was five years older than she was, very emotional, and terribly insecure. He was a threat and a danger to her, and I was very terrified when she began to date him. Very quickly, he had absolute control over her. As I was talking hard to her about getting out of the relationship, at the same time, that particular day, she and Larry were eloping. A few hours later, Michelle called and said she was married. This marriage led to 19 years of severe abuse, and two troubled children. Yet, Michelle was determined to stay the course and do what she could to do what was right.

After the 19 years, she gave up, left the marriage, and later married Gary. She healed from what had happened to her. She found peace and strength. She found her life. She is a woman who gives. She has overcome great obstacles and pain.

Laura was always racey. She sought adventure, and sometimes found it in danger. She was a child that was a great joy and a great worry. The day she graduated from high school, when she was 18 years old, she insisted to be married in a church wedding. She made her own satin wedding dress which cost $25. She married Mark, who was a drug addict and an alcoholic. She believed she could change him. He had a good heart, but he was a sociopath, and the years that would lie ahead for Laura were extremely tough and dangerous.

Many days I was not sure if Laura would be dead or somewhere in jail. I knew she was struggling almost to her death to bring the relationship through. After three years, she had April. She divorced Mark and then remarried him. With that remarriage, she had Melissa. Mark had changed not at all. In fact, the situation became desperately worse. The danger to the children was profound. Finally, Laura finished the final divorce, gathered her faith, and went with me to Jerusalem. She carried that little girl on the donkey in the Palm Sunday Procession. Laura has always taken the hard road, but I want to say adamantly, it has always led to life. Her ex-husband, Mark, spent 12 years in federal penitentiary for drugs and bank robbery.

We grieved much. We could have hidden it. We could have said, "Oh well," but we all faced it, and we faced all of it together as a family. The children were not less than we were. The children were as we were. We were a balanced team who looked for ways to help one another.

As our youngest daughter, Jennie, saw the difficulties of her older sister, and as she had achieved so well in high school, she decided to go to Oregon State University, where she majored in Manufacturing Engineering. She finished college, moved to New Mexico, and found her first engineering job. She was engaged to a high school track friend, Chris. He was finishing dental school. They saw each other once a month either here or in New Mexico. After a year and a half, Jennie moved back to this area. She was able to get a good job. She and Chris were married. Although later they divorced, they remain friends today.

When Jennie was about seven, I took her to the Bible, opened it, and said, "I want to teach you the most important scripture in the Bible." That scripture was Exodus 3:14, "God said to Moses, 'I am who I am." I explained this was the Name of God.

When Jennie was eight and nine years old, I was teaching a two-year complete Bible course at our church. For two years, she experienced the entire course, Old and New Testament. I can remember so well that she would periodically walk around the room. She was the only child in the class. She was listening, and she was to be there. It is part of who she is and the call on her life today.

When she was nine years old, someone I knew, whom she did not know, died. The woman was a young mother that died of cancer. I took Jennie to the mortuary. We sat in the room with the body. I taught her about death, and then we touched the woman's body. I explained the woman was no longer in the body. I had seen her spirit leave. Jennie has never had a fear of death since then, for we faced the fear and death was conquered.

We raised our three girls to be independent and interdependent. They never turned their backs on the family. They learned through their experiences what was right and good. Gradually, they each came to know what was permanently valuable.

Jerry and I struggled hard with personal anger issues. Jerry and I do not waste any time now with anger. Sometimes we feel frustrated, but anger is a waste of time. It does not bear fruit. It makes you dwell in self-pity, and it certainly never was a help to the girls. These young women each had their own struggles. They carried ahead the generations of our family. Those generations have strengthened their generation.

We did not turn our backs on our son-in-laws. We set out to know them, understand them, and respect their struggles. Sometimes they would break and talk. We visited Mark several times while he was in jail. I wrote several letters to him. His mind was consumed as a child is, and unreachable. In the spiritual realm, only God can reach him.

Jennie spent 20 years as an engineer. She was a team leader of engineers, and, for a time, the President of the Engineers Association for the State of Oregon.

Jennie took me to North Vietnam. This was a journey of my heart to honor the many Vietnam veterans I worked with over the years. When I retired, the veterans gave me an encased American flag. The inscription read: "Presented to Bettie P. Mitchell, from the Veterans of the U.S. Military and Public Service and their Loved Ones." I cherish this honor.

When Jennie married Tom Havey, they stood on Tom's family marriage rug. His parents and we stood up with them. Honoring

Christ and family are cherished themes in their home.

After Jennie's divorce, and when her heart was torn in pain, Jerry and I bought a special purity ring and placed it on her finger. Later, before they were married, she gave Tom one as well. I would highly recommend this to all parents. It has brought Tom and Jennie joy and miracles.

One day I asked her if she would be willing to train to take over my work. It was really not my work anyway. She was to take over "The Call." I helped her understand that it was "The Call" she would have to keep, and "The Call" would have to keep her. She pondered this deeply as it felt overwhelming to her. She wanted to be herself, not me. I upheld her that she was right, "You must be yourself and 'The Call' must be yours."

Jennie has trained hard. She has learned painful lessons. She has come into the fullness of the ministry. At my retirement, she was named for this work. She is empowered by the Power of Forgiveness.

Laura is always creative, and sometimes she has the most wonderful ideas. One day she called me and said, "Mom, I think you need to put the slides of Nineveh into large photographs, because people need to know and see what this Call is." Surely she was right. I immediately saw to this being done, and the fruit of that decision has been incredible. No matter where I go with slides, a DVD, or the pictures themselves, others can see the pictures taken the day of "The Call" in 1976. Here are the children on the walls of Nineveh. Here is the child at Irbil. "The Call" has become an echo through the generations. It will be heard by generations to come. It was received as sacred. It is held sacred by our generations, and this responsibility is shared with your generations.

When April and Melissa were young, Jerry and I took a special interest in their lives. They were dealing with the tragedy of their father, Mark, and their losses were profound. We became the ones who kept their lives. We treated them in a way that developed them. We held them to God's purposes for their lives. We travelled often with April and Melissa. We took them each overseas. It was extraordinarily important for Jerry and myself to be there for them.

When she was four years old, I asked April to lead Wednesday group therapy at Good Samaritan Ministries. Can you believe that? The goal was for the people in the group to learn the meaning of having the faith of a child. April was put in the middle of the group and she was responsible for what was to happen. She managed this for almost two hours, and we saw the faith of a child in action. April went with me twice to Africa. Once when she was 11, and again when she was 15 years old. When she was 11, she gave our team's closing speech in Uganda. Although we had a team of eight or nine, we all agreed she gave the greatest speech. From time to time, she worked at the front desk at Good Samaritan Ministries.

April graduated from Linfield College. This was a major achievement as she spent seven years as a drug addict. During this period of time, she became more and more addicted to severe drug use. She saw the whole drug world and experienced all of it. Did we give up? Did we shake our heads? Did we feel bad? We knew that God was with us. Knowing this empowers His goodness and mercy to prevail over all darkness and evil.

April's recovery from drug use was long and hard. She went to two treatment programs, but then something inside clicked and her faith began to move the mountains. When she was in recovery from addiction, she met a man with whom she had gone to high school, Mike Ashmon. She and Mike fell in love. They have a very special relationship. He said, "April, because of your problems with addiction, I will never drink." There is something really special about this. They work together for the common good of the family as a whole.

Today, April and Mike have two year-old Gabriella. April has opened a shop in Lincoln City on Highway 101. It is a resale shop, selling baby and children's clothing and furniture from birth to five years of age. The shop has been successful. We can see April's time at Linfield College bore dividends in her decision-making and life direction when she was free of drugs.

Melissa was always close to Grandpa Jerry. He was her special friend. After Melissa was grown, when Jerry was ill and in the hospital, she came 100 miles to spend the night with him in the hospital. She said she couldn't leave him. Jerry often took care of the little children. Particularly, he did so when I took Laura to the Holy Land to recover from the horror of her time with Mark. On this journey, Laura was given the grace of God, an outpouring of His knowing of her. This journey changed her whole life to live with empowered faith. She would desperately need that faith every single day.

Amanda and part of her family went with us to Egypt and Israel when she was ten. Amanda, the third daughter of Laura and Kerry, has become a horse woman. Since she was 11 years old, she has been buying and selling horses, and working at horse jobs and at fairs. Currently, she works at Government Camp during part of the year. She gives sleigh rides in the winter, and horseback rides in the summer. Her business is really important to her. She loves meeting people from all over the world.

Kerry Ann is Kerry and Laura's youngest daughter. She is a child of great faith. When Kerry Ann was eight, she personally raised money to build a well in Uganda. She presented the gift at the 2002 International Conference. When she was 13, she went with me on a tour to Egypt and the Holy Land. We had a perfectly marvelous, remarkable time together. She is alive and alert in her heart and spirit to all that is happening around her. We walked our journey in faith. She was and is an inspiration to many.

Nic was Kerry's son. Out of high school, Nic joined the Marines and went to Iraq. He struggled to find himself, and now he is finding himself. He is in school to be a helicopter pilot.

In Laura's journey of faith, each of her children, through their individuality, their own story, their own events, and their own opportunities has learned and prospered from their experiences. Faith has won their hearts.

Michelle had two children. Steven was very troubled. He struggled with mental illness and severe addiction. He is sensitive and has a good heart. There came a day that Steven was so manipulative that I said something to him that, again, will probably be a shock to you. It was Thanksgiving. I said, "Steven, I will never give you money again as long as you live, not even if you have cancer of the eyeball." Two months later he called and asked for some money. I said the same thing again. I further said, "Stephen, I will not talk to you for five years." Now, this seems harsh and rejective, but I tell you truthfully, I did not talk to him for three years. Now, he never manipulates us, and he has respect for us. He is clean and sober. He is going to school, and he is finding his road.

Michelle's daughter, Jennye, is very gifted. Again, I took her on a journey to the Middle East, and helped her with the spiritual problems and pain she was going through from all her family had suffered. Jennye has found her road of faith. She has graduated from college. She is working as an interior designer and real estate agent. She married Peter, who is a Portland Policeman, and a Major in the National Guard. They each went to New Orleans and helped after the hurricane. Peter went to Iraq. When Peter was in Iraq, Jennye took responsibility for the care and overseeing of the platoon's family members.

When Mohammad joined our family, we were whole and complete. He became a family member truly from his heart. We have the same way of faith with each of our generational members. We believe in their freedom, their exploration, and their interdependence among the family as a whole.

Mohammad and his wife, Diane, are remarkable parents. I can always hear our daughter-in-law say in these words to each of her children, "Gentle, be gentle."

Our grandson, Gabriel, is in eighth grade. Our granddaughter, Sarah, is ten.

As our two great-grandchildren, Dominique and Gabriella are growing, it is our vision and imperative for the scripture to develop their faith in action. By our faith, our whole family will be saved.

In all seasons and in all times, Jerry and I keep the generations of the past and the generations of the future. I baptized my husband, and we baptized my parents, three of our children, and five of our grandchildren in the Jordan River.

This family has never been exclusive, but inclusive. The doors are kept open. Radical hospitality continues. The trials we have experienced have brought the fruits of the spirit in each of our lives.

And so, not only the generations of this family, but the generations of the world, are part of the divine inclusive story of Jesus spreading His arms to give forgiveness to all of us.

Going back to the scripture I read to my mother in Revelations 22:17, "The Spirit and the Bride say come. Let everyone who listens answer. Come and let all who are thirsty come. All who want it may have the water of life and have it free."

CHAPTER 30

Only As You Are Willing
To Lose Your Life

And now a man came to him and asked, 'Master, what good deed must I do to possess eternal life?' Jesus said to him, '*Why do you ask me about what is good? There is one alone who is good. But if you wish to enter into life, keep the commandments.*'" (Matthew 19:16-17)

Losing your life is losing your selfishness. We must find our true selves.

I was adequately selfish. I have not completely recovered from selfishness. You could never describe me as sweet, or such a loving and gentle person. These, perhaps, are the attributes of saints. I am a lusty, sometimes outspoken, clear and direct person in all of my communication. The key to my life is not what I want, but what my neighbor needs from me!

Nice and good are words we struggle to overcome. They may have played a significant part in our childhood instruction. Now, my favorite words are naughty and bad. Naughty is a very good word. It describes someone who is full of life and not afraid to be themselves. Bad is more deliberate, deeper cutting, and not in favor of others, but mostly in favor of their own opinion. I use the words when they are needed. I often laugh when I say them. It gets the point across.

Dying to self, putting away selfish instincts and the long list of selfish desires is not an easy task. I found there had to be an incredibly important reason to give up my selfish nature, and begin to develop a life of patience.

Many years ago, I decided the hardest scripture in the Bible was: *"But I say this to you, love your enemies and pray for those who persecute you; so that you may be children of your Father in heaven, for he causes his sun to rise on the bad as well as the good, and sends down rain to fall on the upright and the wicked alike."* (Matthew 5:44) I set out on a journey to train in that scripture for ten years. I did not look for another scripture. In all seasons, I looked inside myself for the action of that one command. I had begun radical training.

First, I began to love what I hated. I would not try to love radically, but I radically chose to love what I did not like, indeed, what I often hated.

You might laugh, as I started with foods I didn't like, my menstrual periods, rain, circumstances that annoyed me. I stayed outside the realm of people for awhile. Choosing to radically love these things first, I began to change the way I used my life. My personality was slowly transforming.

I chose to radically love all seasons, preferring none, but seeing the grace and beauty in all of them.

When I was a substitute teacher, I was working hard on this assignment. On the way to school, I would get ready, choosing this radical life of empowering love.

Now there is something strange about my years as a substitute teacher. All of the shop teachers in the school district wanted me to teach for them when they were away. Why was this? How could that be, since I did not know how to use the simplest tool, or turn on any of the machines (let alone turn them off)? Why would any of the shop teachers not want to leave their classes unless I took them?

I could have taken this as a compliment, but instead it was

something I did not like to do at all. Generally, there were three or four rooms with cement floors, machines running all day, things going on that I couldn't quite put my finger on, and a lot of walking around, I had to do. There was a general atmosphere of stress. Why would they choose me?

I know one of the reasons is I radically chose to love teaching shop. If I had to teach shop two to three days a week, the subject I was least prepared for, and least wanted to teach, had to radically love teaching shop! There were life-changing surprises happening inside of me, as I walked the floors of those school shops.

I remember the day I went into a shop and put on one of the shop teacher's long coveralls. I rolled up the sleeves, rolled up the legs, and walked around all day. Loving lifted my heart, it lifted my life, it lifted me out of that selfish, "I like some people, but I don't like others."

Early in teaching and in the ministry, I learned to prefer no one. For in preferring one over another, I was not fair.

Radical me produces very little fruit. It can be the screaming me me's. It may involve anger, disappointment, resentment, and a whole lot of trash in the spirit. I could usually get what I wanted, but I couldn't enjoy it, because somewhere, deep inside me, I knew it wasn't right.

The whole of me learned how unimportant I am. My significance is that I'm human and that I live with the humans of this world. We were created to be together in this, our time. I learned that significance would not be forced in being more important, most important, great leader, or best teacher. The most significant thing about me is that I understand the meaning of Jesus saying, "In the least, I am."

I stopped comparing myself to others, looking around to see if I fit in, or trying to find social acceptability. In losing yourself, you don't find it so important to find yourself. There is more time for laughter, more time for inner peace, and a ton less argument.

One day I decided I would dive off the diving board at the Beaverton Swimming Pool. It is one of the things that I liked the least as a child, getting water in my ears and pressure in my head. It was a bad memory from my childhood. At that moment, I can remember standing on that diving board, then a woman in her 50s, looking down and preparing to make that dive. It took me a long time. I did it! Do I do it again and again? No. When I did it once, I did it always.

Oh, how I hated mice!! I would look face to face with them in the unexpected places where they showed up.

One day we were in a car coming from South Central Oregon towards home. Suddenly, I looked down at my feet, as we were driving along, and there was a mouse looking at me! Of course, I freaked out! My husband stopped the car. I got in the back seat and put my feet up on the seat. Of course, I put our daughter, Jennie in the front seat armed with a stick.

Now, while I was sitting there, I realized that I had to love that mouse. So, I began to think about that mouse in a different way. As I closed my eyes and thought about that mouse, I understood that creature better. In my mind's eye I could touch that mouse, I talked to that mouse, and we became friends with each other. I was dying to self and joining the whole creation.

I hated Mother's Day. Which mother was to be honored? I was the one with all the little children. Then, there was my mother and grandmother confusion. Yet, I hated having no Mother's Day even worse. I hated it when my husband didn't really say, "Happy Mother's Day," or acknowledge me as a mother and a woman.

Then, I decided to radically love my enemy. If my enemy was Mother's Day, then I would radically love it and radically change its purpose and meaning forever. I decided to cook a great family dinner, and to even have nametags at everybody's place at the table. I decided to give each person in the family a gift. I gathered all of the family slides I had taken over the years, and arranged them by concepts. We looked at the slides at the dinner table so no one could scatter or leave.

Now, it took so long to watch the pictures because I had every person at the table talk about and honor the pictures of the individuals. Our first concept was that family is made up of very significant individuals. Then we all saw three or four individual slides of each family member. The stories and purposes of the family were remembered. We went through a whole box of tissue. There were many tears, many healings, and the greatest Mother's Day became all of the Mother's Days. It was finished!

Expectations are dangerous. We set up in our mind what we expect to happen, and feelings are hurt if it doesn't happen. Expectations, perhaps, in a subtle way, are the most dangerous of all spiritual attacks. You see it seems so natural and normal to expect certain things.

Very slowly, I learned to accept whatever state I was in, to be content, and to receive what each day brought as the school of God's lessons.

It did not happen all at once, and I still feel attacks from time to time. Each season of life has its hardships, and in those hardships, we can get very uptight. Suddenly, knowing a better way does not necessarily produce doing things that better way. This is why the Holy Spirit is our teacher and teaches us all things. Don't ever expect the Holy Spirit to stop being your teacher. You will not graduate, you will not finish. You will be taught day by day that selfless love, unselfish living, leads your life to the surprises of God and His praises that will come to your heart.

As a teacher and as a counselor, I have been outspoken. I never find an individual or a group of people to criticize, for I share with them their human burdens. It is something "we" do together, this life. Never think you are alone. We are doing life together, and this life will produce greater togetherness in the time above.

I use colorful language and expressions. This may startle the hearer, the words remain as a warning and a healing. I love colorful language and parables.

Part of me likes swearing because it releases emotions that so desperately need to be. Then I cry out "Father," and immediately my broken heart receives His true tenderness. I am freed from the frustrations and pain I experienced without ceasing the cross of this ministry.

God said I was chosen. He never said I was chosen to be good, to be nice, or to be perfect. I was chosen to learn, to grow, and to participate in the mercies of God throughout the world.

The Word says train hard spiritually. I've often laughed and wondered what that meant. I've often wondered, "What do people do to train hard spiritually?" How hard do I train? How hard do they train? Do we train differently? These are interesting questions. Do we train hard in scriptures we don't like?

"And if anyone requires you to go one mile, go two miles with him." (Matthew 5:41) That reminds me of my husband's 40th birthday. We went on our first back-packing trip up, up, up a cliff in the Columbia River Gorge. Our journey was all of three miles. Jerry packed at least 60 pounds in his pack, trying to provide for every eventuality, and we set out. This was my gift to him for his 40th birthday. Trust me, it was selfless love. I did it, not because I wanted to, and certainly not because I could do it. I want to say quite frankly and honestly, I could not do it, so I did what I could not do!

The first night we camped high up and there was snow. As the Boy Scouts were having a camping experience practically right next to us, we found it very tough for the two of us to stay in a plastic tube tent wide enough for one person.

The next morning, when we came back down and headed for the car, I suddenly collapsed. Even to this day, my husband and I laugh about this. I had gone as far as I could go.

This adventure, this unselfishness led to a backpacking trip around Mt. Hood that lasted four days. It about killed both of us, but out of it came a great adventure. We met an old man with a truck who drove us back up to Mt. Hood. His motor wouldn't start. I laid hands on his motor and his truck made it back up to Timberline.

I'm not particularly drawn to sharing. It doesn't thrill me to share. It isn't something I easily comprehend or do. Being raised an only child for much of my childhood, and having few times when sharing was part of my development, it seemed to be a missing piece. Sometimes I would share if the portions were equal, but I had to learn to give my whole portion to someone else. I had to learn what is fair is not what is divine. Jesus gave His whole life for us. Giving part is as if we were giving none.

Many people say to me, "How do you like retirement?" I would say, "I love it!" It is a new season. It is closer to the time of going to heaven. It is a better training time because I'm not so rushed with the needs of others, but can take time to be trained again. It provides me choices whereas for many years, I had almost none. It provides me quality time with my husband, and usually, we appreciate that.

Retirement is a season, and I radically love all of the seasons. Forgiveness is one of the most powerful forces on earth. We are always trying to forgive. We tend to think that in trying to forgive, it is too much, too big a struggle. We don't know whether we want to forgive, so we analyze for another five months. In another year, and then another two years, and then after awhile, we forget that forgiveness is the issue.

> "*Forgiveness is not a dripping faucet.*
> *Forgiveness is a gushing flow of living water.*"
> ~Bettie Mitchell

I've had enough of drippy faucet forgiving. Do you like a dripping faucet that has to be repaired? Is it something that never annoys you and always feels like the right sound? Why are we so often choosing forgiveness that is so limited in its scope and so poorly crucified to Christ?

One of my favorite scriptures is from the Apostle Paul, "*I have been crucified to Christ and yet I am alive; yet it is no longer I, but Christ living in me.*" (Galatians 2:20)

Selfless love does not make you a non-person. If Christ is living in you, you are a new person, and you overflow with living water. I say again unto you: Forgiveness is not a dripping faucet. Forgiveness is a gushing flow of living water.

I have spent much of my lifetime listening to others complain, not to mention listening to my own complaints. If it is not one complaint, it is many. Complaining has its own scripts and tends to continue once it gets started. What are we complaining about? What is it that we have to complain about that is more urgent than the gushing flow of living water?

As I come to the end of this book, I have finished what I have to say. I have spent this time with all of you. I have also spent this time to see you, hear you, and ponder your life and struggles. We are each challenged to become whole!

I wish so much you would write your stories. I would read them — eagerly. I have learned from you! The Holy Spirit has often spoken through your lives. I wish so much I could learn more from you.

What will you read again in this book? What will you remember the most? What will be your spiritual training? Is the Holy Spirit your teacher too?

Many came to Jesus and stopped right there. They do not know that Jesus came to us!

Amen, so be it! Our lives make a difference to God Himself. Whether you write a sentence, a letter, or a book, you are writing your part of the history of the world.

Jesus said, "*Father, Your Kingdom come, Your will be done, on earth as it is in heaven.*" (Matthew 6:10) We will freely speak. The Lord is listening. Amen, so be it!

APPENDIX

APPENDIX I

CONCEPTS TAUGHT AT A MITCHELL MOTHER'S DAY FAMILY EVENT

CONCEPT 1: The Family is made up of very important people. Show slides of each individual family member separately.

CONCEPT 2: Important people stand behind each family. Show friends and relatives that have added strength to your family.

CONCEPT 3: Families extend and grow in many directions, and each new group adds quality to our lives. This group can include in-laws, marriages that have been added, and pets of the family over the years.

CONCEPT 4: This family is very large. Anyone can be included who wants to be. Pictures of all of the people your family has included over the years.

CONCEPT 5: The family learns from each other. Show slides of family members in learning interaction.

CONCEPT 6: The family needs each other to lean on. Show slides that show the interaction of love and faith in one another.

CONCEPT 7: Eating isn't a big deal, but we've had some great meals together. Food pictures from feeding the baby to the family holiday dinner.

CONCEPT 8: Some of us sleep more than we need to—some of us sleep only when there is nothing else to do—and some of us can hardly sleep at all. Show those great sleep pictures.

CONCEPT 9: Childhood is happy! Childhood is sad! Show and tell about the truths of your children's childhood.

CONCEPT 10: Santa Never Lost His Magic for this Family. The tree before the gifts are open and other Santa stories.

CONCEPT 11: Our happiest times are when we are giving. Show not only the giving of presents, but pictures when you knew the giving came hard in your family.

CONCEPT 12: Dressing up has always been a big deal around us! Party dress, Easter clothes, and Halloween make a fun and contrasting concept grow.

CONCEPT 13: MOM AND DAD. Three Little Girls That Love Each Other. Show interrelations of love in your family that make you a family.

CONCEPT 14: There's nothing we won't try once. Picking up snakes to climbing a mountain can be an exciting concept for life.

CONCEPT 15: We can Be Tough and Take It on the Chin. Show pictures that remind of family hard times, and individual suffering and growth.

CONCEPT 16: We love the Lord. Show slides of spiritual growth from a naked baby, a pregnant mother, an Easter Sunday—this category can grow and grow.

APPENDIX II

WORDS FROM THE TEACHINGS

CHRISTMAS

"Only God can make Christmas good."

"God chooses to spend Christmas with us if we let Him."

"To be allowed to do anything at Christmas is a great gift from God. The true gift is God with us."

CHURCH

"Church means the called, the chosen."

"We tend to go to church and listen to the pastor, but we take little action."

"Are we listening in church with our action ears?"

"When we go to church, we go with every Christian around the world."

"He wants the church bonded all over the world."

"Baptism is about you, not about water."

"The root of the number one sickness in the church is we don't know Jesus. We know about Jesus, but we don't know Him."

COMMUNICATION

"When you seek the last word, it's your pride and ego. And, it ruins the conversation."

"The Spirit of God has to have the last word."

"It's hard to listen to our own spirit while we talk and discern."

"Look into the eyes of our fellow man."

"Three-way communication: when you are fully aware that God is part of the communication. Our challenge is to live in three-way communication."

"Christians have a responsibility to speak to the insides of people."

"Don't be afraid to pray with others. It's the Presence of the Lord that heals."

"Sometimes, agree with your adversary, and laugh a little."

"We are learning not to break communication through stupidity."

"When people ask, they tend to ask for less than they need."

"Asking is humbling."
"We talk about Jesus, but do we walk in His name?"
"Meet with a man with a possible solution, and he will listen. Meet with a man about your emotional problem, and he won't listen."
"Why questions are whiney manipulations."
"Most people's voices are never heard."
"Denial doesn't listen."

COMMUNION
"How do we get communion inside of us? We bring our human cross to the table, and leave the table with Christ's Cross."
"As you go to the table, remember, you are changing crosses."
"Our lives are to receive communion from three tables: the one in the room, the group table, and the world table."

ETHICS
"Every time you open your mouth, your ethics show. "

FAITH
"We tend to walk with a small amount of faith we use every day."
"Crisis demands empowering faith."
"We have to use our faith for it to increase."
"Faith has to do with what you say and who you say it to."
"Faith is personal. You can't have another person's faith."
"Faith, love and obedience are keys to faith."
"We must have intense love for God and others. Intense in Greek means boiling."
"My declaration of faith: I choose to believe that God Himself and what He chooses to provide at this moment is all I need. I am complete in Christ."
"You have to walk in the Faith every step."
"When you stop having faith in someone, you leave them open, and naked, and exposed."

340

"We need to be Mother to the whole world. If our child was killed, we would scream and cry out. But, we don't when others die."

"Can you operate on your faith and not on the reactions of those around you?"

"Indecision will shut down the faithing system."

"Hang on to the little miracles, especially when you are upset."

"You have the angry floor, the sin floor. As you go down to the bottom, you will find the faith of a little child."

FAMILY

"In families, we often give so much importance to some members, and so little to others."

"Men are the head, women the heart."

"A Mother and the unborn child deeply know one another."

"The baby is always aware of the safety of the Mother."

"God says, "Honor your parents so it will go well for you." If we are going to honor God, we must honor the parents He chose for us."

"The first five commandments are about God, Mom and Dad."

"Man gave a sperm. Mom gave an egg. God gave the soul."

"The honor commandment is for all children, not the parents."

"You need to honor even the worst parents, because you need to know how to honor."

"Honoring is like a union: it's continuing, never ending."

"When the family begins to fall apart, stand powerfully for them."

"All of Satan's forces are at work to divide the family."

"Never stop believing in your family."

FORGIVENESS

"People are not forgiving us, because we didn't take God's forgiveness seriously."

"Beg God to feel His forgiveness, and then His forgiveness will

become your life."
"There is no human justice until we walk in divine justice."
"When we say, "I can forgive you, but I can't forget" that is deep bitterness growing in our soul."
"Forgiveness has to be working within us all the time, a well that never runs dry."

GIVING
"All of your needs can be met by giving."
"God is searching for the true giver."
"We want to check up on the result of giving, instead of going on to the next giving."
"We want thanks. We have to give up wanting thanks, and continue to give willingly."
"A big giver with a big mouth is a big disease."
"Measure what you give against what God gave."
"Be eternally useful."
"Always consider the needs of others to be more important than your own. This is about needs, not wants."

GOD ALLOWS
"What God allows is God's business. His plan is the perfect plan."
"Jesus makes Satan look insignificant."

GSM = THE SAMARITAN LIFE
"An organization is not a position, but a responsibility."
"We get courage from learning about each other's crosses."
"God inspires us as we plan."
"The only two things that defeat sin are love and mercy."
"We do weak Kingdom work, if we do it in our own name."
"The Kingdom of God is throughout the Universe."
"The work is done by the least in the Kingdom of God. Jesus said, "In the least, I am.""

"In the parable of the Good Samaritan, actions speak louder than words. Do not argue. Talk little. Give much."
"Look for opportunities for actions. Every time our mouth gets big, we get into trouble."
"Never check-up on your money once you've given it."
"There are not enough Samaritans to accomplish the work needed."
"Be much bigger than resentment."
"If we are passive, we don't win the war."
"Encouragement is the key to others making it."
"Allow God to develop your international citizenship."
"If we feel guilty, the lights go out. And, we get rapid brain."
"As a Samaritan, develop yourself to aid others."
"Don't ask to be blessed. For, you are already blessed."
"Ask God how you can help. Don't look for a quick, easy or convenient answer."

GUILT
"There is no time for guilt. None."
"Guilt is unproductive energy."
"People who sit in guilt, accomplish nothing."
"Guilt creates selfish thinking."
"GUILT IS SELF-CENTEREDNESS."
"Guilt is a life without action to change."

HOLINESS
"You are holy. God made you."
"We must have the faith of a little child. They haven't heard of religion."
"Practical holiness: Leviticus 19:2."
"The exact opposite of practical holiness is self-consciousness."
"All ground is holy if we walk on it."
"God is always aware of us. It is for us to learn, to be aware of Him."
"God feeds, clothes, shelters us and sends protecting angels to

care for us."

"Eventually, we'll lie down, stand, and sit in holiness"

"As we walk in holiness, the protection around us will become greater and greater."

"Holiness empowers the actions of God in your life."

"Let our first words be, when we enter a house, "Peace be upon this house.""

"Our labor is being guests in people's houses. Say, "The Kingdom of God is very near to you.""

"The holy sites are the homes of the people."

"The most horrible thing we can bring into a house is prejudice."

"It is the genuine hospitality of guests that brings changes to this world."

"Jesus chose to be a guest among men. All of His actions say this."

HOSPITALITY

"Fill us with the hospitality of Heaven."

KINGDOM OF GOD

"There are no days off in the Kingdom of God." This is my most repeated lesson, and I have said it often. While many interpret it to mean we must constantly be working, that's not what this is about. It is about not sneaking off and doing your own thing away from the Kingdom of God.

"You can't live in two kingdoms: your own, and God's."

"Your spirit is ageless. Stop thinking about how old you are!"

"We have to pass THROUGH death...not TO death."

"The only important time is one day at a time. Anymore, and you go into anxiety."

"In the Spirit you have power. In the emotions you have no power."

"Never take things personally."

"We need a total change in the system. We must die to the

flesh. We need to prepare to get rid of the sin."
"God gives us circumstances to humble our spirit."
"Give up the fear of man. Give up giving this fear too much power."
"He talks to the lowly and the meek. God wants you, not the pretender."
"Think like from Heaven, not from our small plot."
"Hear yourself breathe. Through the breath, He connects us to Himself."

MARRIAGE

"Power struggle: Are we over, under, or balanced in power with our mates?"
"Your marriage loses its balance when one person quits."
"Marriage is always difficult. You have two sinners wanting their own way."
"Women need understanding and trust. They need to be chosen."
"Women's hearts are based on the husband's integrity."
"We have to start every day with a clean sheet of paper. Forgiveness from the past must be completed. Marriage is not a dirty sheet."
"Key word in a marriage: You will always be more important to me, than what you did wrong."

MONEY

Jesus fed people food and words.
Jesus knew man loves money more than God.
Does our security come from money, or does it come from God?
Money temporarily makes us feel safe.
Jesus took money away from his followers.
"All that I have is for the common good of our fellow man."
"Getting in to other people's business is meddling. Ask their permission, but FIRST, take the plank out of your own eye."
"There is a fine line between being helpful and meddling. Ask

yourself, "What am I getting out of this?""
"Be courageous, correctly."
"Sow not seeds in anger, but sow them in love."
"You have to have a final decision, and don't go back over it. This leads to double-mindedness."

OURSELVES

"We struggle with a terrible weakness…OURSELVES!"
"We do very little pouring oil and wine on people, and too much praising God. We must take pity action in His Name."
"Mostly, we pity ourselves. We're angry that no one else pities us."
"Satan uses our brain like a dartboard."
"We can't be washy wishy."
"Evil is to be confronted and defeated."
"We are addicted to appeasement. It takes a lot of study to look at this."
"Appeasement is not turning the other cheek."
"You can't be successful in a victim attitude."
"God gives us peace deep down. Don't let anyone take it away from you. Choose PEACE, not fear."
"Every minute of the day say, "Father, I trust you" no matter what's going on."
"If we are really a Christian, not playing one, it will profoundly change us."
"Give through the Spirit to another human being."
"I stand for freedom in giving. God taught me to do it."
"Giving in will kill any relationship it touches."
"If you are unteachable, this is sad to God."
"When we question and doubt, then we lose our peace."
"The attacks are in the if onlies. What happens next is fear and confusion come in.
"Doubts make us like a feather floating in the waves."
"Doubt can destroy quicker than anything."
"The only way to conquer pride is to stay needy."

"Our brains are always trying to con. We wander around saying we need to forgive ourselves."

"We often slam the God door with our inflexibility. This shuts down today."

"Self-pity is as bad as an alcoholic binge."

"You must know the battle will be won. The war is usually rooted in our selfishness."

"We have two memory systems: temporal and eternal."

"Our problems aren't healed by our self-image."

"Growth requires radical change and constant discomfort."

"Freewill is the attitude in which we do things."

"Learn to live love in the middle of all circumstances."

"Satan would like to keep you in the past."

"You can never be a reconciler if you don't like your enemies. Liking comes from a well deep within you."

"We are all longing for real friends...no watered down coffee."

"Before you sing, be sure the light is on in you."

"Anger kept shuts down any creative, possible thinking. Our first inclination is to go into impossible thinking."

"So much of what you want is what you are. What we crave and desire is what we are."

"Only in peace will I know what to do today and tomorrow."

"Avoidance methods: staying busy, going silent, hoping it will go away, arguing, giving up. We have to study ourselves moment by moment to see where we avoid."

"Don't have retirement mentality."

"People develop their own self-punishment."

"Doing something unique each day is healing. Create something good. We all have blemishes."

"Sometimes we have the habit of sorrow."

"All of us have certain harming in us."

"If we live in the past, it's like living in a haunted house. You can make no progress."

"You have eight minutes to change a negative thought. Cortisol develops in the brain and shuts down the immune system if

you don't."
"The heart has brain cells. We call this the Mind of the Heart. They are back-up systems in our bodies."
"We are responsible for our own feelings. Don't have someone else be responsible."
"You are responsible to take authority over yourself."

PRAYER

"Prayer is done at the hardest time, not the convenient time."
"Jesus lived a life of prayer. This is why people could touch Him and be healed."
"Always pray for yourself. The Spirit is deeper than your insane wants."
"Do I allow God to question me in prayer? Why are we afraid of His answers?"
"We tend to pick and choose. He wants to reach us."
"Before praying, you have to get ready to pray."
"Prayers are the most important conversations in our lives."
"Remember the fear of God is the beginning of prayer."
"We seem to spend a lot of time telling God what to do."
"Some pray for fifty years and just move their lips. God cares what they think."
"Often God is the one who starts the prayer."
"We can forget God, but God never forgets us."
"God hears our feelings and gives us back strength. He understands how we feel."
"If you are praying for something to happen and it doesn't, this sets you up for depression and problems. Every prayer answered does not have the outcome we want."
"Speak your thoughts to God, and He will change your mind."

REJECTION

"The hardest part of Spiritual Training are the words when all men hate and revile you."
"Be prepared, for when all men revile and reject you as Jesus

said, toughen up and become courageous."
"We are given rejection training. We want belonging training."
"Without rejection training, we can't fulfill the call on our life."
"We must defeat the need to be liked, so we can stand up when rejection comes."
"See rejection in our lives as training for our freedom. Then, justice can come."
"Rejection training is the hardest call for a human being to deal with. We want attention, not rejection training."
"God is preparing to give you something from Him after heavy rejection."

RELATIONSHIPS
"Defense mechanisms totally destroy a relationship."
"Find the humor in the impossible."
"An enabler gives weak assignments."

REMORSE
"Remorse is the area of doing nothing."
"Some of us are professional remorsers."

REPENTANCE
"Remorse is to feel sorry for yourself. It always turns inward. Remorse seems to turn to God, but it doesn't. God requires that we repent."
"Repentance is turning to God. The person also turns away from something that is displeasing to God. You can't fool God.... He knows we can turn."
"Repentance is accompanied by sorrow over your sin. If you don't have sorrow over your sin, you will not know the full reality of repentance."
"Face God face to face. No talking to yourself."
"It's a very grievous sin to be angry and let the sun set on it."
"The one who fights for repentance will have the greater

spiritual peace."
"We should be in constant repentance."
"We are each a chief among sinners."
"We want to take sin to the Cross without pain."
"Our most pressing concern: we need steadfast love, not hot and cold."
"Guilt torments a person. Repentance changes your attitude."

SACRIFICE
"A life of prayer is a life of sacrifice."
"Sacrifice your resentment."
"Most of our unhappiness is our lack of sacrifice."
"It's easier to sacrifice a lamb, than to sacrifice the need to be right."

TEACHING
"You teach love with subject matter, not subject matter without love."
"Teachers don't live off the praises of others."
"Teachers must keep the Father's authority alive."
"Internalizing the Cross will greatly strengthen us."
"Jesus always knew the price of teaching for God."
"The minute you have to have an answer to a question, forcing God's hand, you go into opinion. Every word coming out of the teacher must proceed from the Father. As you hear God, the brain will let go of its thinking. The brain must relax."
"Listen to every word coming out of your mouth."
"Human nature needs assignments. God's assignment to us is eternal life."
"Some people always give an answer. Jesus asked questions."
"The teachings of Jesus were short, especially when he was creating new attitudes."
"Jesus taught by words, pictures, and examples."
"Remember that as we study the Bible, the Bible is studying us."

TESTIMONIES

"Each day, we have an opportunity to give our testimony. We usually blow it."

"Remember when you are speaking your testimony, you are speaking it in front of God."

"Testimony should reveal who God is."

"We need to omit a lot of our words."

WOMEN

"There are two kinds of women: those who try with the Cross, and those who try without the Cross."

"Women tend to pick up too many crosses. Leave each person's cross with them, and pick up your own."

"Be a woman of God, not a woman."

IN CLOSING

Each of these words is given to you. How will you use them? Each word is a whole teaching. Will you teach from the word?

This book can be purchased at:
www.createspace.com/3748949

Made in the USA
Middletown, DE
14 May 2021